FEMALE
&MALE

FEMALE & MALE

SOCIALIZATION, SOCIAL ROLES, AND SOCIAL STRUCTURE

CLARICE
STASZ
STOLL

California State College
Sonoma

WM. C. BROWN COMPANY PUBLISHERS
Dubuque, Iowa

wcb

PRINCIPLE THEMES IN SOCIOLOGY

Consulting Editor

Peter Manning
Michigan State University

Copyright © 1974 by Wm. C. Brown Company Publishers

Library of Congress Catalog Card Number: 73—93840

ISBN 0—697—07519—2

Printed in the United States of America

contents

Foreword   **vii**

Preface   **ix**

Acknowledgments   **xi**

1   Nature   1

2   Culture   23

3   Sexism in America: Statistical Overview   41

4   Sexism in Social Science   57

5   Coming Female and Male   76

6   Being Female and Male   110

7   Surviving: Households, Kinship, and Work   131

8   Coping and Its Consequences   160

9   The Politics of Gender   183

Epilogue   **209**

Methodological Appendix   **213**

Glossary   **218**

Author Index   **222**

Subject Index   **225**

foreword

Reading this book is like reading a detective story and it possesses all the necessary *desiderata:* there is the central enigma of the nature of being and becoming, there is a pride of possible "villains," and there is a hero investigating the clues, piecing them together, drawing inferences and tentative conclusions. One is drawn into this book and into the issues it articulates. What are the biological elements in sexuality? What are the social and sociological elements in sexuality? How do social scientists and others investigate these issues and how are they blinded by the very problem they study? What differences occur in people's everyday lives because cultures socialize people to enforce arbitrary distinctions between "females" and "males"? How does society mystify such distinctions, reify them, and provide people with socially sanctioned justifications for all that passes as sexual knowledge?

Throughout the book there is a voice, a person, a being, who speaks clearly and knowledgeably. There is a great deal of Clarice in this book, her personal feelings, her struggle to understand, her visible commitment to elucidating the very complex issues revolving around sex and sexuality in our society. This struggle with self in the context of a personal intellectual problem speaks very eloquently to me. I believe that the most profound issue which faces scholars of the present generation is that of the relationship between their feelings, commitments, morals and their work.

I think this book makes clear that any resolution of the meaning of socialization and sex roles must involve an understanding of how "mind," "self," "society," and "body" are interdigitated and drawn apart in everyday life. For this latter issue is not an exclusively intellectual question, but involves the entire range of sexual *praxis* in this society. The naive dualism of medicine, its often unrecognized mind/body separation and reification, leads to and reinforces many confusions people presently share about health and illness and about sexuality.

But the needed knowledge is not "medical" alone. It is sociological. I believe that this knowledge is socially significant. Clarice, through careful examination of the available evidence, concludes that the social location of sexuality is still unresolved. Without a clear understanding of what is taken to be true by society's members we cannot solve intellectual problems surrounding the issue of sexuality. That it is now possible to debate the "determinants" of sexuality and sex roles (the law, the medical profession, biology, destiny, culture, self, social relations, etc.) is a development of great significance. Once this debate is opened it is entirely likely that many people will accept the possibility that "sex" is entirely a function of the here and now situation, of the moment. The issue, however, is one of uncovering the total range of possibilities that lie behind the constraints that society has typically placed around intimate human relationships. If the total human situation of a person is understood, it is possible for a person to consider the full range of meanings and choices that sexuality portends, and for us to collectively and individually assemble ourselves as sexual beings again and again.

The situational meanings possible for sexuality are now a part of our politics, and provide leverage for movements which seek to alter or substantially modify our present conventions and understandings of the nature of "sexual" relationships. The impact of scholarly writings such as *Female and Male* is not trivial; indeed, to understand how "sexual politics" is possible, one must understand the extent to which intellectuals, since they have been investigating and meanings and consequences of being labeled male and/or female, have fractionated, destroyed, questioned and thereby made fragile what in Anglo-American society historically has been taken for granted.

Peter K. Manning
East Lansing, Michigan

preface

Being female or being male is a part of everyone's social identity from birth till death. Gender is at the core of what we "really are," just as blood lines tell us to whom we are "really related." It is, like race, an identity few can dispute or change. We have no choice over our bodies, only over our culture's evaluation of our particular body type. In America, the evaluations attached to gender affect individual women and men in every area of life and throughout its course. This book examines the consequences of being female and being male—the roles, rewards, costs, and identities that accompany rather simple biological differences.

I wrote this book as a text for undergraduate students, though it is more than a review of theories and findings. At the time of the writing, it was the only book on the sociology of women and men, so it necessarily refleccts my personal interpretation of the field more than might be found in texts for long-established areas of discipline. It proved to be the most exciting project of my career, primarily because so many questions needed to be answered. I could have attempted a comprehensive review of the literature to date, but I decided that this procedure would be improper because it implies a closure that does not exist. So I have tried instead to write the book as I would teach my own students; to expose them to problems and theories as they are—issues for further consideration or research —and to provide a wide repertoire of techniques, analyses, critical modes, and analytical devices for them to adopt in their own work. This required that I be selective in my choice of topics. For example, chapter seven, *Kinship and Work,* includes a lengthy discussion of blue-collar males, who, I believe, are much misrepresented in social science. Since I could not give equal treatment to white-collar males, I have included a guide to their study in the suggested projects section of chapter seven. I hope to have been comprehensive in covering the issues and approaches to the study of gender identity and sexism. Thus any student or class should be well-equipped for making sense of context matter not treated with in detail here.

The book can serve as a text in courses on the sociology of sex roles, as well as any woman's studies social sciences courses where the man's positions in society is considered as well. It may furthermore be useful in courses on social psychology, social stratification, personality and social structure, or socialization, and in those cases where the instructor would like the material to be interpreted along a theme of personal meaning to all class members.

Each chapter has suggested projects for student or class research. Chapter ten, *Epilogue,* presents my reactions to the contents as a whole, and is perhaps the best statement of both my theoretical and personal biases. A *Methodological Appendix* introduces students to the logic of casual analysis as it applies to the study of sex differences or similarities.

My major intellectual debt in preparing this volume is to Peter Manning, who saw that it could be possible when I was filled with doubts. Since I have always been a solitary scholar, his encouragement, provocation, and criticism over the years has been a primary support in my scholarly work. His advice throughout has enabled me to locate deficiencies in the presentation and shape the volume in a more satisfying way.

Many others provided assistance. My initial interest in sex roles was provoked by my own students at Sonoma State College, and later by J. J. Wilson, originator of Sonoma's Woman's Studies program. Special gratitude is due to my sociology department colleagues, who encouraged me to initiate a sequence of courses in that area during a time when such classes were considered frivolous by many academicians. Ellen Marks and Karen Rogers helped me with the clerical work; Sandra Bem directed me to relevant psychological literature, saving me weeks of research in the process; Mildred Dickeman, David Frederickson, and Sue Branscomb Parker advised me on ethnology and archeology; bits of many conversations with Anne Neel and Cathleen Stasz found their way into the manuscript.

I saw less of my good friends Baillie Kay, Lorraine Duncan, and especially Jim Phillippi, than I wished. Preparing this volume has informed me of the small yet significant costs incurred by the performance of a traditionally male role. And, Kendra, here's your name in print again.

acknowledgments

I wish to thank the following publishers and authors for permission to reprint copyright material:

Statistical Bulletin, Metropolitan Life Insurance Co., Volume 43:3, Feb. 1962.

Judith E. Singer, Milton Westphal, and Kenneth Niswander, "Sex Differences in the Incidence of Neonatal Abnormalities and Abnormal Performance in Early Childhood." *Child Development,* 1968. *39,* 103-122. Copyright © 1968 by the Society for Research in Child Development, Inc.

John Money, "Developmental Differentiation in Femininity and Masculinity Compared." In Farber and Wilson, *Man and Civilization: The Potential of Women.* New York: McGraw-Hill Book Company, Publishers, 1963, p. 57.

Reprinted with permission of Macmillan Publishing Co., Inc., from *The Natural Superiority of Women* by Ashley Montagu. Copyright © 1945, 1953, and 1968 by Ashley Montagu.

Helen Mayer Hacker, "Women as a Minority Group." *Social Forces* 30:60-9. University of North Carolina Press, 1951, p. 65.

Exhibit 9.1 from *Aging and Society,* Vol. 1: An Inventory of Research Findings by Matilda White Riley and Anne Foner, © 1968 by Russell Sage Foundation, New York.

Michael A. La Sorte, "Sex Differences in Salary among Academic Sociology Teachers." *The American Sociologist,* Vol. 6, 1971, p. 306.

Clarice Stasz Stoll, "The Sociology of Sex Roles: Essay Review." *Sociological Quarterly,* Vol. 13, 1972, p. 419.

Hannah Arendt, *The Human Condition,* copyright © 1958 by Chicago University Press.

Table 1 "Sex Differences in Infancy and Early Childhood" (p. 93) from *Psychology of Women* by Judith M. Bardwick. Copyright © 1971 by Judith M. Bardwick. Reprinted by permission of Harper & Row, Publishers, Inc.

David B. Lynn, "The Process of Learning Parental and Sex-Role Identification." *Journal of Marriage and the Family,* Vol. 28, 1966, pp. 466-70.

George Herbert Mead (deceased), *Mind, Self, and Society,* edited by C. W. Morris. Copyright © 1934, 1962 (renewed) by University of Chicago Press.

John M. Roberts and Brian Sutton-Smith, "Child Training and Game Involvement." *Ethnology,* Vol. 1, 1962, pp. 166-85.

Reprinted with permission of Macmillan Publishing Co., Inc., from *Adolescent Society* by James S. Coleman. Copyright © The Free Press, a Corporation, 1961.

Harold A. Mulford and Winfield W. Salisbury, "Self-Conceptions in a General Population." *Sociological Quarterly,* Vol. 5, 1964, pp. 35-46.

Carl J. Couch, "Family Role Specialization and Self-Attitudes in Children." *Sociological Quarterly,* Vol. 3, 1960, pp. 115-21.

Marlaine Loskheed Katz, "Female Motive to Avoid Success: A Psychological Barrier or a Response to Deviancy." Princeton, N.J.: Educational Testing Service, 1972.

From *Occupation: Housewife* by Helena Znaniecki Lopata. Copyright © 1971 by Oxford University Press, Inc. Reprinted by permission.

Ira J. Reiss, *Premarital Sexual Standards in America.* Copyright © The Free Press, a Corporation, 1967.

Reprinted with permission of Macmillan Publishing Co., Inc., from *Husbands and Wives* by Robert Blood and Donald Wolfe. © The Free Press, a Corporation, 1960.

Emma Goldman, *The Traffic in Women and Other Essays on Feminism,* with a biography by Alix Kates Shulman, Times Change Press, Penwell Road, Washington, N.J. 07882.

nature

Some things in life are so constant, so obvious, that it is easy to overlook them. Our curiosities are piqued by the bizarre and sensational, not the simple or everyday events of life. Humans are problem-oriented, and go through the day seeking tasks to complete or injustices to settle. Being animals, they have the basic survival problems of locating sufficient food, shelter, and reproduction in a world of scarce resources. As moral animals they create further problems for themselves in their debates as to the way these needs should best be met. Given the difficulties they face daily, it is important for them to have certain facts of life taken for granted, to serve as an ever-present backdrop. Some events that they can count on include maturation, the constancy of skin or eye color, death, ritual celebrations, football seasons.

Outside of death, perhaps the most important biological constant shared by all is gender identity. Knowing our sex we can make many valid predictions about our lives. Some of these are long-range bets. *He* knows that *he* will not menstruate or bear children, while *she* knows that *she* has the potentiality for both. Others are more immediate. She knows that the construction men she is about to pass will gaze at or make remarks to her. He knows that he should open the door for the woman ahead of him in the corridor. Many of these events are not sure things, but they are very good bets nonetheless. Decisions can be made and actions taken with these probabilities in mind. A surface ordering of social life results, for "everyone knows" what to expect of a man or a woman in particular situations, just as "everyone knows" what to expect of people of certain races or age memberships.

It seems natural that men and women should behave differently throughout their lives. They are after all so different. At least, that is what seems to be so, for we have always known it to be so. Men work and women tend the home; even some of our primate cousins follow this pattern. Commonsense suggests that had nature meant us not to be different,

1

we would all be the same. But did nature intend so? If she did, then biology should prove the simplest explanation for the many patterned differences in the social behavior of men and women. So any open-minded sociologist must consider the potential reasonableness of such an explanation outside the traditional sociological realm.

Sex Differences in Humans

The terms "male" and "female" are biological words for the two sexes. Traditionally, "male" applies to the *active* organism who seeks out and penetrates the passive "female" organism (de Ropp 1969).[1]

Typical of higher mammals, the male human is identifiable at birth by his penis, an appendage in the lower abdomen for urination and copulation. The female is recognized by the labia or lips which enclose her separate orifices for urination and copulation. The first obvious difference we encounter is that there are special organs for copulation. The most general reason for copulation in nature is the reproduction of the species. In the human, this requires a union between one male sperm cell and one female ovum, which is best effected by the entry of the penis into the vagina where the sperm are ejaculated. Let us trace the biological lives of a female and male human from this point through to death.

The act of conception is a complicated process, so much so that only one in 100 acts of copulation without birth control will result in a conception. The ovum, which matures once each monthly cycle, lives a mere day after its release from the ovary; sperm cells survive two days. Furthermore, the sperm and ova must be healthy, and the chemical balances of the female must be favorable to the sperm's viability.

Sperm and ovum each bear twenty-three chromosomes that carry the hereditary particles determining the child's fate. In the sperm, half of the cells have the merest remnant of a full chromosome at the position that determines sex. This is known as the Y chromosome, and determines that the child shall be male. The other half have quite large, well-upholstered chromosomes, known as X chromosomes, and determine that the child shall be female. All ova have X chromosomes. Hence, sex is determined by the sperm.

Although there are equal numbers of "female" and "male" sperm cells, many more males are conceived than females, with estimates running from 130 to 180 male to female conceptions.

---

1. This distinction is applied to one-cell species where no differentiated sex organs exist. To call the active, penetrating organism "male" is purely arbitrary, for among many species higher up the phylogentic order, the male is neither more active nor does he penetrate.

During the first month of life, the fetus is sexless. Two processes produce sexual differentiation; one concerns the gonads (sex glands) and the internal accessory structures. The anaglen for both male and female are present at first. At the proper point in development one set regresses and atrophies, while the other proliferates and differentiates. Thus for a period of time male fetuses have remnants of female organs and vice versa. (See Money 1965 for diagrams of these processes.)

Externally a different process takes place. In the sexless state the fetus resembles a female. A genital tubercule resembling a clitoris sits at the head of a groove or opening. Labioscrotal (lip-like) swellings surround the opening. When sexual development begins, if the child is to be a male, the tubercule becomes a penis and the outer opening seams itself shut. If the child is to be female, there is simply a refinement of the external appearance already present, with the tubercule shaping itself into the clitoris.

These changes occur in the third month of pregnancy. The presence of the Y chromosome triggers off a spurt of androgen from the mother. Androgen is a male hormone which in this case encourages the development of male organs and structures. Without this hormonal charge, the fetus develops into a female. As shall be discussed more fully below, if for some reason a fetus with a Y chromosome does not receive the androgen stimulation, then the child will develop like a female. Nature's scheme is to make a female, with males being special elaborations of them (Money 1963).

Because so many changes are needed to produce a male from an essentially female body, malformations are common. The genital cleft may not close. The testes may not descend fully on their long trip through the abdomen. The space the testes travel through may not close fully, leaving a proneness for hernia. Along with these developmental problems appear to be other biological deficiencies, for many more male fetuses are spontaneously aborted, and premature males have a higher fatality rate (see fig. 1-1). By the time of full-term birth, so many more male fetuses than female fetuses have been lost that the sex ratio is almost equal. For example, currently in the United States 106 male human babies are born for every 100 female.

Furthermore, the male child is more likely to be sickly than the female. The Y chromosome is believed to be at the root of many male disorders. Four disorders have already been traced to genes which occur only in some Y chromosomes, and hence can be passed only from father to son. These are barklike skin, dense hairy growth on the ears, keratoma (hard lesions) of the hands and feet, and a webbing of the second and third toes. More serious are the numerous conditions which occur because protective genes are missing in the Y chromosome. Mothers pass these on to sons only, because their daughters have genes in their X chromosome that typically dominate the recessive mutant gene. Hemophilia and color blindness are two well-known disorders of this type. Table 1-1 lists some conditions due largely to sex-linked genes and thus found mostly in males.

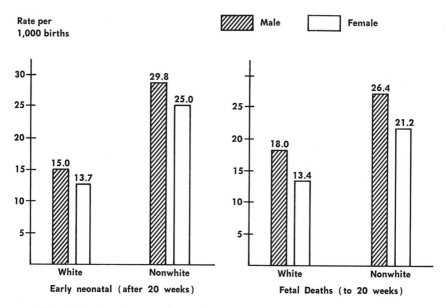

Figure 1-1. Annual perinatal mortality rates (by color and sex) United States 1958-1959.

Source: Statistical Bulletin, Metropolitan Life Insurance Company, Volume 43, February 2, 1962.

Infancy

For the past fifty years child development researchers have charted a variety of sex differences, many of which are observable even among newborn infants. Many of these studies are longitudinal, that is, trace the growth and performance of the same child over a period of time. The brunt of the research suggests that the male begins life at a disadvantage.

A more recent example is the study by Singer, Westphal, and Niswander (1968) based upon developmental data on 15,000 babies born in one year in Buffalo, New York. As table 1-2 shows, the boys were born in worse condition, as measured by the Apgar measure of vital signs (a

Table 1-1
Conditions Due Largely to Sex-linked Genes Found Mostly in Males

Table 1-1
Conditions Due Largely to Sex-linked Genes Found Mostly in Males

Absence of central incisor teeth
Aldrich's syndrome (chronic eczema, middle-ear disease, etc.)
Anhidrotic ectodermal dysplasia (maldevelopment of sweat glands)
Cataract
Cerebellar ataxia (loss of muscle coordination)
Color-blindness—red-green type
Day blindness
Defective hair follicles
Double eyelashes
Epidermal cysts
Glaucoma—juvenile type
Hemophilia
Hurler's syndrome (dwarf stature, bone disease)
Icthyosis (scale-like skin)
Mental deficiency of certain types
Mitral stenosis (stricture of bicuspid valve of the heart)
Myopia
Night blindness
Optic atrophy (wasting of the eye)
Parkinsonism
Peoneal atrophy (wasting of muscles of the legs)
Progressive deafness
Retinal detachment
White occipital lock of hair

Source: Montagut (1970, pp. 77-78).

test of infant health), and were considerably more likely to have one of the 187 abnormalities listed on the neonatal summary form. At eight months a psychologist tested the infants using several standardized scales of infant development. The boys scored significantly poorer on all scales except the social-emotional. At twelve months a neurologist or pediatrician examined the infants. Again the majority of males exhibited abnormalities, while only a minority of females did so. These differences remained in samples of four-year olds.

In explaining these differences, the investigators candidly conclude:

Details of the mechanisms behind sex differences are obscure. Possibilities include: (a) the presence of deleterious genetic material on the Y chromosome, (b) the relative lack in the male of beneficial genetic material on the X chromosome, and (c) immunologic incompatibility between the male fetus and his female mother (Singer, Westphal, and Niswander 1968, p. 109).

Table 1-2
Early Sex Differences
(15,000 Buffalo Children)

Measures	Percent Abnormal		
	Male	Female	x2
Neonatal Condition			
Apgar (6 vital signs)	4.4	3.5	14.75*
Neonatal summary (187 items)	71.1	25.1	41.0 *
8-month Bayley Scales			
Mental	7.9	6.8	9.11*
Fine motor	15.0	11.0	64.54†
Gross motor	15.7	12.7	33.98†
Social-emotional	7.7	9.4	16.81†
Final diagnosis	15.5	12.5	26.25†
12-month exams			
Neurological	8.9	7.8	8.17*
Summary (248 items)	65.0	26.6	39.8 †

* p .01
† p. .001

Source: Singer et al. (1968), Table 1.
Source: Singer, Westphal, and Niswander (1968, p. 107).

A fourth possibility is that the testors expect boys to be less normal. Perhaps the lore of child development research has sensitized examiners to score boys more poorly. Or perhaps the boys, being more highly valued in our society, receive more careful examination, so that possible defects can be corrected early. Yet one could just as well argue that, given the widespread attitude that females are inferior, the examiners would score girls lower. Sex differences of the direction found here have been found too repeatedly on different samples and with other measures not to attribute them to biology. This is not to imply that the differences are large, for many are not. Similarly, the correlations are typically not very strong; in other words, one will find many exceptions where a girl or boy does not exhibit his or her "typical" behavior. Nonetheless, given both a boy and girl baby, one could make bets on the following:[2]

2. These findings have accumulated over years of child development research. For detailed summaries of studies and references, see a general child development text. Three notable sources on sex differences in young children are Anastasi (1958), Bardwick (1971), and Maccoby (1966).

1. The boy will generally display a greater activity level from birth. He will cry more, awaken more, move more. His metabolic rate will be five to six percent higher than a girl's. The boy will be larger, have more muscle mass, and maintain this size difference throughout life. This size advantage will not display itself in tests of performance or ability, except where strength is involved. The boy will develop more slowly than the girl.

2. The girl will be more sensual even as an infant. She will be sensitive to a wider range of stimuli than the boy, prefer complex music while the boy prefers the simple; be more sensitive to pain; display a readier response to visual stimuli than the boy. The girl will have a more acute sense of smell which will increase following puberty.

3. The infant girl will fixate earlier on the human face and respond more to social stimuli. She will look to other humans as a source of satisfaction more than the boy, and learn to cope with discord verbally. The boy will resist others demands and cope with discord through physical activity.

4. The girl will speak earlier, read earlier, and count earlier. If one of the babies has a speech defect, it is likely to be the boy.

5. During early childhood the boy will more often grab toys, attack others, ignore danger, refuse to listen to orders or requests to comply, laugh, and jump around. The girl is more likely to play quietly, exhibit withdrawal, seek praise from adults, and be less quarrelsome. Thus the male seems to have a lower threshold for frustration, while the female is more fearful.

6. The girl will tend to score higher than the boy on intelligence and aptitude tests during the preschool years, though by late high school the boy may be scoring higher. In some tests of spatial ability, the boy is likely to score higher. The girl will possibly do better on some tests of creativity and verbal skills. The findings in this area are not totally consistent, and the magnitude of difference in scores is not large.

That these developmental differences are not sizeable is evidenced by the fact that the girl and boy will be very much alike for the most part. Girls may speak earlier, but not so much so that it is noticeable to parents, pediatricians, or teachers. Similarly, to describe boys' play as "typically physical and active" it not to omit that it may also be quiet or withdrawn. Someone watching children at play will not see all the boys playing actively or all the girls quietly conversing. Perhaps only if one observed for long periods of time and kept careful records of activity would a pattern of sex-typed play behavior emerge. Many of the differences described here are based upon repeated observations, thousands of subjects, with measures that are rather refined.

Hypothetical data: Glockenspiel counts eye blinks in 18,346 infants on the third day of life and discovers that on the average the males blink .415 times more often than the females. She reports that this difference is "statistically significant." If we charted the distributions of eyeblink frequencies, we could find any one of the following situations:

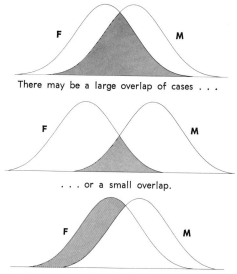

There may be a large overlap of cases . . .

. . . or a small overlap.

There may even be cases of males who blink less frequently than females.
Probability statistics are such that any of these situations is often possible. We need to ask Glockenspiel how much **variation** there was in the samples as one clue to identifying the underlying distribution. Also, because the difference is "statistically significant," this does not mean it is "socially significant." That is for you to decide.

Figure 1-2. Hypothetical sex differences.

Figure 1-2 illustrates how a "difference" cannot be taken to mean a categorical separation of the groups under study. One has to know the general distribution of the traits under study before one could, for example, say "most girls speak earlier than boys." This error is prevalent in mass media and even in textbooks. A scientific study is cited as showing that a difference exists, while the amount of overlap is ignored. Unfortunately, studies themselves too often emphasize the fact of the difference though, as in the case of the Singer et al. data (table 1-2, p. 6), it may be a matter of a mere percentage point.

The distributions in figure 1-2 also remind us how any statement of difference refers to the class of members of the sex, not to the attributes of any one individual member. No individual female child ever had a mean age-at-first-word-spoken, although the class of "female children" has. The error of confusing the attributes of a group with those of the individual members is one committed very often with regard to sex differences, as we shall later see.

Puberty

Toward the end of the first decade of life, certain pituitary hormones will stimulate the child's development toward that of a mature adult of her or his sex. Prior to this time the boy and girl do not differ much in appearance, except for the genitalia, overall size, gross skeletal structure, and fat distribution. Puberty brings both external and internal changes that emphasize the nature of sex identity and sexuality.

Externally, the secondary sex characteristics are elaborated. Some of these are rather superficial, such as the hairline recession, beard growth, and larynx enlargement of the male, the breast development of the female, or the characteristic pubic hair growth patterns of each. Other changes are less apparent though more important in terms of physical performance and skill at various tasks. The extra fat layer of the female thickens, leaving her with a rounded appearance and more insulation than the male. Her hip bones widen, while the male's rib cage and shoulders expand considerably. The male adds muscle mass in contrast to the fatty weight gain of the female. His long bones grow for a longer period, which accounts for his generally taller height. In contrast to the male's straight arms and legs, the female's arms hang with angles at the elbows and a slight knock-knee bend in the legs. These muscular and skeletal changes are evident in the different manner in which adult men and women run, throw objects, or lift things. Their relative strength, leverage system, and stamina direct each to use their bodies in slightly different ways for efficiency.

The most obvious internal change is the development of the sex glands and organs. Menstruation begins in the female several years after the physical changes marking puberty and it will be even later before the menses and ovulation are regular. Similarly, the prostate gland develops fluid that can be ejaculated during orgasm for several years before mature sperm are a component of that fluid. By mid-teens most American males and females are fertile.

Puberty marks the time when the sex hormones are activated so as to affect mood and behavior. Prior to this time they seem to be of little matter. In normal children of both sexes there is scarcely a detectable amount of androgenic (male) hormone until puberty, at which time the level spurts upward for *both* sexes. If the child is a female, there will be a spurt in the estrogen level as well, which will establish itself in a cyclic pattern.

Maturity

The female "cycle" has been extensively studied, so much so that Bardwick (1971) concludes:

> Regular, predictable changes occur in the personality of the sexual-
> ly mature woman, and these changes occur in spite of individual
> personality differences and may even be extreme; they are a conse-
> quence of endocrine and related physical changes.

The *content* of the emotional state is a function of the psyche and the real world of the individual—the *direction* of the change is a function of the physical state.

Many studies have correlated emotional changes with the estrogen and progesterone levels of the different phases of the cycle. There is extensive evidence of what is popularly known as "premenstrual tension" during the period when both the estrogen and progesterone levels have dropped. Women score higher on measures of irritability, hostility, anxiety, and depression during this time. In the most careful study of this type, Ivey and Bardwick (1968) asked normal females at various points in their cycles to relate recent experiences they had had. A sensitive scoring device enabled the researchers to identify and tabulate current, real anxieties. References to death, mutilation, and separation were characteristic of the premenstrual phase, while self-satisfaction was more common at ovulation. When women are on birth control pills, which hold hormone levels relatively constant, anxiety and hostility levels are correspondingly constant (Paige 1969). That high levels of estrogen are important for positive moods can be seen in the proven value of prescribed estrogen as therapy during menapause when the drop in this hormone can cause numerous troublesome bodily ailments.

Although many women may experience an increase in feelings of hostility and anxiety during the premenstrual period, they will vary considerably in their response to these moods. Though it is true that a woman is more likely to commit murder during this time, it should be remembered that compared to men, women are very unlikely to murder at all. Women engaged in ego-satisfying work report far less discomfort and emotional disarray during their cycle than women in boring or stultifying jobs. Looking at a roomful of women one knows well, it is still virtually impossible to predict off-handedly where each one is in her cycle. Only with time and detailed, refined measurements one could do so if it mattered.[3]

Less well known is the male cycle, partly because so few studies have been done on male endocrinology. Testosterone is the androgenic hormone most closely associated with male activity. Its most important effect appears to be sexual arousability. (This is so even for the female, whose ovaries produce the hormone at a much lower rate than the testes). For males, it appears that only a minimal androgen level is necessary for sexual arousal. Men deficient in androgen increase sexual fantasy and activity in direct proportion to the administered dosage. This is not to place all of sexual arousal with hormones; it is only to indicate their necessary contribution if arousal is to occur (Money 1965).

Testosterone levels are found to be highest in early morning and lowest after midnight, with the physiological and mood effects occurring several hours subsequently. The high period is marked by a feeling of well-being, energy, decreased need for sleep, with the low period marked by irritability and dissatisfaction. Over a month the hormonal output ebbs and flows like the woman's, with similar changes in mood. The exact details of the process have not yet been well charted, though there is sufficient evidence to date to suggest that the correlation between hormone and mood exists for man as well.[4]

While all adults experience the hormone cycles appropriate to their sex, not all will be involved with reproduction. For the female, the fertile period lasts as long as mature ova are being produced, which in Western societies can be for thirty or forty years. Fertility for the male lasts much later in life.

Conception occurs through copulation of two fertile partners. Copulation in the human appears to serve as a basis for intimacy more than a purely biological act of reproduction. Unlike other animals, the female is potentially capable of copulation at any point in her cycle, not simply at the point of ovulation. The male is similarly responsive, as most male

3. Of course, in our society "pre-menstrual tension" matters greatly and the "fact" of its existence is used as one rationale for excluding women from many opportunities. I do not recall ever reading of cyclical swing in studies of primitive societies—another indication that our culture has turned a minor physiological process into a process of serious import.

4. Our knowledge of male physiology in this area is shockingly small. A primary reason is that women in modern society are expected to be responsible for birth control. Our extensive knowledge of the female here reflects a political belief that the woman should be manipulated. This is curious given that our superficial knowledge of the male body suggests that manipulation of his body may be simpler and have fewer side effects.

animals are. Logically, either sex may make the initial advances toward copulation, though cultural practices may set a direction or limitation.

The human male does not need the consent nor the arousal of the female in order to maintain his erection and complete copulation. This contrasts with other animals. For example, male monkeys mount only females who present themselves according to ritual. Or if a domestic cat does not respond with certain responses to a mounting male, then he will lose his erection and not be able to penetrate her. Since in the human, learning has replaced species-wide rituals of sexual behavior, females have no universal social cues that could automatically dampen male interest. Often, her only recourse is physical force, which is seldom effective. Furthermore, neurological research (MacLean 1965) has identified that the structure in the brain concerned with penile erection is immediately next to that concerned with aggressive behavior. Neurologists hypothesize that this may explain the human male's capability—not found in other animals—to be sexually aroused during violence, or to commit violence during sexual arousal.

If the female is impregnated, she will carry a child in her uterus for a nine-month period. As a mammal, she can feed the child through her milk. The male has no biological role in child development beyond conception. No logical reason exists why the male should not have developed milk-supplying breasts at some point in evolution, but this did not turn out to be the case. Contemporary man's breasts today are useless in child care.

The female grows considerably throughout her abdominal area during pregnancy and appears to be clumsy. This is not the case, for her skeletal structure and muscles permit her the mobility and strength to perform her usual tasks. Childbirth can occur unassisted although it is more favorable to both mother and child to have some aid in withdrawing the baby. Labor is not very long, sometimes only a matter of hours, particularly if the mother has had a previous child. Child bearing is made more hazardous if the mother reproduces frequently or if her nutrition has been poor. No adult male dies in the reproduction of the species.

The human infant is helpless at birth and requires care for a number of years before it is able to meet its own needs. *Any* adult human could satisfy these needs. Nevertheless, there have been arguments as to whether the female has a drive to nurture young. Although some (e.g., Bardwick 1971) have suggested that hormones, specifically progesterone, may relate to this psychological state, no research has been done, even on a preliminary level.

When the female reaches late middle-age, both estrogen and androgen production decline, while ovulation ceases. This period, menopause, is characteristically fraught with numerous somatic ailments, with depression a frequent accompaniment. Few women lose normal functioning as a result of these changes though. The body also masculinizes in small ways, for the effect of the androgens always present in the woman's body can now be stronger. The female is now prone to diseases characteristically prevalent in the male, such as cardiovascular distress. Estrogen decline is also a possible cause of skin aging, atherosclerosis, and the bone disorder known as osteoporosis.

The androgenic hormone levels in the male also decrease gradually, although the testes may function to produce viable sperm throughout life. Prostrate trouble and some psychological ailments are common in male aging, but these have not to date been related to hormone output. As with the woman, sexual activity in old age has no known relationship to hormonal activity. Estrogen levels do not change much in the male, so some appearances of feminization may appear (Moore 1968).

The male is likely to die at a younger age than the female. During his lifetime he is more prone to accidents and debilitating diseases. (We will see detailed data on this in later chapters.)

It can be argued that men are exposed to more risk and stress than women, but much evidence counters this possibility. In an intriguing study, Madigan (1957) presented data on the longevity of a large sample of Catholic nuns and Catholic brothers, groups who for many years had been living the same life style. The sex differences in mortality rates resembled those of the general population. Furthermore, working single women live longer than working bachelors. Other research has found that housewives work longer hours under no less stressful conditions than working men. Women have fewer fatal accidents in the home, even though they spend considerably more time there. Men suffer more from infectious diseases during epidemics than women. These and other data argue for the view that the female has a superior capacity for survival.

Cross-species Research

In discussions of the nature of humankind, scientists and philosophers frequently look beyond our species to others. Unfortunately, we are such an eccentric species that only recently have we begun to observe and catalogue the behavior of other species. *Ethology* is the discipline concerned with the research of different animal species as they exist. Wickler (1972) has described the comparisons marking the work in this field. One is of the relationships species exhibit, such as how a behavior pattern functions and changes during evolution. The transferral of feeding patterns to courting behavior in some bird species is an example of this comparison. Another example is abilities, such as reproduction or fighting. For example, to understand the reasons for pair-bonding, it is necessary to study species that are quite different from one another. Only through study of diverse species, that is, cases where monogamy has been invented independently of intra-species contacts, can one begin to locate the conditions leading to monogamy.

All ethologists would not agree with that last point. For example, the works of Morris (1971) or Tiger and Fox (1971) generalize from the behavior of primates only to the nature of man. At first glance, it seems reasonable that we should learn much from study of our evolutionary kin. There are several problems here. One is that man is the only hominid left on earth, so there is no species within his class for easy comparison. Studies have indicated that our closest kin, the apes and gorillas, have developed highly specialized behavior patterns peculiar to their species and environment. If one includes the other primates, such as lemures, marmosets, or monkeys, then it is extremely difficult to make many generalizations about the "nature of man." Popular notions about "monkey behavior" confound our understanding. It is now common knowledge that many baboon tribes have social structures with a strong male at the lead. Before making any statements about what this means for human behavior one has to ask why data about one primate alone would be meaningful, particularly given that this stratification is not universal even for baboons.[5]

Generalizations from other species, even primates to man, must be made with caution. Ethology often lacks data on more than one or two species for a given topic, and even then there is no sure logic for extrapolating to human behavior. Nonetheless cross-specie comparisons provide insights to human behavior, if only by pointing out areas where man is unique or shares a pattern in common with other animals. Whether his behavior is natural or not may be beside the point.

Sex and Sexuality   One feature that man shares with virtually every living organism is sex—that is, the differentiation into a female and male organization. The forms sex takes on in other species is quite different. Only in higher mammals does one find highly developed sex organs like the vagina or penis. The typical mating in amphibia and birds consists of a pressing together of the cloacae, the bodily outlet for wastes.

5. There is accumulating evidence that primate social structure is considerably influenced by habitat. Species once thought to have a small elite polygynous male ruling group, such as baboons or howler monkeys, have been seen to form very different social structures. Population density, food sources, and geography are several of the variables that encourage different primate organizations (Eisenberg et al 1972).

Some animals (such as the snail) are hermaphrodites. The sex organs are in the head and each partner in the copulation acts as male and female simultaneously. In other species, the same animal can serve as the male at one point in time and the female at another. Some oysters are male one season and female the next; members of one worm species are male until their length reaches twenty segments at which point they become female. In many species, reproduction occurs without copulation; the sperm and ova from either sex partner meet externally (de Ropp 1969).

From these examples it can be seen that perhaps the only cross-species commonality with regard to sex is that two sex types exits. They may not exist for the same individual; hence, *masculinity* and *femininity* are *relative states* throughout their lifetime. There is no body structure common to each sex (except for the fact of bearing ova or sperm which is not true for the simplest organisms). The structures for reproduction vary considerably, with the means for reproduction similarly displaying different patterns. Going up the phylogentic scale, one can say however that specialized organs for reproduction have evolved such that mammals have elaborate sexual structures that overlap less in function with other structures—such as those for waste disposal. Secondly hermaphroditism or changeable sex identity is less frequent as one moves up the evolutionary scale. Why nature has moved this way is a puzzle biologists and philosophers have few insights about.

Several other findings from ethology are enlightening for a perspective on man's nature. One concerns secondary sex characteristics. The form and extent of differentiation in appearance between the sexes takes many shapes. In the insect world the reproductive female is often much larger than the male. Among many birds the male is more colorful. Some animals are so alike in appearance that experienced zoologists have difficulty distinguishing the sexes.

In mammals, prehistoric forms manifested frequent similarity between male and female. One interesting conclusion from research on this topic is that a characteristic formerly belonging exclusively to male individuals (such as antlers) appears also on female animals at a later stage of evolution. Thus we find the sexes of higher mammals becoming alike in appearance (Buytendijk 1968).

The research on the effects of hormones offers an interesting counterdevelopment. If a young male animal is castrated, it undergoes a clear feminization in appearance and behavior. A capon differs little from a hen. On the other hand, spayed females do not move towards masculine direction, but rather display an arrested development, retaining immature external characteristics and behavior. Here is further illustration of nature's inclination toward the female form.

Behaviorally, the sexes of many species display several characteristic activity patterns, although again one cannot say that there is one pattern fairly common to the male or the female. Infant care is a good example. In many lower animal species, the young receive no care and never know their parents. Among birds, brood-tending is often shared rather equally by both parents. Mammals are more noted for the female's association with young, but there is considerable range across these species with regard to the amount of time and care the female exhibits. Even among primates there are females that scarcely bother with their infants. Furthermore, it is characteristic of most primates and many other species that the male participate in some form of what could be called fathering. This latter fact is often overlooked or underemphasized in discussions of gross behavioral differences.

Compared to other species, one uniqueness stands out—the human female's sexuality. Only the human female has an intricate organ, the clitoris, with no apparent purpose other than serving sexual pleasure. The human female also has breasts that are large even when she is not lactating, with the nipples serving as a locus of sexual pleasure. The human male uniqueness—if there is any—may be the frequency with which the male uses his penis for sexual pleasure. Part of this activity relates to the lack of estrus or mating period in the human female, so the human male similarly displays a year-round arousal ability lacking in other species.

Sex: Category or Continuum?

Looking over the data from biology and ethology, two opposing trends may be noted. One is how it is possible to group species into two types by sex identification and predict certain characteristics of development from these categories. On the other hand, there is evidence of much variability within categories, so much so that the differences between male and female are of a gross nature often contradicted by specific cases of men and women. The outstanding sex differences have to do with sexual and reproductive behavior, which constitute very little of animal's life activities. Of secondary importance are the biological weaknesses of the male and general activity patterns. That the sexes are not very different should not be surprising, for both share forty-seven chromosomes of the forty-eight and both bear "feminine" and "masculine" hormones.

Further evidence that "male" and "female" are not to be considered mutually exclusive categories in the human species is available. Common sense has it that all babies are born either male or female, perhaps because common sense is based upon the notion of the categories being absolutely distinct. This is simply not the case. Children are born who bear physical manifestations appropriate to either sex; if identified as such, they are called hermaphrodites (although unknown numbers are undetected). Any of the following variables are involved in this configuration (Money, Hampson, and Hampson 1955).

1. Chromosomal sex. A person may exhibit the characteristics of one sex (e.g., male) yet test chromosomally as female (XX).
2. Gonadal sex. The sex glands may not be fully active. Gonadal tissues may display both ovarian and testicular cells.
3. Hormonal sex. The hormones may not develop in the direction that a mature female or male display.
4. Internal accessory organs. These may be ambiguous or display features of both sexes.
5. External genital appearance. What is actually a clitoris appears as a penis, or a genuine penis resembles a clitoris. Testicles may be so atrophied as to be unapparent.

These anomalies generally pattern themselves to fit one of a variety of identified hermaphrodites.

When these persons are born, they are almost always identified at once as "female" or "male" generally on the basis of external appearances. This societal assignment is known as *gender identity*. Money and his associates studied 110 such individuals to see whether the individuals' own feelings about their identities correlated highly with any one of the physical characteristics. None did. Many individuals were living satisfying and fulfilling lives as members of one sex category when almost all the physical evidence placed them in the other sex category. This was true even of people who looked like normal members of one sex entirely, yet had been raised as members of the other sex. Money (1955) concludes:

> One is confronted with the conclusion, perhaps surprising to some, that there is no primary genetic or other innate mechanism to preordain the masculinity or femininity of psycho-sexual differentiation . . . The analogy is with language. Genetics and innate determinants ordain only that language can develop and differentiate provided that the sensory and motor capacities are intact and that communicational stimulation is adequate, but not whether the language will be Nahuatl, Arabic, English, or any other. Psychosexually, also, genetics and innate determinants ordain only that a gender role and identity shall differentiate, without directly dictating

whether the direction shall be male or female. In fact, the expected
norm of reaction may be completely reversed by factors that come
into play after birth.

Thus Money argues that many psychosexual differences are to be regarded
as environmentally conditioned or culturally learned. He does not agree
that all sex differences can be reduced to culture, however, for he believes
that such data as the sensory capabilities and activity displays of each sex
are cross-cultural. Nonetheless, the hermaphrodites provide evidence that
much of what appears to be sex differences are not biologically linked.

In passing, one criticism of this research must be noted. Diamond
(1965) doubts that the human's sexual identity is not predetermined by
birth as it is with other animals. He disputes that data from clinical or
"abnormal" cases can tell us about normal development. Most people are
not hermaphroditic. Yet Diamond's argument is also disputable because
however strange hermaphrodites might seem, the fact that *assigned* gender
identity supersedes all other physical characteristics of sex identity cannot
be swept aside. Furthermore, these cases are "abnormal" only because we
view them as such—the actual distribution of anomalies in the human
species is unknown. If only a tiny minority of people are hermaphroditic,
the fact of hermaphroditism can not be called abnormal except in a statistical sense. Finally, there are cases of individuals who physically are members of one sex, yet live satisfactorily as members of the opposite sex.

Curiously, another instance of unusual psychosexual development,
one studied by Money, offers support for Diamond's thesis. Transsexuals,
persons who believe themselves to be trapped in the body of the wrong sex,
form the case in point. Their belief is so strong that many undergo surgery to change their bodies to the desired sex. (Transsexuals have been
noted even in societies lacking modern medicine where painful primitive
surgery is needed to achieve their goal.) Female transsexualism is very
rare with estimates running from one-third to one-eighth as common as
males (Stoller 1968). Following medical therapy, transsexuals usually
have few problems that can be related to their sex change. Indeed, the
physical change marks noted psychological relief for most.

What could cause this deep psychological need? One constant
throughout the literature is the absence of any clear familial, social, or
physiological cause. Money has discovered transsexual desires in children
and at all class levels. Bardwick (1971) theorizes that the cause relates
to fetal development. Perhaps males predominate among transsexuals because central nervous system changes toward masculinity do not occur
when they are supposed to. Hence the male feels trapped in the female
body. This interpretation is consistent with Diamond's view of psychosex-

ual differentiation. On the other hand, Stoller, who had once emphasized biology in this syndrome now argues that the problem may be more cultural. Males have a more difficult time with their sexual identity because they must separate from the mother onto an appropriate male figure. Thus one can expect (as one finds) more male sexual ambiguities in all areas, such as fetishism, transvestitism, and so on.

Is sex a distinct category or a variable upon which individuals can be placed? The answer requires very specific definitions of what we mean by sex. In some cases, such as asking people (gender identity), we can place an individual in one of two categories. In other cases, such as reproductive capacity, there are three categories: male, female, neuter. There are correlates of sex-at-birth such as activity level which suggest basic differences. But if we were to line up all children by activity level, many females would be more active than some males, so the difference is not considerable.

How important is biology in sex? We don't know yet. There simply haven't been many studies to guide us; even the experts disagree. It looks as though its role depends upon both the biological component and the issue at hand. Thus we know that a specific hormone level is needed in adult males for sexual arousal, but having that hormone level is not enough to ensure arousal. We know that hormones affect moods and feeling states cyclically in both men and women, but we also know that behavior cannot be predicted well from these cycles. We don't know how much of what could be called "femininity" and "masculinity" are shaped in utero if at all.

Sexism

Looking over the biological and ethological data, it is striking how few established sex differences exist. Perhaps the only constant is the aggressiveness of the male, and even this is disputable, for it depends on what behaviors one calls aggressive. Parenthood, whether female or male, is lacking in some species, just as jointly shared parenthood appears in others. Among mammals, the child requires lengthy care from both parents and "maternity" can be reduced to a matter of childbearing and breast feeding. Size differences and likelihood of survival are among the few clear distinctions between male and female.

Human males and females are clearly more similar than different. Both can perform the same physical activities, except for the very few tasks where extreme strength is needed. In any case, the brain would help a female to use some tool to be as strong as a male without a tool. Both walk, talk, make love, enjoy a sunset, sing, laugh, create stories, admonish children, toil, make sacrifices, enact evil, and die.

Some philosophers have argued that without sex there would be no death, for a species would procreate through individual divisions. Once egg and sperm enter in, inevitable death results, because colonies of individuals develop within the old which rupture and die. Yet with sex comes the possibility for new combinations of individuals, greater adaptability, and individualization.

Philosophical and biological debates may be enticing, but they ignore a most curious and obvious problem. *Man acts as if there are differences between the sexes.* You may note that "man" is being used instead of "human" for the first time in this discussion. The switch is intentional. Man, the male of the human species, has seemed intent to emphasize male-female as though it were a distinct categorical system. This is not all. Being social animals, humans evaluate categories and activities. And men have become the principal definers of what are the basic human categories in all societies. Very often they have argued that their way is "the natural way," one superior to "woman's way"; when, in fact, we have seen that nature offers very little in support of this proposal. The belief in the superiority of the male principle is the basic element in any *sexist* ideology. Here is the problem for sociologists: within the framework of biology—which seems to be relatively unimportant for many issues—why are women and men so different? And why do men dominate history? Man is a creature of nature only if society enters into nature's conspiracy. Most of the time he seems to. Let us see why.

SUGGESTED PROJECTS

Note: The projects here and following subsequent chapters may be most helpful to you as examples of the styles of questions you can explore on your own. The suggestions for readings are merely recommendations for a first place to look. You will also have to go to the journals (with the help of *Sociological Abstracts*), check the card catalogue at the library, or confer with your reference librarian as to government documents and other relevant data sources.

1. Has the information so far affected your own identity as a woman or man in any way? Start a journal that covers the time period that you are dealing with this book as a document on personal changes that result from the information you encounter here and in class discussions. Your first entry should state your current definitions of "femininity" and "masculinity," your attitudes toward various "women's liberation" aims, and your sense of yourself as a woman or a man.

2. Is "man" naturally aggressive? Some current works have answered affirmatively: Robert Ardrey, *The Territorial Imperative* (New York: Dell, 1971), Desmond Morris, *The Naked Ape* (New York: Dell, 1962) and *The Human Zoo* (New York: Dell, 1970), Konrad Lorenz, *On Human Aggression* (New York: Harcourt Brace Joanovich, 1966), and Anthony Storr, *Human Aggression* (New York: Atheneum, 1968). One dissenter is

Irenaus Eibl-Eibesfeldt's *Love and Hate* (New York: Holt, Rinehart & Winston, 1972). Examine such a work for yourself and see whether you agree or not. Look up reviews in the popular press and in professional anthropology journals as well. (The *Book Review Index* is a useful guide here.)

3. Do those who believe the sexes are biologically different also believe that women are inferior? Can you design a sample survey that would measure these two attitudes? What kind of sample would you need? (Most social psychology texts will have chapters on attitude measurement.)

4. How well-informed are people on the biology of sex differences. Does education matter here? Will people in some occupations (such as social science teachers, doctors) know more than those in others (such as English teachers or lawyers)? Or is there another variable you think might predict knowledge here? Draw up a short test based upon material presented in this chapter and do a pilot study on your hypothesis.

REFERENCES

Anastasi, Anne. *Differential Psychology.* New York: Macmillan Publishing Co., Inc., 1958.

Bardwick, Judith M. *Psychology of Women.* New York: Harper and Row, 1971.

Buytendijk, F. J. J. *Woman: A Contemporary View.* Glen Rock, N. J.: Newman Press, 1968.

de Ropp, Robert S. *Sex Energy.* New York: Delta, 1969.

Diamond, Milton. "A Critical Evaluation of the Ontogeny of Human Sexual Behavior." *Quarterly Review of Biology* 40(1968):147-75.

Eisenberg, J. F.; Muckenhirn, N. A.; and Rodran, R. "The Relation between Ecology and Social Structure in Primates." *Science* 176(1972):863-74.

Ivey, Melville, and Bardwick, Judith M. "Patterns of Affective Fluctuations in the Menstrual Cycle." *Psychosomatic Medicine* 30(1968):336-45.

Maccoby, Eleanor E. *The Development of Sex Differences.* Palo Alto, Calif.: Stanford University Press, 1966.

MacLean, Paul D. "New Findings Relevant to the Evolution of Psychosexual Functions of the Brain." In *Sex Research: New Developments,* edited by John Money, pp. 176-96. New York: Holt, Rinehart and Winston, 1965.

Madigan, F. C. "Are Sex Mortality Differentials Biologically Caused?" *Milbank Memorial Fund Quarterly* 35(1957):202-23.

Money, John. *Sex Research: New Developments.* New York: Holt, Rinehart and Winston, 1965.

―――. "Developmental Differentiation of Femininity and Masculinity Compared." In *Man and Civilization: The Potential of Women,* edited by Farber and Wilson. New York: McGraw-Hill, 1963.

Money, J.; Hampson, J. G.; and Hampson, J. L. "An Examination of Some Basic Sexual Concepts: The Evidence of Human Hermaphroditism." *Bulletin of the Johns Hopkins Hospital* 97(1955):301-19.

Montagu, Ashley. *The Natural Superiority of Women.* New York: Collier, 1970.

Moore, Mary E. "Physical Changes.' In *Aging and Society,* by Matilda White Riley et al. New York: Russell Sage Foundation, 1968.

Morris, Desmond. *Intimate Behavior*. New York: Random House, 1971.

Paige, Karen E. "The Effects of Oral Contraceptives on Affective Fluctuations Associated with the Menstrual Cycle." Ph.D. dissertation, University of Michigan, 1969.

Rosenberg, B. G., and Sutton-Smith, Brian. *Sex and Identity*. New York: Holt, Rinehart and Winston, 1972.

Singer, Judith E.; Westphal, Milton; and Niswander, Kenneth. "Sex Differences in the Incidence of Neonatal Abnormalities and Abnormal Performance in Early Childhood." *Child Development* 39(1968):103-22.

Stoller, Robert. *Sex and Gender*. New York: Science House, 1968.

Tiger, Lionel, and Fox, Robin. *The Imperial Animal*. New York: Holt, Rinehart and Winston, 1971.

Wickler, Wolfgang. *The Sexual Code*. Garden City, N.Y.: Doubleday, 1972.

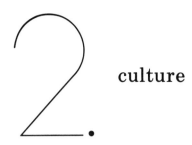

culture

When asked why there are sex differences, one common answer is that men and women are biologically different. We have seen that the evidence does not support this statement very strongly however one interprets it; in particular, biology fails to show that women are "inferior" in some way to men. Another typical explanation is that society causes the differences. That is, one can show that in virtually every society men and women are expected to act in sex-specific ways. Each generation passes these differences on to the next with minor modification. This argument holds the supremacy of nurture over nature and is more appealing to those who presume that society is somehow more easily changed than biology. The position also assumes that human animality is a minor variable in explaining human behavior.

Many attributes distinguish humans from other species. Humans have the capacity to produce the necessities and comforts of life on a level far more variable and adaptable than any other species. Our fantastic brain allows us to develop and manipulate complex symbol systems for communication and memory. The extended juvenile period allows an individual human many years to acquire skills before she must take over responsible adult decisions and performances. With each generation, certain types of knowledge can be compressed so that successively more can be learned at an earlier age than previously. Our enormous brain capacity and the facility of our human hand allow the construction of many tools and the performance of tasks unattainable by other species. Humans are more creative in the areas of art, music, and dance than other species. We are the only animals to have a literature, a repertory of ballets, an encyclopedia of knowledge, a history. We have inventive humor; we feel deep despair, joy, and ecstasy. We are the only moral animals in that we evaluate one another's behaviors according to standards that are relative to our own cultures or groups. We wage wars for other than simple territorial or survival reasons. We copulate for other than procreation. Given the wide variations in capacity and ability among our members, we are the most individually unique of any animal. All of this is a way of elaborating that humans are social animals who survive best through cooperative effort.

Given our physical and psychological needs for others, humans band together. Groups of humans, if they are to be more than transitory meetings, maintain themselves through rules of order, rituals, cultural commonalities, shared language, and other devices of social structure. These structures are neither fixed nor taken for granted by everyone concerned. People fight over the establishment of these regulatory principles; rules exist in both the ideal and the real sense. Sex roles and the ideologies supporting them are one set of such principles common to all societies. There is no society without some differentiation of labor and other activities by sex, as well as a supporting common sense theory as to why the division should occur. Some of these divisions are so pervasive, so deeply-rooted into early human history that the role of nurture looms very large indeed.

Biology has played a role in the choice of distinctions made by various cultures around the world. The assignment of a child to one of two categories at birth on the basis of external genitalia seems an obvious way to sort out group members for future identification purposes. Similarly, in a culture that includes several racial strains, skin color would be another useful device for locating someone in a meaningful social space.

The special characteristics attached to each sex has added other bases for distinctions. For example, size has often been associated with power or strength in many societies. Far back in history this may have helped the males, who were more than likely the larger members of a population, receive higher status. Size would be one of the characteristics used in determining a preference system of males for reproductive purposes. Consequently, over generations the males would become even larger—"proof" that they were naturally superior with regard to strength. (Large males are not universally preferred, as shall be observed later in this chapter.)

Another example is the role of the menses. One cannot help but wonder what beliefs about the sexes there would be if men also had bloody emissions of several days duration instead of colorless nocturnal emissions. Or what if the human female's menses, like that of other primates, were sparse and hardly visible? The fact of monthly bleedings has been the basis for rituals in many cultures that resulted in women's being temporarily excluded from daily affairs, feared, becoming objects of disgust, and so on. The menses is typically a sign of defilement, though presumably a culture could have made it a symbol of female uniqueness or power. Reproduction and lactation are similar biological circumstances that have provided the basis for special definitions and responses to women.

So important are these gender distinctions in our society today that they are an important criterion for determining what a person really "is." No one can belong to a bisexual or hermaphroditic category. We "rehabilitate" children born with hermaphroditic characteristics and force them to take one or the other sex. It does not occur to us that there could be a third category. Transsexuals, those who actually change their sex, receive less public approbation than the transvestites, those who only take the garb and social display of the opposite sex. Homosexuals confuse and disturb many people because the "natural" form of intimate and sexual attraction is supposed to cross sex lines—to bring the complementary parts of humanity together. Even in athletics, sports figures are examined to establish proof that they are what they claim to be.

Biology provides many givens for a culture to explain, react to, and modify. It is easy to understand why categories of distinctions by gender have pervaded all cultures. But why has this resulted in universal systems of sexism? Apart from the fact that males are usually held to be superior and more powerful, are there any other prevalent gender-based distinctions across cultures?

Prehistory Rewritten

As we separate the species today, humans have been on earth for about twenty million years. The first upright, large-brained human, *homo erectus,* emerged about a half million years ago, while modern *Cro-Magnon* is perhaps fifty thousand years old. During these years, not only our physiques evolved, our social and emotional repertoires were patterned as well. Until a few thousand years ago, the species typically existed in small tribes of fifty or so. Agricultural and industrial civilizations represent the remaining one percent of history.

We know too that the history of earliest man was influenced by major changes in the earth's climate. At first there were lush forests and an ample food supply. During the Pleistocene period, a drought caused forests to shrink considerably in size. When we look at human fossils in the middle Pleistocene period (about 14 million years ago), we find the first evidence of cooperative hunting bands. Tiger (1970) has argued that these climactic changes with their accompanying consequences upon social organization form the basis for present-day sex differences.

Specialization in hunting widened the gap in behavior between the sexes and set up genetic packages that fostered the differences even further:

> Two consequences would follow the fact that females would nor-
> mally be pregnant or nursing their infants virtually all the time.
> (1) Most adult females would be unable to participate in the hunt.
> (2) Any who did take part would be at least marginally more prone
> than their sisters to loss of offspring, miscarriage, and early death
> by accident. . . . A female hunter would be less fleet, generally
> less strong, possibly more prone to changes in emotional *tonus* as
> a consequence of the estrus cycle. . . . Also, they could interfere
> with the co-operative nature of the group by stimulating competi-
> tion for sexual access (Tiger 1970, pp. 58-9).

In time, the type of body favorable to hunting—the tall, lithe, muscular
male—would have the greatest survival opportunity and would also become
valued for mating purposes. Similarly, the wide-hipped female would
produce more offspring, also wide-hipped, than her slender sister.

Morris (1971) has added another dimension to this explanation. He
claims that many sex differences have evolved for purposes of sexual signalling and arousal. Some parts of our bodies are "genital-echoes," so that
the fleshy pink lips of humans supposedly mock the female labia; similarly,
the large female breasts mock the buttocks. Female shoulders and knees
are soft-looking and hence mimic the buttocks in a more subtle way. Similarly, human males have large, exposed penises to serve sexual signalling.
Morris has an intriguing explanation for the need to mimic buttocks. Since
humans changed the rear-mounting copulation to a face-to-face one, frontal
signals were useful as arousers. All of these changes were to encourage the
male-female pair bond, to make it more rewarding by making sex sexier.

In an elaboration of the view, Tiger and Fox (1972) argue that we
are still "man the hunter, incarcerated, domesticated, polluted, crowded,
and bemused." They argue that the recent modern civilizations have done
nothing to the basic wiring of the human animal. Like any animal, humans
have wired into themselves a *biogrammar,* a repertoire of signals (postures,
gestures, movements) to communicate what the animals feel and what they
plan to do. We behave in regular and predictable ways, regardless of our
cultural backgrounds, because we share a common evolutionary history.
This history, they claim, is a hunting history. We are wired for the desires,
excitements, emotions, fears, and social relationships that were needed to
survive the hunting way of life.

The social essence of this biogrammar is as follows: Humans are
political creatures (unlike other social animals) and politics in its essence
concerns breeding, for breeding determines who will share the scarce resources in the future. Reproduction in humans is more than an act to
perpetuate the species; it is also a sign of status for the male.

> Politics is about genetics, not sex per se. The more powerful
> animal gets a better chance to perpetuate himself genetically than
> simply a better chance to indulge in sybaritic excesses . . . A dom-
> inant male moves more freely, eats better, gets more attention, lives
> longer is healthier and less anxious, and generally has a better time
> than a lowly and peripheral animal.
>
> . . . . While all males get a chance to copulate, only the more
> dominant get a chance to breed. This is the point around which the
> social system evolves: Who does the breeding? (Tiger and Fox
> 1972, p. 28).

Where are the females in all this? Fated by their reproductive organs, it
would appear, to be instruments at the hands of the men.

Tiger and Fox suggest that the females form much of the reason for
cohesiveness in the society. Males who do not make it in the status system
are outcast, while females are bonded to one another through their roles
as mothers and nurses. Furthermore, the mother-child bond is the bedrock
of social order. Adult male-female relationships can be transitory and the
social order will continue. This is not the case with mother-child. Tiger
and Fox have argued that kinship and marriage evolved so that the mother-
child bond could be protected from the capricious, fragile nature of adult
female-male ties.

Another consequence of the hunting biogrammar is that males prefer
all-male groups for certain tasks, notably politics, defense, discipline, and
control. Politics, with its posturing, threat, chicanery, bonhomie, and pom-
posity, appears so because it reflects the personal interactions of an all-
male activity. Similar patterns can be found in executive washrooms, locker
rooms, in womanless bars. If the men are off alone, then the women have
each other, the children, and other men, such as the elderly.

Tiger and Fox do not say much about the possibility of female bonds.
Like any proper member of Western society, their theory is weighted toward interest in male behavior.

This theoretical perspective results from a synthesis of both primate
and archeological research. The preceding summary fails to indicate the
detail of the arguments, and the wealth of data. Many ideas seem very
reasonable, as though one's own hunches or common sense had somehow
been sanctified by scientific imprimatur. Here is precisely where these
ideas have come under attack, by feminists who claim that theories such
as these are merely dressed-up political tracts on behalf of male supremacy.
Any social science theory can be interpreted as having a political meaning,
and it is for the reader to judge the implications of this and other ideas presented in this volume. Most important here is that many people, including

competent social scientists, subscribe to this interpretation of early history, at least in part. It permeates our culture from romantic tales such as Jack London's *Before Adam* (New York: Ace Books, 1906) to Flintstone cartoons and prehistoric monster movies.

In recent years detractors have begun to document problems with what could be called the "hairy-chested" view of early humankind. One theory, popularized by Morgan (1972), disputes the importance of both man's hunting activities and sexual arousal needs in the development of physical differences. She attacks the model on many grounds for it leaves many questions unanswered. For example, there are no human fossils yet found from the period of the Pliocene drought. Where were our human ancestors at that time? If we became bipedal to run fast for hunting, does it follow that four legs are faster than two? Why did only one ape species develop hunting weapons, given that other apes fight well enough to obtain food without them? If man became naked because hunters ran better without hair, then why are "stay-at-home" females not hairier than males? If sexual signalling devices were needed to make pair-bonds more cohesive, then why is it that many species of animals are much more monogamous than man and lack these sexual appeals. Doesn't the increased sexiness of one female add to a male's interest in other females? Why do men have fleshy red lips? And so on.

Morgan elaborates the *aquatic theory* of human evolution, which argues that we took to the water during the long drought. Where else was there to go when the trees no longer offered protection from larger predator carnivores? The water provided ample sustenance, and encouraged humans to develop characteristics of aquatic mammals. Thus our fur disappeared; what hair remained grew in the pattern found on swimming mammals, not primates. We developed a fat layer not found in our ape relatives. Hair remained on our heads for infants to cling to. Breasts enlarged similar to other aquatic mammals who can feed while floating on their back. The theory elaborates many other distinctions between man and other apes, such as facial expressions, tear ducts, noses, and so on. The female's vagina withdrew further into her body to protect it from water and sand; in fact a protective covering, the hymen, was added. Similarly, fleshy buttocks added protection for setting on rocks and barnacles. Sexual attraction, according to Morgan, had nothing to do with it. As for the male penis, it grew large for the simple reason that it could no longer reach its goal. Even then, man found it necessary to approach from the front because the pitch of the vagina made rear approaches difficult.

As for social structure, Morgan argues, the "Tarzanists," as she calls them, conveniently overlook studies of primates that do not fit their model.

With regard to hominids, they ignore the existence of another early man who was apparently more versatile than *homo erectus,* the hunter. Furthermore, these theorists ignore that man is omniverous, not carnivorous. Perhaps the men did go off to hunt, but they were equally dependent upon the women for vegetation. Men could not have enslaved women by withholding food.

Morgan suggests that food, not children, tied women to the home. We know that in existing remnants of primitive tribes the men do not spend much time in hunts. Rather, once a supply is stored, they spend their time dancing, gossiping, and making decorative objects. Women have been tied to food of the soil, thus spending hours daily at gathering, planting, cultivation. The farmer's work, even today, is never done.

Morgan's attack is most provocative in her explanation as to why humans are physically unlike other apes. Yet her argument fails with the others on similar grounds. One is that in explaining physical sex differences, both sides ignore the role of hormones. Male baldness is related to testosterone, just as female fatty breasts are an effect of estrogen. Women high on testosterone also bald just as men who are given estrogens form breasts.

Both theories are weak with regard to evidence. Morgan and others have noted the deficiencies in the hairy-chested theory, yet her ideas are similarly lacking in evidence. The aquatic hominid has yet to be discovered, and our knowledge of all the early hominids is fragmentary. There is so little evidence that we do not even know, as Tiger and Fox presume, whether there were physical size differences between males and females. (We often lack bone fragments to even identify the sex of fossil humans.)

Another problem with both explanations is their overconcern with physical features and social order to the neglect of culture. In neither viewpoint do we sense that the men and women talked, drew, danced, joked, loved, and so on. Yet information is available, if not on earliest man, at least on the earliest civilizations.

Evolutionary anthropologists once proposed the theory that matrilineal social organizations formed the primary human's social organization. Bachofen, the thesis' original proponent, argued that the study of ancient authors, myths, surviving customs, place names, and language all point to form a pattern that points to the existence of matriarchy prior to patriarchy. Considering language, the oldest words in the languages of Indo-European peoples are those that relate to what was woman's work: spinning and sewing, agricultural terms, food preparation, and so forth. Women's names are usually associated with the history of the founding of cities. Is it not possible that women in actuality planned and built such cities? The earliest form of ancient myths credit women with the inventions and discoveries. Similarly, the first religions deified women, not men, as early man's cave paintings illustrate.

Engels (1972) reiterated this thesis in his treatise on *The Origins of the Family, Private Property, and the States.* He argued that women reigned in primitive times because they dominated the household. Descent was through the female line, so a father's children did not receive his property. Engels suggests that somehow maternal law was overthrown. Early marriages, such as those found in communal living groups, were easily dissolved by either party and the child belonged to the mother. With the advent of private property and wealth, the primacy of the male overthrew the mother's right to her children. Engels refers to those Greek civilizations where it was explicitly stated that the exclusive aim of monogamous marriage was to make the man supreme in the family and to propagate children of his own. Monogamy ensured that the children were indeed of his own seed.

Thus marriage has moved from a matter of sex-love, a natural bonding, to an unnatural one of economics:

> Monogamous marriage comes on the scene as the subjugation of one sex by another; it announces a struggle between the sexes unknown through the whole previous prehistoric period . . . The first class opposition that appears in history coincides with the development of the antagonism between man and women in monogamous marriage, and the first class oppression that coincides with that of the female sex by the male. Monogamous marriage was a great historical step forward; nevertheless, together with slavery and private wealth, it opens the period that has lasted until today in which every step forward is also relatively a step backward, in which prosperity and development for some is won through the misery and frustration of others (Engels 1972, p. 128).

A careful reading of Engels shows that he does not condemn marriage or monogamy in toto. Rather, he disapproves of the system of monogamy as it actually occurs, a system of controls over the woman, though not the man. As a result, there is an inherent contradiction in the family, where the appearance of equality is subverted by the fact of female subjugation. The first condition for the liberation of the wife would be to "bring the whole female sex back into public industry, and that this in turn demands the abolition of the monogamous family *as the economic unity of society*" (Engels 1972, p. 138, emphasis added).

MATRI-WHAT? A NOTE ON TERMINOLOGY

Anthropologists have a technical vocabulary to assist in the description of a society's kinship relations. Sometimes journalists and nonprofessional readers misinterpret these studies because they fail to understand the meanings of words prefixed by patri- and matri-. Here is a key.

Residence of a family is identified as patrilocal (a couple resides with the husband's family or community), matrilocal (with the wife's kin) or neolocal (without relevance to kin), as in America. Residence is not necessarily a basis for predicting woman's position in a society.

Descent refers to principles of family identification and authority. In patrilineal families, children descend from the father's line. In matrilineal families, the mother's line reigns, though often authority is vested in male relatives. Matrilineal systems do not mean that women are equal to or more powerful than men. In bilateral systems, lineage is traced to both families, as in America.

Authority and dominance within the family unit can be patriarchal, matriarchal, or shared. Legally, American families are patriarchal, though in terms of everyday decision-making, they are not necessarily so.

"Matriarchy" and "patriarchy" are also used to describe the general locus of power by sex in a society. American society is described as patriarchal because most positions of authority are held by men. This does not mean that power in all types of relationships is held by men, nor does it exclude the possibility that residence and descent can be located in the female line.

How valid are these "Great Mother" theories of society? In the century since Bachofen presented his thesis, considerable debate has resulted. Many contemporary anthropologists do not consider the evidence in support of these theories to be very strong. They point out that woman has always had the "natural" subjugation brought on by childbearing and child rearing, while the men have always been foremost in the economic, political, and intellectual life of society. Reed (1970) criticizes this view as being presumptive. How can we explain matrilineal descent systems if the woman has not at some time held a special meaning for a group? Can we ignore the documented evidence of woman's extensive contributions to early science, medicine, agriculture, and religion?[1]

As one looks at this controversy, it seems that the question being debated might not be so important as it seems. In recent history, men have

1. Two source books for research on matriarchal societies are Diner (1965) and Davis (1972). Diner discusses the various theories in detail, as well as provides case studies of Amazon and female-headed societies. The Davis book has become popular among feminists, which is unfortunate because she uncritically accepts her hundreds of sources at face value. Nonetheless, her work is useful as a guide to literature on the topic.

reigned supreme around the world. What the researchers of the past have found that cannot be disputed is that women were not just dull, passive, primitive homemakers. We even know now that Amazon (all-female) societies existed in Africa and South America. Numerous matriarchal tribes prevailed in many parts of the world. Few Americans are aware that many North American Indians fit this pattern, with the consequence that there were female chiefs, priestesses, magical persons, as well as numerous restrictions on men's activities. In many matriarchal societies men held the political titles, though the women actually controlled the economy, family, and other tribal activities.

Given the variety and scope of the data, we can not presume that men have always been the leaders, prime movers, and innovators in society, as they appear to have in recent Western (and much of Eastern) history.

On the other hand, there is not much support for the notion that matriarchal societies always preceded patriarchal ones, and that matriarchal societies are more primitive. In his survey of 250 societies, Murdock found that matriarchy occurs at all levels of societal complexity. The forms of social organization, indeed, appear to show a striking lack of correlation with levels or types of technology, economy, property rights, class structure, or political organization (1948, p. 187). In other words, woman has an important history of contributions in many types of societies. That her history has been lost does not mean she has not been powerful. Today in some societies, both primitive and complex, women are not domesticated servants of men, nor do the men resemble the hairy-chested hunter of Western mythology.

History Rewritten

If our ideas concerning our origins are based on creative conjecture and hodgepodge data, then what can we learn from the anthropologist's code of information on recent and contemporary human societies? Here one can ask, are there nearly-universal patterns of sex-role patternings across societies? For example, if only men hunt, then one must consider seriously that there is a specific biogrammar for the sexes with regard to this activity.

Although anthropology has much information relevant here, it is not easily retrievable, for few studies are available that collect and organize the material. Until recently much anthropology concerned the study of one or two societies, and the problem of comparing societies from many sources is a relatively recent interest. Mead's (1935) classic study shocked many because she detailed how the expectations concerning what is male or female could take very different forms, depending upon the culture being studies. The mountain Arapesh tribe women and men both were gentle and unaggressive in their actions. The cannabalistic Mundugumor women disliked childbearing and children, and were as fierce and angry in their personalities as the men. The head-hunting Tchambuli men were given to adornment, artistic interests, and gossip while the women briskly went about their child rearing, fishing, and marketing in an efficient manner. Consequently, the traits known as masculine in one culture may be considered feminine in another, and perhaps considered inappropriate to either sex in a third.

Yet Mead's sample consisted of three fairly primitive societies, hardly a convincing base in light of the 2,000 societies known to anthropologists. Given that anthropology has no immediate proofs or disproofs of universal sex differences, let us examine briefly some commonplace attitudes or claims in this area.

"Women are weaker than men because they are smaller." This is erroneous for relatively simple reasons. First, there is a sizeable overlap in weight and height of the sexes, so that while the average for women may be lower, a large proportion of them are equal to many men, if not larger. Cross-culturally, recent evidence suggests that males are larger because they are fed better. During the Biafran famine of 1970, most cases of malnutrition were girls, who were less favored by the Nigerian society (Oakley 1972). Also, there are societies where the sexes have similar physical appearances, such as Bali, possibly because they do similar labor. Finally, this statement presumes that strength matters very much in assigning roles, whereas human's capacity as a tool-maker is what has discredited the "survival of the most powerful" as a force in their evolution.[2]

"Childbearing is dangerous; it weakens the women and inhibits them from arduous tasks." When women died young at childbirth, as was the case in Colonial America, it more likely resulted from poor nutrition and the effects of exhaustive physical labor. Kennedy's (1972) study of mortality in Ireland over a century found that the female death rate was related closely to her position in society. With recent public health and electrification (hence, some domestic labor-saving devices), female mortality

---

2. Another variable often overlooked is the role of genetic preferences in mating. Many of the seemingly natural sex-differences we see around us are the result of cultural pressures that last through generations. Individuals who meet the culture's standards for their sex are more likely to mate and perpetuate those physical characteristics. In some societies, such as Burma, this has meant the perpetuation of preferences that de-emphasized the physical differences between the sexes. In Western countries, the preferable female has been the small one, the preferable male, the large one.

dropped. Maternal mortality is related to age at parturition, and is thus higher in societies where women marry young. In numerous societies, women do hard physical labor throughout their pregnancies, but American beliefs are to the contrary. Housework in America is a demanding job, yet few pregnant women have been denied *that* opportunity, yet they have been excluded from paid responsible non-physical jobs.

"Given that we are mammals with very dependent infants, children need mothers." Some societies would find this most curious. Bororo or Arunta women would be amused, for they recognize that breast milk can come from many women, not just the mother. Many famous American men were wet-nursed by hired help, often of a different race, yet did not suffer noticeably. Similarly, there are societies where child rearing is not attached solely to the mother, as occurs in modern industrialized societies. The father, the mother's brother, a group of unrelated adults, or some representative of the state may bear responsibility. Mother and child may provide the first social bond for a society, but the bond need not be the only one, nor long-lived, if history is any proof.

"Women are more suited to the domestic needs of society." Some would argue that this is true because women must stay at home with children, but we have already discredited that argument. In fact, women jealously guard the home in some of those very matriarchal societies where they are not expected to be full-time mothers. Why? Often because the housework is so valued that women wouldn't permit men to do the "important" work. Thus the fact that women do housework in so many societies has two explanations. One is that they have no other role; the other is that they prefer it so. Of course, not all societies find women in domesticity. Nonetheless, one must face the fact that women are almost always the food-preparers and provide much of the clothing (except in those few societies where women were more powerful than men). Men perform these tasks more as a special circumstance than on a regular daily basis.[3]

"Men, being more active and exploratory, form the economic life of society." Part of the issue here is what one means by "economic." In America forty-two million women are "irrelevant" to economists because they provide unpaid labor as housewives and volunteers. In less affluent societies women bear additional burdens, a common task being food

---

3. Feeding patterns also exist in other animals in ways that suggest their contribution to adult bonding and intimacy. In many bird species, partner feeding is the prerogative of the male; in many insects, feeding between equals is a basic source of cohesion. In some mammals, the request for food is a sign of appeasement, again a contributor to social cohesion. Seen in this light, woman's contribution as a food-preparer and presenter is not a trivial one.

production. For example, Europeans who tried to colonize Africa ignored that women were often the agricultural experts and instead taught the men who previously had worked at other tasks. Agricultural reform in Africa has often meant loss of women's rights to land and work (Leavitt 1971). In industrialized societies women have formed an increasingly larger proportion of the paid labor force. Even in highly patriarchal societies—such as Muslim areas of Africa—women are expected to be traders even though the job often requires leaving home for some time (Oakley 1972). Thus one can say that "generally men meet the economic needs of a society" only by subscribing to a very narrow model of economics. Women make significant contributions to the production and distribution of goods and services though possibly without monetary benefits.

"Being more aggressive, males must handle military and political issues." This argument too is deceptive. It is true in that in recent history, men have dominated the formal positions of power and managed warfare. Women have been relegated to the sphere of informal influence and persuasion. Even then only women connected to the leaders, usually by kinship or marriage, have had this opportunity. Women in politics in modern societies form the vast network of those who work to elect men. Women have participated and died in recent wars. They served as guerillas and infantry persons, *not* as officers. Antiquity may have had its Amazon armies, but for the most part warfare is indeed a man's gaming arena— except when it comes to the casualties. However, not *all* men participate in war or politics. This is often reserved for certain groups of men.

"Given sexual physiology, males are the aggressors in sex." This idea is wrong for mammals as a class. When female rodents, carnivores, ungulates, or primates are having a receptive period, they may actively seek out a male and stimulate him physically to increase his interest. In many human societies, there are beliefs that only men should take the initiative in seeking and arranging a sexual affair. However, the behavior within these societies often violates expectations. There are some societies where the women is expected to initiate an affair and does so (Ford and Beach 1951). This attitude is likely a common one among Americans, but the cross-cultural evidence all points to its erroneous nature. As with many beliefs about men and women, it appears to represent wishful thinking more than reality.

Looking at historical humanity, there is yet less evidence for theories of man-the-hairy-chested-hunter and women-mother-sex-goddess. Variability in sex differences across cultures is so extensive that the activities assigned to men and women in one culture may be reversed in another. Even gross physical differences as we see them in America do not hold elsewhere. If women are the primary food-preparers in most cases, this is one small activity among hundreds performed in a society. More profound in terms of its consequences to humanity is the male predominance of formal politics and military life. Even here we must realize that this seems true only of the more complex, recent societies. In many small cultures women have ruled; no one fought wars—men or women. The aggressive male is not a universal type.

Western Culture Rewritten

The claims discussed in the preceding system would seem reasonable to persons knowledgeable only of American or European society. The tendency to generalize to humans in general is one expression of *ethnocentric* or culture-bound beliefs. It is difficult to imagine a society where a man takes care of his sister's children, where child care and domestic work carry high prestige, where women bear arms in battle, where men wait for women's sexual advances, or where men and women spend their days sharing all tasks together. Yet there have been and are humans for whom these practices are both preferred and practiced. We balk at seeing these other forms of social organization as normal, natural, or even real, because our own ways are so familiar. Furthermore, our society is among the largest and most powerful, which encourages us to believe that we have indeed found Nirvana and the superior way of behaving.

No wonder that so many were surprised by the apparently capricious appearance of a woman's rights movement in the sixties. After all, aren't modern Western women among the most fortunate in the world? Haven't they labor-saving devices, the longest life span, the smallest families? People will admit to certain inequalities between the sexes (e.g., unequal wages) yet conclude that these are soluble and not serious. Women *will* get their rights for Western history is the history of freedom, isn't it? Just a smattering of historical sophistication argues otherwise.

Western society is rooted in the earlier civilizations of the Greeks, Romans, Jews, and Scandanavian-Germans. The early forms of these civilizations suggest periods of feminine influence and even rule. For example, in the early versions of Greek myths, goddesses are significantly more active, creative, and life-giving than gods. As men increased their power in Greek society the myths underplayed the previous feminine strengths. Sullerot (1972) has identified the common elements of patriarchy realized in the late stages of Greek, Roman, and Judaic culture:

1. The wife was considered a breeding machine.
2. The wife was the husband's property. She was "purchased" and could

be killed by the husband if she committed adultery.
3. Women were confined indoors and given domestic tasks.
4. Women could neither own nor dispose of property.
5. Women had no civic role.

As can be deduced, property was a basic organizational focus of these societies.

In the rural economies of early Britain, France, Scandanavia, and Germany, women were less restricted. They were raised with boys, enjoyed property rights, and participated in religious and political roles. Their work was often segregated from the men's, but it was respected and remunerated.

Christianity became a unifying force for these disparate cultures and some (e.g., Figes 1970) have argued that Christian ideology is the root of contemporary sexism in Western society. True, the religion made god a man—and a man god—but it did not so clearly relegate women to a minor role, as the history of Mary-worship testifies. The structural patterns of patriarchy already existed in the more urban cultures; so as the northern rural cultures urbanized, the patriarchal practices supplanted earlier egalitarian ones. Christian ideology was so rich that later religious persons could select and emphasize those ideas most compatible with patriarchy. Thus the role of women is altered by economic development. For example, agricultural wages of men and women in Europe changed as follows (Sullerot 1972, p. 35):

> 12th century—female earned 80% of male wage
> 14th century—female earned 65% of male wage
> 15th century—female earned 50% of male wage
> 16th century—female earned 40% of male wage

The sixteenth century was a period of humanism and affluence and also one of feminist fervor in several countries. This increasing gap between female-male wages can be documented in other eras. It is true of the United States at present, in spite of recent wage equalization legislation.

The daily lives of men and women were more similar until two centuries ago. They might work at different tasks, but they would work close together, if not at home. Both worked whether peasants, trade-persons, or aristocrats. Social class distinctions made a greater difference with regard to rights and amenities than sex. Today class still matters, though the class system is more fluid, but sex (or race) is more relevant to life chances. Five centuries ago a poor man and woman shared equal wretchedness. Today a non-white or a woman of any class suffers the consequences of inferior status.

Women in America enjoyed fewer rights compared to their European cousins of any time, partly because the industrious, hence patriarchal persons predominated. British common law with its *pater famalias* set standards for our legal system. Few women participated formally in religious or political offices. American women at least in the eastern and southern colonies were domestic women. The adventurous rural settlers numbered many independent, courageous women who worked the same tasks as men, defended their homes and provided leadership. As the West became more "civilized," however, they considered gloves more proper than calloused hands.

The urbanism and industrialism of the late nineteenth century introduced contradictory forces on woman's role. The daughters and wives of migrants were forced to work for family survival, which encouraged the attitude among middle-class Americans that respectable women did not work. Education did become a proper activity for the more fortunate women, while only a few occupations were acceptable, namely teaching, nursing, and with the advent of the typewriter, clerical work. Jobs were temporary expedients until marriage, motherhood, and domesticity. The poor woman's plight was doubly-aggravated because after work she was still responsible for such duties as soap making, food growing, sewing of all clothes, cleaning, etc. So strong was the belief in woman's domesticity that it was poor work conditions, not the burdens of home life that spurred many feminist activities.

And what of the men? They were driven out of the home, forced to leave the house and family, hence to lose the responsibilities and benefits of kin relations. The company and boss became so powerful that a man was to define himself through job success, not leisure satisfaction, paternal skills, or arts.

Men run government and military as they always did, but they also control the major corporations, the universities, the media, the formal arts. In the sexual arena, until very recently, women were passive objects of men's whims. Today women are still objects, though they are allowed to have some pleasure while they are being used. The American male is presumably a political animal, even in the bedroom, but he has been separated from the youth and women in the process.

As this is being written, there appear daily articles and books relating to sex roles and political activity. We know that the country is facing potential changes on many levels. A strong sentiment against military power is expressed in all segments of society. The education level is very high. Leisure time is increasing. Ecological concerns are affecting industries, jobs, urban planning. Social science can report only on where we've been.

Let us see what the life situations for today's women and men in America are.

SUGGESTED PROJECTS

1. Are you curious as to what contemporary sex roles are like in another society? A good place to start for references, if not conclusions, is Georgene Seward and Robert Williamson's *Sex Roles in a Changing Society* (New York: Random House, 1970). Also, many United Nations bulletins and publications will have material on this topic, so check with your reference librarian here.

2. Ethnography, the description of culture, is a prominent technique in social science. One excellent collection of ethnographies relevant to sex roles is Denise Paulme's *Women of Tropical Africa* (Berkely, Calif.: University of California Press, 1971). If you would like to try your hand at ethnography, first see what you can learn about "field research." One particularly useful book here is James Spradley and David McCurdy's *The Cultural Experience* (Boston: Little, Brown & Co., 1971), a guideline that includes studies written by undergraduate students.

3. In "A Conflict Theory of Sexual Stratification," (*Social Problems* 19 [1971]:3-21), Randall Collins argues that the human sexual drives and male physical dominance are at the base of sexist stratification. I (the author) criticized his view in a rejoinder (*Social Problems* 20[1973]: 392-395). Which position do you prefer? Scientists disagree as a matter of course. Why then did this debate warrant a written response?

REFERENCES

Davis, Elzabeth Gould. *The First Sex*. Baltimore: Panguin Book, Inc., 1972.

Diner, Helen (Berta Eckstein-Diner). *Mothers and Amazons*. Translated by John Philip Lundin. New York: Julian Press, 1965.

Figes, Eva. *Patriarchal Attitudes*. New York: Stein and Day, 1970.

Ford, Clellan S., and Beach, Frank A. *Patterns of Sexual Behavior*. New York: Harper & Row, Publishers, 1951.

Gough, Kathleen. "An Anthropologist Looks at Engels." In *Woman in a Man-Made World*, by Nona Glazer-Malbin and Helen Youngeson Waehrer. New York: Random House, 1972.

Kennedy, Robert E., Jr. "The Social Status of the Sexes and Their Relative Mortality in Ireland." In *Readings in Population*, by William Petersen. New York: Macmillan Publishing Co., Inc., 1972.

Leavitt, Ruby R. "Women in Other Cultures." In *Women in Sexist Society*, by Vivian Gornick and Barbara K. Moran. New York: Basic Books, 1971.

Mead, Margaret. *Sex and Temperament in Three Societies*. New York: William Morrow and Co., 1935.

Morgan, Elaine. *The Descent of Woman*. New York: Stein and Day, 1972.

Morris, Desmond. *Intimate Behavior*. New York: Random House, 1971.

Murdock, George. *Social Structure*. New York: Macmillan Publishing Co., Inc., 1949.

Oakley, Ann. *Sex, Gender, and Society*. New York: Harper and Row, Publishers, 1972.

Reed, Evelyn. *An Answer to "The Naked Ape" and Other Books on Aggression.* New York: Pathfinder, 1971.

———. *Problems of Women's Liberation: A Marxist Approach.* New York: Pathfinder, 1971.

Sullerot, Evelyne. *Women, Society, and Change.* New York: McGraw-Hill Book Co., 1971.

Tiger, Lionel. *Men in Groups.* New York: Random House, 1970.

Tiger, Lionel, and Fox, Robin. *The Imperial Animal.* New York: Holt, Rinehart and Winston, 1972.

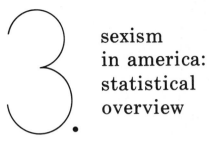

sexism in america: statistical overview

Strictly speaking, there are no such things as "sex roles," though the term is often referred to in social science. It concerns the complicated process in society whereby children separated by gender at birth become girl-boy, woman-man, feminine-masculine. It concerns the distribution of rewards and opportunities by gender, as well as the expectations placed upon each. It means to examine the differences between men and women as well as the consequences of these differences for individuals. This is very different from what "sex role," strictly speaking, implies. A role is the pattern of behavior associated with a position (or status) in society. Statuses provide a basis for social identity. Gender (not sex) is one basis for identity. To speak of a "sex role" is to miss the complexity of how gender identity systems operate in real life.

Benoit-Smullyan (1944) has offered a conceptualization of social positions that is useful here. *Status* refers to relative position in a hierarchy. The most common status systems studied by sociologists are economic (wealth), political (power), and reputational (prestige). *Locus* refers to the social positions that arise from the function an individual's performance provides for a group (e.g., the sister in a family, the student in a school, the worker in a factory). *Situs* refers to an "aggregate of persons socially distinguished by any common characteristic except status and locus." Simple examples are race, age, geographical identities—and gender. These three concepts describe social structure. From the perspective of the individual, we can speak of related terms. *Personal status* refers to one's rank in a hierarchy, *role* to the position one plays in a social situation, and *identity* to the situs categories one bears. Figure 3.1 illustrates the interplay of these systems.

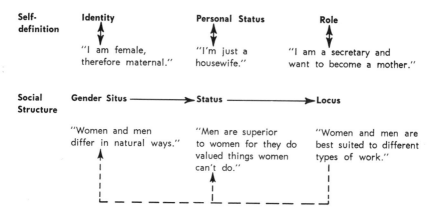

Figure 3-1. Gender, stratification, and self-definition.

Gender is a situs category that provides a basis for personal identity from birth. The culture supports beliefs and expectations that persons within one gender category will behave in a similar, predictable way. The criteria applied may be either real or imaginary, in the sense that they may or may not correspond to objective characteristics of the persons so distinguished. Thus, regardless of situation, women in our society are typically expected to be more passive than men, less analytical in their reasoning, more conccerned with sexual appeal, less physically agile, and so on.[1] This system of beliefs influences an individual woman's conception of femininity as it applies to herself and other women. However, in developing her conception of femininity, the woman will also take into account her other identity categories—her race, ethnicity, religion, age—all of which further delineate the meaning of "woman." Given these multiple bases for identity, it is difficult to argue that there would be one female "role" in a society as pluralistic as ours. This is one reason for arguing against the idea of sex roles per se.

The status system in our society is such that a male is usually considered to be superior in rank to a female. Also, gender is one determinant of the social roles an individual may be permitted to play. The most obvious example is the economy, where one finds most workers are in jobs predominated by one sex.

---

1. Many sociology books make the point that gender is an "ascribed" status; that is, a position filled by virtue of individual qualities. They contrast these statuses with "achieved" ones, those filled by individual accomplishment. Situses come under the ascribed category as these terms are defined. I prefer Benoit-Smullyan's conceptualization because it distinguishes between status and function.

The lines in figure 3.1 suggest a logical order that appears to underlie these relationships. The dotted lines remind us that the process has feedback; that is, it is self-reinforcing. Thus, if men are seen primarily in positions of high rank or in certain types of occupations, then this fact supports the notion of natural differences.

The process described here resembles what Merton has defined as the "self-fulfilling prophecy," which is

> . . . in the beginning, a *false* definition of the situation evoking a new behavior which makes the originally false conception come true. The specious validity of the self-fulfilling prophecy perpetuates a reign of error. For the prophet will cite the actual course of events as proof that he was right from the very beginning (Merton 1957, p. 423).

In chapter one, it was shown that the biological or "natural" sex differences are not very great, and in chapter two many popular ideas concerning the division of labor by sex were repudiated. Sexist ideologies nonetheless prevail.

This process occurs on several levels of social behavior. On the interpersonal level, or micro-order, it influences the way people define both themselves ("I am a man, therefore I should be domineering") and others around them ("She's behaving too aggressively"). As the famous sentence by W. I. Thomas (1928 p. 572) explains, "If men (women) define situations as real, they are real in their consequences."[2] When humans interact, they do so on their understandings of what is going on and what is to be done. The meanings attached to social positions, in this case gender, are one component of their view of social reality.

When one moves up to the level of informal groups, expectations concerning gender pattern themselves further. Knowledge of the sex composition of a group of people would be sufficient for placing good bets on a number of predictions. Consider: in mixed work groups, who would offer advice, remain silent, provide supportive statements, speak up first, be touched by others? How would you characterize the differences in interaction (e.g., cooperativeness, formality, warmth) of all-male in contrast with all-female groups? Of course, these predictions would not hold in specific cases because many other features of the situation would come into play as well, such as the group task, member personalities, and so on.

---

2. Thomas' dictum does not apply so well to women, except insofar as women view themselves as passive or subordinate and act accordingly. If a woman defines herself as strong or powerful, she comes into conflict with the reality of the sexist social order that denies her the opportunity to express these attitudes.

When we consider the overall social order, again we can expect and do find patterns that reflect the daily interactions of societal members. The participation of women and men in various activities will be reflected throughout data on the power structure, the leisure sphere, religious life, and every other institutional area. These distributions hint at the welcoming and supportive opportunities, as well as the closed or forbidding activities that individual women and men face.

In America today sexist processes have resulted in a society where segregation of individual activities by gender pervades virtually every institution—the family, leisure, work, politics, education, the arts, religion. Fair-minded persons can point to the division of labor and the exclusion of women (or men) from various activities as support for policies that perpetuate such practices. They are not being prejudiced in the sense that the facts permit them no other conclusion.

Merton uses examples from racial and ethnic prejudices to illustrate his argument, but the analogy to sex bias holds as well. In fact, prior to Merton's article, Hacker (1951) detailed the numerous ways in which women can be considered a *minority group,* which is defined as

> . . . any group of people who because of their physical and cultural characteristics, are singled out from others in the society in which they live for different and unequal treatment, and who therefore regard themselves as objects of collective discrimination.

According to Hacker, one can show this objectively, by pointing to the many instances of discrimination against women in our society. The definition also has a subjective element, that is, a woman's own recognition of her minority status. One could argue that until the recent feminist revival, few women held minority group status in the subjective sense either because they were blind to the treatment or persumed that they warranted it.

Looking closely at Hacker's definition, men could also be defined as a minority group. They are singled out as being inappropriate for child rearing and housekeeping. Today, some men sense indignation that being allowed to work full-time is as much a trap as is full-time housework for women. Something must be wrong with the definition of "minority group" if both men and women can be so categorized. Many social scientists would point out that minority group membership is transmitted by a rule of descent that affiliates succeeding generations and that the minority group members tend to marry within their group. Neither of these characteristics applies to women or men. Nonetheless, much that is written about minority groups, such as the effects of prejudice upon self-conception, would be applicable to women as well.

Hacker agrees further that the sex role structure in our society is analogous to a *caste system.* Berreman (1960) defines caste as "a hierarchy of endogamous divisions in which membership is ascribed at birth and unalterable." Women's condition is ascribed at birth, but the rules of endogamy do not apply. That is, women are not—for obvious reasons—prohibited from marrying out of their "caste" which consists of all other women. A more precise term to apply to women as an indication of their inferior status would be to call them a "subordinate class." Class divisions do not have rules concerning marriage, as minority group and caste divisions do.

Nonetheless, one can also identify *castelike characteristics* among women. Individuals in the low castes are considered to be inherently inferior, regardless of their behavior. Whether racially or religiously based, caste systems are very stable because they maintain themselves with little effort. The inferior caste member accepts her fate, which means she avoids taboo contacts and displays deference to high caste persons. Considerable economic interdependence binds the group with the benefits (economic, sexual, prestige) going to the superior group. As Berreman notes, "high caste persons gain, *by virtue of their status alone,* deference from others, constant reinforcement of a feeling of superiority, and a permanent scapegoat in the lower castes."

Hacker (1951) elaborated the many similarities between the status of blacks and women as table 3-1 outlines. The relation has historical roots, for the legal status of slaves was borrowed from that of women and children who were under *patria potestas* (subordinate to the male family head). That both minorities once acknowledged the commonality of their positions is evidenced by the cooperation between abolitionist and woman's suffrage groups in the decades prior to the Civil War. Furthermore, the historical movement from a pre-industrial, paternalistic society to technological capitalism and imperialism has affected the status of blacks and women in similar ways.

Of course, the analogy does not hold perfectly. Women can always use marriage as a vehicle for social status (though not freedom). Furthermore, compelling needs drive men and women towards one another; racial minorities cannot call upon the leverage of sexuality or reproduction in their struggles. Hacker argues too that women's privileges exceed that of blacks. This is a moot point because more than half of racial minorities are female, and they suffer doubly for this position. Also, to ask "Who is more

Table 3-1
Castelike Status of Women and Blacks

Blacks	Women

HIGH SOCIAL VISIBILITY

a. Skin color, other "racial" characteristics
b. Sometimes distinctive dress patterns

a. Secondary sex characteristics

b. Distinctive dress

ASCRIBED ATTRIBUTES

a. Inferior intelligence, smaller brain, less convoluted, scarcity of geniuses
b. Freer instinctual gratifications. More emotional, "primitive," and childlike. Imagined sexual prowess envied.
c. Common stereotype "inferior"

a. ditto

b. Irresponsible, inconsistent, emotionally unstable. Lack strong superego. Women as temptresses.
c. "Weaker"

RATIONALIZATIONS OF STATUS

a. Thought all right in his place
b. Myth of contented Negro

a. Women's place is in the home
b. Myth of contented woman— "feminine" woman is happy in subordinate role

ACCOMMODATING ATTITUDES

a. Supplicatory intonation of voice

b. Deferential manner
c. Concealment of real feelings
d. Outwit "white folks"
e. Careful study of points at which dominant group is susceptible to influence.
f. Fake appeals for directives; show of ignorance

a. Rising inflection, smiles, laughs, downward glances.
b. Flattering manner
c. "Feminine wiles"
d. Outwit "men folk"
e. ditto

f. Appearance of helplessness

DISCRIMINATIONS

a. Limitations of education— should fit "place" in society
b. Confined to traditional jobs— barred from supervisory positions
c. Deprived of political importance
d. Social and professional segregation
e. More vulnerable to criticism

a. ditto

b. ditto

c. ditto
d. ditto

e. e.g., conduct in bars

Source: Hacker (1951), p. 65.

opposed?" is to raise a political issue that cannot be settled simply by gathering a set of statistics.[3]

Politics permeates the study of sex roles, however, one tries to "stick to the facts," focus on "theories, not values," or "avoid rhetoric." As Shapiro (1971) has noted,

> The selection of concepts in the definition of a problem is a political process, for this selection determines what is to be changed, what is to be ignored, and in some cases, who the change agents and who the status quo defenders are to be.

Take a simple question, such as "Why do fewer women go to college?" This problem takes for granted that it is more valuable for women to go to college than other activities. It implies a change—to see that more women do go to college. It ignores that perhaps too many men are going, that men would find other activities more satisfying or more useful in their performance of adult roles. The answer to this question in broadest terms would point to the parents and teachers who dampen girls' motivations, as well as to the colleges themselves, whose admission policies are obstructionary. Thus these elements are posed as defenders against those who value college education for women. And the fight is on.

The American "Social Order"

Social scientists are no less without fears, opinions, and prejudices than anyone else in their society. As we shall see in the next chapter, American social science has not been immune from the sexist attitudes and actions of some of its members. Sometimes we take such comfort in the obvious that we overlook some obvious questions for examination. For example, attitudes about housewives are generally derogatory. They are "just housewives," and therefore not worthy of study. (The first in-depth exploration of housewivery was conducted by Lopata and appeared in 1971.) Yet there are fifty-two million "just housewives" in this society about whom we know almost nothing except what media and "common sense" tell us. Accordingly, we may accept erroneous everyday ideas as true and use them in our explanations or theories. For example, many sociological studies presume that the male subjects have a desire to succeed

---

3. Those in power have at their hands the "divide and conquer" strategy to keep minorities from working collectively. They force racial minorities, ethnic groups, and women to compete with each other for scarce resources and encourage conflict as to which group is "most deserving."

or win, when in fact there is little data to support such a presumption.[4] For these reasons, anyone interested in "sex roles" must begin by correcting the taken-for-granted ideas.

It is worthwhile to test some of your own presumptions. Considering only the United States in recent years, are the following statements true or false?

1. Men outnumber women until middle age, at which point stress diseases take their toll.
2. Suicide rates are much higher for women than for men.
3. About two percent of all families consist of a male head who is widowed or divorced.
4. Only about one percent of single parent families are headed by men.
5. Women are overrepresented in mental hospitals and chronic disease institutions.
6. Fewer girls graduate from high school than boys.
7. The typical male worker today has a white-collar job.
8. Half of all women workers are in clerical jobs.
9. Black women have a lower unemployment rate than black men.
10. A man with only eight years of education earns on the average more than a woman with college experience.

If you have a good grasp of what's generally true of women and men in America today, then you will have answered all but the last question "false." Let us look at the supporting evidence to get a sense of the present social order.

Figure 3-2 presents the population distribution according to sex. Typical of industrialized countries where the death rate has been reduced, the American population has many young people. This is because so many persons have survived to become parents. Partly too, the sizeable youth categories represent an increase in fertility during the fifties. This trend is no longer present. During the late sixties fertility showed a considerable drop for reasons such as contraceptive technology and new values concerning family life. Consequently, we can expect some increase in the median age of the population in the future.

With regard to sex, it is clear that there is a surplus of females in adulthood. By age sixty-five, there are only seventy-two males for every 100 females. Why should this be, given that males outnumber females at birth (around 105 to 100)? The causes of death provide one indication,

4. Data to support this presumption is available in studies of male college students— the very people we would expect to exhibit this attitude. But the majority of American men are not young men with "a bright future ahead."

as shown in table 3-2. At all ages male mortality is higher than female, partly due to greater biological susceptibility to physical disease or weakness. More apparent though is the role of accidents, which take toll of youth. For example, between ages 15 to 24, 65 percent of all male deaths are accidental, while only 40 percent of female deaths are. In later years, notably ages 45 to 64, heart disease strikes down the men. These data hint at the costs of being male in our society.

How do these people live? Two-thirds do live in intact nuclear families, as table 3-3 shows. Yet about 8 percent are in families with male heads,

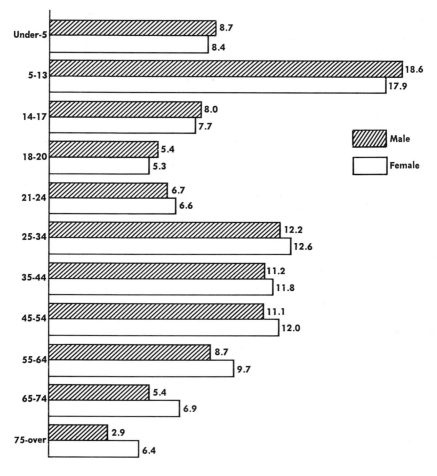

Figure 3-2. 1970 population (in millions).

Source: Department of Commerce, Bureau of the Census, *Current Population Reports.*

Table 3-2
Mortality from Leading Causes, by Age, United States, 1962

Cause of Death	Death Rates per 100,000	
	White Males	White Females
Age 1-4		
All causes	92.7	79.8
Accidents	31.3	22.7
Malignant neoplasms	11.2	9.2
Influenza and pneumonia	10.6	9.4
Congenital malformations	10.5	11.5
Age 5-14		
All causes	49.6	33.0
Accidents	23.4	9.9
Malignant neoplasms	7.7	6.4
Congenital malforations	3.4	3.1
Influenza and pneumonia	2.0	2.1
Age 15-24		
All causes	139.5	54.3
Accidents	90.2	21.0
Malignant neoplasms	10.4	6.6
Suicide	8.7	2.9
Homicide	3.9	1.7
Age 25-44		
All causes	250.5	141.5
Accidents	65.4	16.5
Diseases of heart	63.3	18.0
Malignant neoplasms	32.9	42.9
Suicide	19.8	8.5
Ages 65		
All causes	7,175.0	5,211.9
Diseases of heart	3,384.5	2,419.2
Malignant neoplasms	1,090.5	707.7
Vascular lesions of central nervous system	932.8	895.8
Influenza and pneumonia	248.0	174.9

Source: Riley et al. (1968, p. 196).

and 22 percent in families with female heads. The data discredit the thesis that black families are matriarchal, particularly given that many white families are female-headed. The solitary life is much more a female phenomenon, with twice as many women as men living alone or with non-relatives. This can be expected given the demographic imbalance in the population.

Table 3-3

Households, Families, and Individuals, 1970

Living Unit	Number		Percent
Primary families	62,875		
Nonwhite			
Husband-wife		3,627	6.0
Male head		813	.5
Female head		2,187	3.5
White			
Husband-wife		40,781	65.0
Male head		4,367	7.0
Female head		11,099	18.0
Unrelated individuals	11,092		
Male		4,709	32.0
Female		7,559	68.0

Source: Department of Commerce, Bureau of the Census, *Current Population Reports,* Series P-20, P-25.

Table 3-4

Institutional Population, 1960 (in thousands)

	Male	Female
Institutional population	1,118	769
By type of institution:		
Correctional institutions	330	16
Mental hospitals and residential		
treatment centers	336	294
Tuberculosis hospitals	46	19
Chronic disease hospitals*	25	17
Homes for the aged and dependent	188	282
Homes and schools for the mentally		
handicapped	95	80
Homes and schools for the physically		
handicapped	13	11
Homes for dependent and neglected children	41	32
Homes for unwed mothers	1	3
Training schools for juvenile delinquents	34	12
Detention homes	8	3
Diagnostic and reception centers	1	—

* Excludes TB and mental.

Source: Department of Commerce, Bureau of Census; U.S. Census of Population: 1950, Vol. IV, Part 2C and U.S. Census of Population: 1960, Vol. II, Part PC (2)-8A.

Not all people in our society live freely in households, some are institutionalized. The inmate populations presented in table 3-4 illustrate again some possible costs of sex roles in our society. Why do males outnumber females in prison institutions by over twenty to one? Similarly, why are boys the predominate sex in juvenile delinquent institutions and homes for dependent and neglected children? Why is this, given the common belief that boys are more valued by parents than girls? Only one institutional setting, the aged homes, have a predominance of women.

Statistics on school enrollment from the Census Bureau state that girls and boys alike attend school (and drop out) at about the same rate. More white males attend college, however, and many young women who do attend fail to graduate. At the professional school level, white men compose the great majority of the student body. Universal education to age sixteen appears well to have served girls, who not too long ago were excluded from public schools in America. Yet while higher education favors white males, even the majority of this group does not attend, let alone receive a college degree.

The work force data in table 3-5 reflect these educational facts. A full third of all women workers hold clerical jobs. The majority of men work not in offices, but in factories or out-of-doors, while very few women work in these settings. One-fourth of the men (mostly white) are in affluent positions as professionals or managers. Although many women are listed in the top "professional-technical" category, most are actually in such

Table 3-5
Employed Persons, by Major Occupation
Group and Sex, 1970

Occupation	Women	Men
	(29,667)	(48,960)
White-collar		
Professional/technical workers	4,928	6,842
Managers, officers, proprietors	1,321	6,968
Clerical workers	10,233	3,481
Sales workers	2,091	2,763
Blue-collar		
Crafts persons/forepersons	332	9,826
Operatives	4,303	9,605
Nonfarm laborers	136	3,589
Service workers	6,427	3,285
Farmworkers	525	2,601

Source: Department of Labor, Bureau of Labor Statistics.

poorly-paid positions as that of lab assistant. Many are teachers. For minority persons the opportunities are further limiting. White women are twice as likely to hold white-collar jobs than nonwhite, who instead must become service workers. Similarly, black men hold the poorer paying blue-collar jobs, and are very unlikely to have prestigious white collar positions.

Women are 40 percent of the current work force, but their incomes are considerably lower than men's. Many men's jobs though are so low-paying that women's work, however little the resulting income, may be necessary to meet middle class family needs. Consider these median house-hold incomes (1969 data):

Husband working, wife at home	$ 8,879
Husband and wife working	11,629
Female head of household	4,822
Unrelated male	4,134
Unrelated female	2,397

A woman supporting herself on her own, as well as those families where women head the household, live austere existences.

Although women may now have education equal to men, once in the labor force this experience appears to count little. The most surprising information on this count is presented in table 3-6, which shows median

Table 3-6

Median Income by
Educational Attainment, Sex, and Race (1966)

Educational Attainment	Women		Men	
	White	Nonwhite	White	Nonwhite
Less than 8 years	1,055	932	2,945	2,376
8 years	1,416	1,303	4,611	3,681
1 to 3 years high school	1,960	1,698	6,189	4,278
4 years high school	2,700	2,475	7,068	5,188
1 year college or more	3,519	3,964	9,023	5,928

Source: Department of Commerce, Bureau of the Census. Current Population Reports, P 60.

income by educational attainment, sex, and race. Men, regardless of race, earn twice as much as women of similar educational attainment. In fact, white and nonwhite men with only eight years of education earn *more* than women with some college experience. Comparable gaps occur in unemployment rates, so that of all groups the black woman has the greatest likelihood of being unemployed.

Earlier we saw that the modal household was the intact husband-wife nuclear family. Mythology would have it that the women in these cases are at home all day, particularly if there are children. This is not quite true. In fact, the proportion of mothers who work has increased steadily from 28 percent in 1940 to 42 percent today. In even the lowest participation group, that of white mothers with children under three years, almost one-fourth of all such women are bringing income into the family.

Most men and many women spend their adult lives as workers, and both sexes are very likely to spend part of that time married. In old age, particularly after age sixty-five, the employment period ends in our society. Older women are more likely to be widowed than older men. Because men are outnumbered by women and many men are married to women under sixty-five, widowed females constitute a major portion of the female aged population. Among older people over sixty-five, about seven out of every ten men (but fewer than four out of every ten women) are married. Men do not live as long as women either, so the world of old people is very much a woman's world.

Breaking the Cycle

The preceding section hints at the consequences of sexist (and racist) ideologies. White males receive more education, higher positions, and more remuneration than other groups in society. Men who fail are more likely to be institutionalized than women. Men die earlier and suffer more disability. Women who marry frequently face the extra burden of work in low-level occupations in addition to their household and child rearing tasks. If a marriage fails, the woman continues to bear these tasks, though with fewer resources. The joys of old age, such as they are, remain for women to share with one another.

These facts are time-specific, a slice in history, so it is incorrect to presume that they are a mirror of our own future lives. Twenty years ago, for instance, many fewer married women were in the labor force. Working women earned salaries more comparable to their male counterparts.[5] As for the future, we can observe recent events, some of which may imply long-range trends, others of which are brief social responses.

---

5. Students always question this statement. Labor statistics show that the gap between men's and women's salaries has increased in recent decades. Women are comparatively worse off now.

In other words, the self-fulfilling prophecy does not continue unabated in all social institutions. There is no inexorability about its direction. The resurgence of feminism in recent years represents one of various concurrent trends that can counteract, interrupt, and even reverse the old patterns.

Some notable trends are as follows:

1. *Changes in education.* An increasing proportion of women are going on to college, and we know that the liklihood that a woman will work relates to her educational level. Hence, we can expect the proportion of women in the labor force to continue to increase.

2. *Revised labor patterns.* There has been a steadily decreasing work week in many occupations, which means more leisure time for workers. Perhaps for men this will mean greater participation in family activities.

3. *Decreasing birth rate.* The number of children people expect to have and the actual rate of birth have been falling. This means a woman will have even fewer years of her life committed to childbearing, if she desires to do so full-time.

4. *Alternative family forms.* Sexual attitudes and beliefs about the family structure are such that variations from the double standard, monogamous marriage model are more visible. In some sectors of society cohabitation is preferred to marriage. Communes, affinity living units, group marriages, and marriage with infidelity are more apparent than a decade ago. Thus the role model of husband and wife is not the only acceptable male-female bonding structure.

5. *Feminist influences.* The various activities of the woman's movement have increased many women's subjective awareness of themselves as minority group members. Consequently, in daily interactions certain women purposefully react to this situation by violating cultural ideals of femininity. These brief interpersonal events can accumulate and reverberate to change all those involved.

6. *Legal changes.* Political activity by women has already produced laws that affect work, property rights, and such. The Equal Rights Amendment, if passed, requires the removal of descriminatory patterns toward either sex in all areas of life.

7. *Technological changes.* As biological research continues, various ways of controlling human propagation could be realized. These include the implantation of embryos from one woman to another, test-tube babies, one-sex reproduction, and so on. Similarly, medical research may make breakthroughs in preventive medicine for those stress diseases now inflicting men.

There are yet other trends you might think of as relevant here. It is difficult enough to gauge the impact of any one of these factors on sex roles in America, let alone grasp their combined influence. Also, it is easy to overlook the mass of structural patterns and processes that operate to perpetuate sex roles. Indeed, the remainder of this book in a sense is an explication of the counterplay of the various processes pushing away from and pulling toward the state of "sex roles" or as I prefer to state, gender identities, as they exist today.

SUGGESTED PROJECTS

1. The statistical overview emphasizes the basic institutions of work and household. How do American women and men behave in other areas, e.g., voting patterns, participation in voluntary organizations, expression of religious beliefs or sexual behavior? A good place to look for the answers to these questions is in the *Sociological Abstracts*.
2. What is the situation for women and men in your state with regard to work, household, income, mortality, and such? Find out by locating data in state government reports. First, though, make some predictions about the distributions, taking into account your state's age distribution, economy, urbanization, and ethnic or racial minorities.
3. There are many theories and studies concerning prejudice toward minority groups, e.g.,Theodore Adorno et al., *The Authoritarian Personality* (New York: W. W. Norton, 1969), Milton Rokeach on race prejudice, *The Open and Closed Mind* (New York: Basic Books, 1960). You will find these and others discussed in any textbook on minorities. Select one theory or set of studies and draw conclusions as to its applicability toward understanding prejudice toward women.

REFERENCES

Benoit-Smullyan, Emile. "Status, Status Types, and Status Interrelations." *American Sociological Review* 9(1944):151-61.

Berreman, Gerald D. "Caste in India and the United States." *American Journal of Sociology* 61(1960):120-27.

Hacker, Helen Mayer. "Women as a Minority Group." *Social Forces* 30(1951): 60-9.

Lopata, Helena Z. *Occupation: Housewife.* New York: Oxford Book Co., Inc., 1971.

Merton, Robert K. *Social Theory and Social Structure.* Rev. ed. New York: The Free Press, 1957.

Riley, Matilda White, et al. *Aging in Society.* New York: Russell Sage Foundation, 1968.

Shapiro, Michael J. "Social Control Ideologies and the Politics of Education," unpublished manuscript, 1971.

Thomas, W. I. *The Child in America.* New York: Alfred A. Knopf, Inc., 1928.

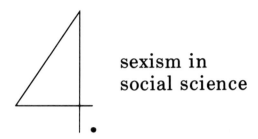

sexism in
social science

Presumably, we can now examine the sex differences that social science has established, the theories on their origins, and the meanings of the social patterns for individuals. Unfortunately, this cannot be attempted without precaution and warnings. To dive into the "facts of things" would be to assume that the facts are available and that they are meaningful in themselves. For the study of gender and sexism no such presumptions are possible.

In America, faith in science and scholarship as a basis for truth is strong. Humanistic forms of knowledge, such as literature and art, are considered by many people to be vague, "soft," and outside the realm of logic. An argument used here would be that one hundred persons could read a novel and each would describe its message differently. Even if a consensus formed as to the essential meaning of the artwork, some would say there would still be disagreement as to the validity of the point. For many persons an argument is proven through a scientific procedure, not through poetic imagery. Scientific knowledge must meet certain criteria, e.g., it should be public and the methods of obtaining the knowledge should be reproduceable. In this manner, presumably, a finding can be verified more than once and theories can be debated in an open, free exchange of scholars. In many cases of data collection, modern statistical techniques guide scholars in deciding upon the meaning of data, such as whether a sex difference is "real" and not due to chance elements in the sampling. Finally, scientific proofs rest upon the traditional canons of logic, whether deduction or induction.

What many of us with faith in science ignore is that the *tradition works in the long run only*. It refers to a process of activities that may involve many persons in numerous locations for a lengthy time period. In doing her work, a scientist will attempt to be honest to the model. When theorizing, she will endeavor to encompass the various viewpoints and supporting data as logically as possible. When collecting data, she will take care to design studies that are reproduceable and comprehensive. She is fallible, however, and working with limited resources, so errors always occur. Her peers will pick up on some of these errors, seek to correct them, make more of their own (as well as new discoveries), and so the search for "truth" continues.

Persons knowledgeable in scientific activities have recognized this problem for some time. They are aware that no one study can provide an "answer," except for very rare instances. Consequently, scientific texts, especially in the social sciences, are replete with qualifying phrases: "possibly," "given available data," "for middle-class Americans it appears that," and so forth. Though this difficulty will affect us here, it is not so serious as another.

Science encompasses numerous social activities and these activities are predicated upon the social world at large. A scientist approaches her work not as a culture-free computer, but as a socialized member of her society. She has received specialized training that directs her to hold certain values (such as empricism over supernaturalism). Her peers are not faceless critics, but similar persons whom she will work beside, debate with, present papers to, and socialize with. Her research requires resources, which means she must legitimate the value of her work to others in society who control funds. Finally, her work may become the focus of political activity for others in society who seek scientific knowledge in support of their rhetorics.

Being creatures of American society, one perspective permeating much social science to date is sexism. Just as many early sociological writers found "logical" and "scientific" reasons to support racist ideologies and policies, so can one find numerous instances of preference for the masculine principle. Yet, we shall see, it is a sexism that supports not men as a class, but only those men who meet certain ideals of masculinity, primarily white, professional masculinity. This sexism is present in two ways. The social organization of social science is sexist (and racist). Thus, the production of social science knowledge, those "truths" it has produced to date, are bracketed by sexist ideology. To read a review of material on sex differences without these forces in mind would result in naive conclusions, misinterpretations, and a failure to see errors of omission in work to date.

The Practical Organization of Sociology

As most elementary texts will inform you, the founding father of sociology was Auguste Comte. He made the breech from philosophy that established the basis for the sociological discipline as it is known today. Almost every sociologist would agree that Comte is a rightful patriarch, or possibly Karl Marx. Yet when the author was in graduate school, she discovered the writings of one Germaine de Staël, an intellectual and political leader in France decades before Comte. Her writings included contributions to political sociology and the sociology of literature. She developed a concept of "national character" similar to one found in contemporary sociology, and elaborated ideas with observations from her own travels. It can be argued still that Comte deserves the patriarch's position, for he conceptualized the separate discipline of sociology. That alone is no reason to ignore de Staël in the classical literature of the discipline, yet her contributions are not at all recognized.

Here are some names every professional sociologist encounters in his or her training: *Auguste* Comte, *Emile* Durkheim, *Karl* Marx, *Max* Weber, *Georg* Simmel, *Edward Alan* Ross, *Thorstein* Veblen, *Bronislaw* Malinowski, *Vilfred* Pareto, *George Herbert* Mead, *Charles* Cooley, *William I.* Thomas, and so on. Books on the history of sociological thought leave the impression that only men have contributed to the discipline. This is true if one defines the discipline as consisting of a body of scholars who meet in formally organized settings, such as professional associations, and who publish for a specialized audience of peers. One would have to exclude the sociological writings and speeches of such literate political activists as *Emma* Goldman, *Charlotte* Perkins Gilman, or *Elizabeth* Cody Stanton on this account. But to be fair one would also eliminate some notable male theorists as well, Marx being an outstanding example.

Studies of citations in sociology verify that works by women are not referred to in the professional literature. For example, Bahr et al. (1971) studied the authors cited most frequently in studies of race and minorities during the period 1944-1968. Of the twenty-eight most frequently cited authors, none were women. Hacker's (1951) paper on women, now recognized as a major contribution to the area, was not recognized by specialists. Indeed, the specialty most single-mindedly ignored all but "Negroes." White ethnic groups, other racial minorities, and women for the most part received only passing mention. The most frequently cited authors were white, with the one outstanding exception of E. Franklin Frazier, a most notable black scholar. Women such as Florence Powdermaker and

Ruby Cox have authored articles and books in this area, but they are infrequently cited.

Where have all the women gone? Are they really so unimportant? One obvious answer is that women have, in fact, not contributed much to social science because few women have become social scientists. This is true if one eliminates the social activists and considers only the more "reputable" professionals, most of whom have been attached to colleges and universities. Entry into these occupations has typically required postgraduate education, and until recent decades comparatively few women were able to earn even a Bachelor's (sic) degree. Currently, women comprise about 20 percent each of the anthropology and sociology professions and 25 percent of psychology. Though not large minorities, these figures suggest that there should have been some noticeable imprint by women in recent years.

Let us examine this idea in detail as one means of exploring the role of women in social science. First, we must operationalize what we mean by "contribution." If we take sociology as our focus, one useful measurement of productivity would be an article in the *American Sociological Review,* which has been shown repeatedly to be considered the most prestigious of all the sociological journals (Glenn 1971). The large majority of papers submitted to this journal are not accepted. We can see how many women have had articles published there in recent years. If women are contributing equally to men, then about one in five articles should be by women. Here is some relevant data:

1. In 1966, 2.7 percent of all articles ($N=57$) were female-authored.
2. In 1968, 2.5 percent of 46 articles.
3. In 1970, 3.3 percent of 49 articles.
4. Out of 210 contributors to the 152 articles for these three years, 13 were women.

Why did so few women produce articles for this journal?

One immediate interpretation is that journal policy and organization may play a role. The journal's editorial board has always been virtually all-male. So have the numerous other sociologists invited to criticize a paper for the editors. For example, in 1971, 261 persons reviewed papers for the journal. *Eight* were women, and half of these were married to sociologists. This suggests the presence of a "buddy system" whereby men refer to other men (or wives of professional men) for advice.

Why should this matter? The reviews are anonymous, i.e., the authors' names are deleted from papers. One reason could be that certain topics, such as social theory and social stratification, are more prestigious. These topics seem to be studied more by male sociologists. Thus a paper on marriage and the family will not appear as "relevant" for the journal as a new mathematical model. Given limited space, the editor may see the latter as "naturally" more appealing.[1]

This explanation is completely speculative, for we lack any data on referee and editorial decision-making processes. Let us take a more conservative tack and suggest further that women (1) aren't submitting available articles to the journal, (2) are not preparing articles, or even (3) are preparing less competent work than men.

The last is easily disposed of on one ground. If proportionately fewer women manage to earn a Ph.D. in sociology, then as a group they are likely to be superior to male sociologists in intellectual achievement. This has been shown in studies of graduate students. For example, Rossi (1970) discovered that women graduate students in sociology had better academic records than men. Presuming this has been the case in the past, we cannot attribute the underrepresentation of women authors in the *ASR* to less competence.

In some cases women may indeed be submitting articles to other journals. In 1971, of sixty-one authors of articles in *Social Problems,* 10 percent were women; of sixty-one authors of articles in the *Journal of Health and Social Behavior,* 13 percent were women. Contributions to these journals, however, do not carry much weight when sociologists are evaluating one another's performance (such as when someone applies for a job). Also, more women were coauthors of articles than the men. That is, if an article has only one author, it is very likely to be a male. Women *do* publish, though not in the most prestigious locations.

The most thorough study of the comparable contributions of men and women was by Simon et al. (1967), who compared a sample of female and male Ph.D.'s in social science. The women were less likely to hold the rank of full professorship, have tenure, or to have ever received a research grant. *They were as productive as their male counterparts* with regard to publishing, consultation work, and professional society involvement. In fact, married women outproduced both the men and their single sister

---

1. Editors do make the final decisions, with referee comments serving only as a guide, not a directive. Given the large supply of papers, some editors in the past may have thoughtlessly turned down acceptable (to the referees) papers by unknown women from small schools in favor of a better known man from a larger university. Having once edited a journal for several years, myself, I am aware that such "inappropriate" choices are made. During my tenure, I tried to seek out good material from persons in the smaller schools, but I knew that an entire journal with only "lesser" schools represented would affect the prestige of the publication.

colleagues on many measures. This data presents the theme that academic women in the social sciences receive less rewards than men for the same professional productivity and commitment.

When one considers the obstacles that academic women work under, it is a wonder that they produce at all. First, while "publish-or-perish" is a rule of promotion in many universities or colleges, it does not apply to women. As Simon's data showed that women who publish are not so assured of promotion. Furthermore, a productive academic woman does not receive the financial rewards that accrue to her male counterparts. La Sorte (1971) found that in one 1968 sample of sociologists (a nonrandom selection), women earned $1,700 on the average less than men. One reason is that fewer of the women had Ph.D.'s and thus were concentrated in the lower academic ranks. Surprisingly, the greatest inequities were for those women who have made a full commitment to the profession. Table 4-1 shows that the wage differential *increases* as women move up the academic ranks, as they earn the Ph.D., and as they engage in research or administration.

Furthermore, for women sociologists to publish is to do so without much personal or financial support. We already saw that fewer women receive research grants. Here is an indication of the solitary position they are in as scholars. Rossi (1971) discovered that women in sociology in 1968-9 were:

1. 43 percent of college seniors planning graduate work in sociology
2. 37 percent of master's candidates
3. 30 percent of Ph.D. candidates
4. 27 percent of full-time lecturers or instructors
5. 14 percent of full-time assistant professors
6. 9 percent of full-time associate professors
7. 4 percent of full-time professors
8. 1 percent of graduate department chairpersons
9. 0 percent of the 44 full professors at the major elite departments

The answer for this attrition lies in the professional organization of the discipline. Epstein (1971) has identified many of the impediments to a woman's (or other minority member's) full participation in a scholarly discipline. First, many women are simply not recruited for professional training. This is not so likely in the social sciences as in other disciplines, but bias does exist. Young women aspiring to graduate work in social science can get in if qualified, though not to the most prestigious school nor with the aid of a fellowship.

63

Table 4-1
Salary Differentials of Sociologists by Gender for Six Variables

Variable	Wage Differential*
Academic rank	
Professor	$1,100
Associate	600
Assistant	400
Instructor	400
Academic degree	
B.A. or M.A.	600
Ph.D.	1,000
Second work activity	
None (teach only)	300
Research	1,600
Administration	2,000
Other	1,700
Years of professional experience	
1 to 9	1,200
10 or more	1,800
Geographic region	
West	1,300
North central	2,000
South	1,600
East	1,600
Age	
39 or under	1,300
40 or over	2,300
All sociologists	1,700

*The figure given is the difference in the average salary for a male sociologist.
Source: LaSorte (1971, p. 306).

Once in training a protege system operates to train students in specialties. Since graduate department faculty are most likely to be men, young women students have difficulty locating sponsors and relating well to them. The man may believe that she will not have a serious commitment if she marries—even though academic women marry less than other women.[2] Both may have secret fears over sexual features of the relationship. Will his wife be jealous? How will it look if she goes out for a drink with him, a

2. Of course, male professors do not question their married male students' commitments. This illustration provides a good test for identifying sexism. Are special standards applied to the judgment of one sex that would seem absurd if applied to the other?

common activity between male-sponsor-male proteges? She cannot share in the sports that tie the social bonds of many men in academic departments.

Once on the job market she will again find herself at a disadvantage. The prestigious schools will not hire her, and the less prestigious ones will hire her at a lower rank than a comparable male. Married women at this stage may interrupt their career a few years for their family or work part-time. If they are married to academic men, anti-nepotism rules may prevent them from accepting jobs at the same institution. A typical solution in this case is for the woman to have to locate a job at a school nearby (usually one lower in resources and prestige) or to be unemployed. The many unemployed female social scientists have yet to be singled out for study, though their stories would best corroborate whether Epstein's hypotheses about attrition are valid.

Since women do not make the elite institutions, they are excluded from "the club context" prevalent in academic disciplines. They do not know, meet, or socialize with the most creative, powerful, or resourceful members of their profession. At professional conventions their meetings with these men are as likely to be tinged by sexual politics as by professional exchange. But they are less likely to even attend these meetings (Fava 1960), so chances for valuable colleague relations are few. The club context is important because informal referrals and recommendations underlie such assignments as journal editorships, nominations to offices, job assignments, positions on grant review committees, introductions to book publishers, and so on. Women are excluded because they are not known. A man "in the club" can then point to the absence of women as a reason why he should not encourage a women student or turn down the grant of a woman from an obscure college or hire the stolid married male over the extraordinarily creative single female. They overlook how women produce as much as men even though they are at schools with high teaching loads, in spite of few research funds, without the emotional support of colleagues, and for many, with the second full-time job of housewife or mother.[3]

Until recently the professional associations reflected the club context. Men held the offices, worked on committees, and edited the journals. To the surprise of many, several social sciences have found themselves faced by a revolt in the ranks. In 1969, a woman's caucus at the annual Amer-

3. After this chapter was completed, the American Sociological Association published a report on *The Status of Women in Sociology: 1968-1972*. All of the issues I discuss here are corroborated by the research on which the report is based. In fact, my discussion only hints at the daily challenges to status an aspiring or fully professional female sociologist faces in her work.

ican Sociological Association meetings gave birth eventually to a second professional organization, Sociologists for Women in Society. Psychology has had a similar uprising, as have anthropology and history, though less formally. The women sociologists, like fellow blacks and Chicanos, found that previous informal maneuverings had produced few changes in the career opportunities of women. After several years of considerable activity, the changes are yet to be very observable. Rossi's 1968 statistics still hold —women are not getting promoted or rewarded as much as white males (Jackson 1972). (The data show that this applies to the other minorities as well, a further indication that racism also underlies the profession.)[4]

As this is written, some changes are visible. Several women were nominated for and received major offices in national and regional sociological associations. More women have received committee appointments. But these are highly visible, relatively powerless positions. So long as academic women are not hired by major universities, are ignored by publishers (Stoll 1972b), refused research grants, and hired at lesser salaries, the women will be left out of the club.

That there is discrimination against women cannot be denied now. Does this mean though that all male social scientists are productive and well paid? Not at all. The fact is that many men are also not members of the buddy system. The most recent study on sociologists' publication productivity by Larson et al. (1972) reiterates the findings of earlier research. More than half of the Ph.D.'s in twenty major departments granting Ph.D.'s had not published an article in any of twelve journals during the ten-year period studied. Although no separate analyses were made by sex, the departments studied have few women anyway. Consequently, it is reasonable to conclude that the findings describe the male sociologist at top schools. As one verification of the "buddy system" model, Larson et al. discovered that the most productive sociologists were trained at a small group of elite schools. These are the same schools that continue to have few, if any, women on their graduate faculty.

4. Jackson's data show the following proportions of sociologists:

	1970	1972
Women	9%	12 %
Black	3%	3 %
Asian	......	0.5%
Chicano	......	0.1%
Indian	......	0.1%

All are disproportionately in the lower ranks.

Since most social scientists are male, the faculty of "lesser" institutions—as the powerful men define them—are predominately male. "Publish or perish" keeps minorities out of elite schools, but it does not apply to men in the coterie. The elite departments each retain men who are unproductive. If questioned about their retention, typical responses are that these men are "good administrators," "serve as sources of cohesiveness," "are too nice to fire."[5] Racial minorities and women do not enjoy such support. As a committee of anthropologists discovered, there is a "more vigorous application of promotional criteria to women than to men (American Anthropologist Newsletter 1973).

What we don't know about is the feelings of those men who have "failed" by elite standards. Are they different in background from the coterie at the top? Are their intellectual ideas—like the women's—in conflict with those of traditional social science? What does the discipline lose when it disenfranchises a large number of men, most women, and racial minorities? How useful and valid is the knowledge promulgated by a select group of white males who have made the elite of their discipline, given that the discipline seeks to explain the behavior of *all* social beings—poor and rich, nonwhite and white, female and male? Here we enter into what is known as the sociology of knowledge—how the social organization of a discipline subtly shapes its intellectual thought.

Sexism in Social Science Intellectual Activity

The women and other minorities who are organizing within their social science disciplines do so for more than career self-interest. Their revolt is also aimed at the intellectual activity of social science: the questions that are raised, the issues that go ignored, the assumptions that underlie social theory, and the use of subjects in research. Sexual prejudice exists not only in hiring, promotion, grant awards, and professional elections, it also affects what Durkheim would call the "collective conscience" of the discipline. *Ethnocentrism,* the belief that one's own culture is superior, and *parochialism,* the inability or refusal to see beyond one's own immediate surroundings or concerns, may feed and in turn be reinforced by sexism. American social science can be held on account in many ways here. It was several years after completing her Ph.D. that the author realized how little that study taught her about how the social beings who compose a society:

5. These are actual reasons given to me over the years in conversations with male colleagues at prestigious schools.

As a *graduate student* in the mid-sixties, I recall half-joking to
friends about the need for a book called *The Sex Factor,* which
would collect and analyze correlates of gender identity. The problem was not to be taken seriously in those pre-Woman's Movement
days when "sex" was a variable to be controlled, not studied out-
right. We all knew that it "made a difference" but we never
bothered to study how it mattered. Parsons' (1942) "Age and Sex:
Structure in the United States" was mysteriously appealing to me
then (and remains today a stand-out in the sex roles literature).
Meanwhile, in courses I read about sociological theorists (all men),
criminals (male only—not enough females to count), occupations
(men again, except for nurses or social workers), socialization
(affective and instrumental robot parents), and politics (remember
Political Man?). My methods text was authored by a woman, but
what can a methods book teach about sex roles, except that sex is
one of those variables you can often control on . . . (Stoll 1972a,
p. 419).

This experience hints at how the content of sociology excludes the study of
women. The problem is much more subtle.

Consider language. The author refers to the book *Political Man,* Lipset's (1960) classic contribution to political sociology. Anthropologists
have discovered that language tells much about a culture's concepts of time
and space, its taboos, its social and familial hierarchies. English retains
more vestiges of sexist attitudes than many other tongues (Strainchamps
1971). Academic style reflects this bias in obvious ways. We have only
to consider the clumsiness of a non-sexist title to Lipset's book: Political
Human, Political Person, Political Individual. The phrases sound out of
tune with our ears. The social science bookshelves abound with titles such
as *Social Problems of Urban Man, Man and Men, Man in Society, From
Man to Society, Roles of Man, Systems of Man, Casual Groups of Monkeys
and Men.* As we shall soon see, the titles are accurate in being specific to
one sex. Nonetheless, in themselves they reinforce the idea of males being
the important members of society. The word "man" is meant to encompass
"woman," just as in the everyday world men circumscribe and define the
women.

Within the body of social science writings, it is customary to refer to
"he" at a referrant when giving examples. Here are some quotes from one
of the best-selling texts in introductory sociology:

If a student comes to college with a definite vocational objective in
mind, he has an instrumental orientation.
The more isolated an individual is from his immediate primary
group , . . . the greater his distress.
Sometimes an executive is criticized as authoritarian because he

shows lack of concern for the opinions or feelings of his sub-
ordinates.

In policy-planning, the planner participates in setting goals for
urban change, but he does so in cooperation with other experts
(Broom and Selznick 1973).

There is no reason why some of these statements, since they are purely for
illustration's sake, should not use the pronoun "she." What the authors
reinforce implicitly by using only a male pronoun is the belief that only
males are (should be) students, executives, and planners.

This may seem a trivial point to some, but it is probable that our focus
on "man and men" rather than persons is one reason why the world of
women is excluded from social science books. So infrequently are women
taken into consideration that they traditionally receive a special heading,
"women," in indexes. The heading "men" is not needed because the books
deal in fact with men, so that would be superfluous.

Perhaps the most outstanding example of how language limits a social
scientist's world view is an acclaimed book, *The Human Condition* (Chicago: Univ. of Chicago Press, 1958), which happens to be one of the few
theoretical treatises authored by a woman, Hannah Arendt. Consider this
quote from the chapter where Arendt sketches her focus:

> The *vita activa,* human life in so far as it is actively engaged in
> doing something, it always rooted in a world of *men* and *man*-made
> things, which it never leaves or altogether transcends. Things and
> *men* form the environment for each of *man's* activities, which
> would be pointless without such location. . . . All human activities
> are conditioned by the fact that *men* live together, but it is only
> action that cannot even be imagined outside the society of *men*. . . .
> *Man* working and fabricating and building a world inhabited only
> by *him*self would still be a fabricator, though not *homo faber: he*
> would have lost *his* specifically human quality and, rather, be a
> *god*-not to be sure, the Creator, but a divine demiurge as Plato
> described *him* in one of *his* myths. Action alone is the exclusive
> prerogative of *man* (Arendt 1958, pp. 24-5, emphasis added).

Reading the book, one soon realizes that Arendt takes the word
"man" literally to apply to males. Her concern is with active men, and
since only men (males) are active, the world of males is all that she considers. Women are relegated to four mentions in several hundred pages.
Ironically, in these references Arendt mentions the enslavement of women
by men in power, yet she fails to see how her own analysis is premised on
that very sexist ideology. That an astute, brilliant woman can ignore wom-
ankind in her own work testifies to the success of sexist ideology in social
science thought.

Women have been ignored by researchers as well. History as a discipline can be characterized as having had a collective forgetfulness about
women. It has refined history of men, first, by neglecting the female institutions; second, by emphasizing masculine activities such as economics or
politics; and third, by omitting to mention women who did contribute in the
male sphere. American historians in particular have very successfully eradi-
cated woman's contribution to the culture and growth of this society.

In sociology and psychology, studies of research samples have shown
that women are less likely to be included in surveys or experiments. The
results of the author's examination of three volumes of the *American Sociological Review,* as presented in table 4-2, show considerable use of all-

Table 4-2

Sample Characteristics of American Sociological Review Articles [a]

	Year of Publication		
	1966	1968	1970
Sample type:			
Male only [b]	34%	38%	56%
Female only	16	8	0
Both sexes	44	42	31
Not determinable	6	12	16
Total	100	100	100
	(32)	(24)	(16)

a Only research studies are included in the count.
b This includes cases where the sex composition is implicit, e.g., famous scientists,
ministers.

male samples. In some cases this happened because only men composed
the group under study (ministers, executives, scientists). However, in
many cases there was no logical or expressed reason for studying only men.
Studies of women-only samples tended to be in the area of fertility. In
many of the studies with both sexes included, sex differences were mentioned or treated superfluously in the data presentation.

Unpublished research on psychology by Prescott, Foster, and Schwabacher noted the underuse of women subjects and explored the reasons for
it. Curiously, they found that studies of men only generalized their results
to both sexes, while studies of women restricted their conclusions to females
as a group. Some investigators included both sexes in pilot studies, yet used
only male subjects in their major experiments for no given reason. When
the authors of single-sex studies were questioned by mail as to their sample
choice, most stated "availability." Prescott, Schwabacher, and Foster's

conclusions apply to sociology as well: are studies of women being unreported because they produce negative results, i.e., fail to support current psychological theories? If a discipline combines a lack of concern about half its population with a tendency to overgeneralize about the other half, can it be called scientific?

Women are not only ignored by social science, they are misrepresented. Male theorists, being unacquainted with data on women, and lacking woman's experience, appear to use social stereotypes in discussions of women. Weisstein (1969) has described how the major contemporary theorists in psychology encourage a view of women as nurturant, maternal, concerned with attractiveness, and passive. Examples abound, from Freud's "anatomy is destiny" to Erikson's oft-cited claim that woman's "somatic design harbors an 'inner space' destined to bear the offspring of chosen men." These ideas are so well-accepted that clinicians believe that a healthy woman is one who conforms to the stereotype (Broverman et al. 1970). Thus persons who rely upon psychological theory in their counselling of individuals adapt the built-in sex stereotypes as true, when there is no evidence in fact.

Data in support of these theoretical ideas are scarce, partly because women are not studied to begin with. When they are, it is oftentimes possible to find cues that the researcher discovered what he wanted to see because he left no room for other possibilities. Erikson's (1950) research on children at play is a case in point. He asked boys and girls to construct "a scene out of an imaginary moving picture." He gave photographs of the scenes to two other psychologists to verify the presence or absence of towers, streets, enclosures, and such. The boys built high-low objects much more often than the girls, who built enclosures. What was wrong with this study? Consider the following quote from Erikson's report:

> One day, a boy arranged such a "feminine" scene, with wild animals as intruders, and I felt that uneasiness which I assume often betrays to an experimenter what his innermost feelings are. And, indeed, on departure and already at the door, the boy exclaimed, "There is something wrong here," came back, and with an air of relief arranged the animals along a tangent to a circle of furniture (a masculine arrangement) (Erickson 1950, p. 101).

It seems obvious from this scene that the boy picked up Erikson's discomfort with this "feminine" arrangement. Why else the relief? Erikson argues that virtually *all* the boys built what he saw as appropriate male models. That so many youngsters behaved precisely as he had hoped they would only points to Erikson's considerable interpersonal skills in directing behavior.

This example of *experimenter bias* is particularly applicable to the study of sex roles. Sex identity is so visible that it is difficult to conceive of ways to measure sex differences that are not somewhat predetermined. If one hires research aides who are unaware of the purpose of the study, there is still no guarantee that they will not use their own stereotypes to influence subjects unwittingly. Similarly, if we ask someone to observe and count types of playground play by sex, we cannot be sure how often our assistants will balk at counting or ignoring "inappropriate" behavior, as Erikson wished to do until his subject complied.

The area of sex-role measurement by use of self-rating adjective scales further illustrates problems of bias. Lenney's (1972) comprehensive review of these inventories show how most share similar faults. The major one is that they presume there to be two sex roles, male and female, which are opposite one another. A male who scores low on "masculinity" is automatically high on "femininity" and vice versa. A good example is Terman and Miles' (1936) seminal research on sex and personality. They compiled various tests, including word association, attitude inventory, interest analysis, ink-blot identifications, and general information. In developing the tests, they looked for items that would distinguish male and female. The scores place respondents in either a "masculine" or "feminine" location. The test results are blatantly predictable. For example, women have more knowledge about domestic items.

Many M-F inventories similar to that of Terman and Miles have been developed. What is interesting is that the *scales correlate poorly* with one another. This result is especially surprising in light of the fact that many of the same items appear from one test to another. What can we conclude from this? Possibly "masculinity" and " femininity" are very complicated personality constellations not measured well by simple tests. More likely though, the very idea of masculine-feminine is presumptuous. The scales are not very useful because they do not measure a viable phenomenon in our society. One critic (Goldberg 1971, p. 234) recommended "the substitution for past M-F scales of the following single item: 'I am male. True or False?' "[6]

Bem (1973) is the first investigator to design an inventory that does not make the usual assumptions. She argues that many individuals are "androgynous." That is, they do not define themselves in terms appropriate only to their own sex, nor do they limit their activities to sex-typed behavior. Her attitude scale, the *Bem Sex Role Inventory,* includes both

6. Note how Goldberg's suggestion shows a preference for the male! The most nonsexist form of this inquiry would simply leave a blank to fill in next to "sex."

a masculinity and a femininity scale that yield independent scores. Consequently, a respondent who scores low on "femininity" is not automatically high on "masculinity." (Future work will examine whether the scale actually picks out those who are androgynous in daily life activities.)

If social science is sexist in its omission of the study of women, its notions about men reinforce the sexist beliefs that men are active, rational, and intellectual. A useful illustration is this comment from a social psychology textbook:

> There is often talk of certain professions for which women are better or worse suited, such as medicine or law. In this context Erik Erikson makes the perceptive observation that the matter has been wrongly put; one should not ask whether women can be lawyers but rather whether there is a feminine way to be a lawyer as well as a masculine way. To the extent that one can be quietly pervasive, appeal to the juries' empathetic tendencies, convey one's feeling about a situation, women should be equally as proficient as male lawyers, who are more likely to act in an aggressive, forceful, if not browbeating manner (Grossack and Gardner 1970, p. 270).

This argument is interesting because the writers suggest that men and women are equal, though different. They imply that men are "aggressive, forceful, even browbeating." What evidence is there for this belief? The remaining chapters here will not provide much support.

Certain aspects of the man's world have been ignored by social scientists. Studies of child rearing virtually ignore the father. Studies of husbands omit discussion of love, comfort, and other emotional dimensions of the relationship to the spouse. (Sex is not overlooked however.) Only recently has research appeared on the "average" middle-class male, his life concerns, his attitudes, his dreams and disappointments. Rather, much research on men views them as functionaries—workers to be motivated, voters to be swayed, angry poor to be appeased. Their gender is irrelevant. They are cardboard images, not persons with feelings, pains, or pride.

Women are similarly treated in sociological research. Consider the area of social stratification. Sociologists presume that men are the participants in the distribution of power, wealth, and prestige. Studies with female respondents will use "husband's occupation" as the basis for measuring a woman's class. Note how this approach is self-reinforcing. Since women are presumed to be unimportant, they are proven to be so.

Another illustration is research on marriage and the family. Heiskanen (1971) sampled articles from the journal *Marriage and the Family* and discovered that about one-half of the studies were of middle-class couples. The most popular topics were of marital roles and adjustment, i.e., the perpetuation of the present nuclear family. Virtually unstudied were unwed mothers, divorced persons, employed wives, househusbands, and nonnuclear, nonlegal family forms. Heiskanen notes that books on the family mention the variety of forms yet discuss only the middle-class structure because it is the one for which we have data! Again, another instance of scientific "knowledge" reinforcing itself.

We shall find many other examples of sexism in social science throughout this volume. Let us note again the major points.

1. Women have been excluded from and ignored by the small group of male sociologists who produce ideas about society.
2. Social theorists often write as though it can be taken for granted that there are two bi-polar sex roles in our society.
3. Much social science research can be characterized as *androcentric,* that is, focused upon the activities of men. Yet stereotypes of masculinity may bias these findings.

What this means for our explorations of sex roles here is some difficulty in finding evidence. There are many studies of men at work, but few of men at home. Some surveys will be of women only because only women are at home when the interviewers visit. Some studies examine both men and women, though operate from such a stereotyped perspective that many relevant questions are not even raised. For many topics, we shall have virtually no data at all.

Given these complications, the author shall focus on problems where the data is available enough to sketch some insights. Many studies of sex differences will not be included, either because they are so poorly designed as to be useless, or because they are the only study of a topic available. Studies will be looked at closely so the reader can draw additional conclusions to the ones given. So let us, at last, begin our selective review of sex differences in America.

SUGGESTED PROJECTS

1. What is your favorite topic or specialty in sociology? To what extent and in what ways has it been permeated by the sexist patterns described in this chapter? Refer to textbooks, specialized journals, and information in *The American Sociologist.*
2. See if you can locate a "lost" woman scholar in sociology. Write an essay in support of her contributions, along with her accompanying bibliography. See if you can get her work included on the readings list of the appropriate course in your department.
3. If you understand the material on sexism in the social science professions, you should be able to draw a diagram of the various underlying processes

or list a set of interrelated hypotheses. Choose another occupation or profession and see whether data is available to test your scheme. Try to explain any discrepancies that result.

4. Choose one of your current social science texts and describe how you would rewrite parts of it, reorganize it, or add material in order to make it less sexist. Send your comments to the author and the publisher for response. What do they think of your recommendations?

REFERENCES

"Statistical Data on Occupational Status of Women in Anthropology Departments." *American Anthropological Newsletter* February 1973.

Arendt, Hannah. *The Human Condition.* New York: Doubleday & Company, Inc., 1958.

Bahr, Howard M.; Johnson, Theodore J.; and Seitz, M. Ray. "Influential Scholars and Works in the Sociology of Race and Minority Relations, 1944-1968." *American Sociologist* (1971):296-98.

Bem, Sandra L. "The Measurement of Psychological Androgeny." Department of Psychology, Stanford University, Palo Alto, California, 1973.

Broom, Leonard, and Selznick, Philip. *Sociology: A Text with Adapted Readings.* 5th ed. New York: Harper and Row, 1973.

Broverman, Inge; Broverman, Donald; Clarkson, Frank E.; Rosenkrantz, Paul; and Vogel, Susan R. "Sex Role Stereotypes and Clinical Judgments about Mental Health." *Journal of Consulting and Clinical Psychology* 34(1970): 1-7.

Epstein, Cynthia Fuchs. *Woman's Place.* Berkeley, California: University of California Press, 1971.

Erikson, Erik. *Childhood and Society.* New York: W. W. Norton & Company, Inc., 1950.

Fava, Sylvia Feis. "The Status of Women in Professional Sociology." *American Sociological Review* 25(1960):271-2.

Glenn, Norval. "American Sociologists' Evaluations of Sixty-three Journals." *American Sociologist* 6(1971):298-303.

Goldberg, L. R. "Personality Scales and Inventories." In *Advances in Psychological Assessment,* edited by P. McReynolds. Palo Alto, Calif.: Science and Behavior Books, 1971.

Grossack, Martin, and Gardner, Howard. *Man and Men.* Scranton, Penn.; International Textbook Co., 1970.

Heiskanen, Veronica. "The Myth of the Middle-class Family in American Sociology." *American Sociologist* 6(1971):14-18.

LaSorte, Michael A. "Sex Differences in Salary among Academic Sociology Teachers." *American Sociologist* 6(1971):304-7.

Larson, Richard F.; Petrowsky, Marc L.; and Vandiver, Joseph S. "Journal Productivity of Ph.D. Sociologists." *American Sociologist* 7(1972):9-11.

Lenney, Ellen. "The Measurement of Masculinity and Femininity: A History and Criticism." Department of Psychology, Stanford University, Palo Alto, California, 1972.

Lipset, Seymour Martin. *Political Man.* New York: Doubleday & Company, Inc., 1960.

Parsons, Talcott. "Age and Sex Structure in the United States." *American Sociological Review* 7(1942):606-616.

Rossi, Alice. "Status of Women in Graduate Departments of Sociology, 1968-1969." *American Sociologist* 5(1970)1-12.

Simon, Rita James; Clark, Shirley Merritt; and Galway, Kathleen. "The Woman Ph.D., A Recent Profile." *Social Problems* 15(1967): 221-36.

Stoll, Clarice Stasz. "The Sociology of Sex Roles: Essay Review." *Sociological Quarterly* 13(1972a):419-25.

———. "Feminist Thoughts on Publishing." *SWS Newsletter* 2(November 1972b):11-12.

Strainshamps, Ethel. "Our Sexist Language." In *Woman in Sexist Society,* edited by Vivian Gornick and Barbara K. Moran. New York: Basic Books, 1971.

Terman, Lewis, and Miles, Catherine Cox. *Sex and Personality.* New York: Russell & Russell Publishers, 1936.

Weinstein, Naomi. *Kinder, Kuche, and Kirche as Scientific Law: Psychology Constructs the Female.* Boston: New England Free Press, 1969.

5. coming female and male

Somewhere in America a woman becomes pregnant. She tells the father of the child, and they discuss possible names. Because names in our country serve as a basis for gender identity, few names are appropriate for both girls and boys.

A frequent question the prospective mother will be asked is, "What do you want, a boy or a girl?" She may answer, "A girl, because they're easier to raise." Perhaps she'll say, "It doesn't matter, so long as it's healthy," while secretly retaining a preference. The unknown gender provides mystery to the process, a motive for maintaining interest during the long gestation period.

The child is born. The doctor says to the mother, "You have a lovely girl (a sturdy boy)." The baby is wrapped in a pink or blue blanket and entrusted to the care of women nurses. Some friends will give presents of yellow clothes—a sexually neutral color—while others will bring just-purchased color-appropriate items. The lives of both parents, if they are living together, will be affected; but the woman will learn that her life is more changed in day-to-day ways.

The child is helpless. Someone must feed it, attend to its wastes, keep it safe from injury, carry it from one place to another. In a few years, it will be able to feed itself, properly dispose of its bodily wastes, avoid dangers, and walk around. It will also be able to communicate with others, distinguish itself from others, and expect things of others. In yet a few more years, it can be trained to acquire the skills to take care of itself as an adult and to contribute to the society.

It will become a unique adult. So difficult will it be to find a match for itself, that it will invest much time and resources in seeking compatriots, friends, or lovers. These activities are true for any baby, regardless of sex, race, or class. These processes are what compose *socialization* of a person.

Socialization by definition implies a model of behavioral change. First, one considers what persons are to be studied; sometimes these people are designated by the term *socializee*. Then one asks what *outcome* is to be studied; and what socializing *agents* in society that are possibly responsible for the change. Sometimes these agents are conceptualized as persons who occupy certain positions via-a-via the socializee, such as parent, teacher, friend. Other analyses look at the structures or institutions wherein socialization occurs. Obvious examples are the family, the school, the church, and the less formal culture of play and games. When agent and socializee come together, many types of interaction are possible:

1. An agent can *reward* through love, praise, money, privileges, etc. The rewarding of valued behavior is one way of reinforcing it, so that at some future point the socializee will perform the behavior without reward.
2. An agent can use *incentives* of love, praise, and such to encourage a person to perform in some valued way.
3. An agent can *distract a socializee* from continuing an activity that is disapproved of. This is a nonpunitive way to react to "wrong" behavior.
4. An agent can *discipline,* whether by ridicule, denial of privileges, physical injury, or the withholding of support. If punishment is consistent, then in time the socializee will learn to avoid the behavior.
5. An agent can *specify the rules* that govern the many situations where she or he is not present to react. In this way a moral order of ideas and symbols is communicated.

Socialization, in fact, is a lifelong process, for individuals move through many settings and relationships as they age, each with its special demands and requirements. Whenever a woman enters the work force or a man becomes a father, each must learn new tasks, attitudes, and shift from past preferences and behaviors to new ones. The process can be more subtle, an example being the shifts in age situs from youth to adulthood through middle age to old age. For the life of the individual, these socialization periods often mark periods of personal difficulty and challenge, as shall be seen in later chapters.

Let us limit ourselves here to youth and consider how babies develop into "female" and "male." Notice that the question assumes that there are such categories. After criticizing social scientists for this type of presumption in the previous chapter, why should we consider it here? Perhaps a better way of stating our question is—how do individuals learn about the *expectations* a society attaches to being female or male? What matters is not that we prove that there are two sexes, but rather that we show the extent to which an ideology influences the lives of youth. Consequently, we should not expect boys and girls to grow up very differently. After all, they are being exposed to many other ideologies as well—racial, class, religious, patriotic. Gender is just one basis for identity throughout life, and hardly anyone makes it the sole basis for their identity; just as race, ethnicity, or religion are not the sole standards.

First we must define exactly what societal expectations in America are attached to gender. Some opposites come to mind such as passive-active, emotional-rational, gentle-tough. These *ad hoc* categories are unsatisfying because they appear to exaggerate the case. If girls are supposed to be emotional and boys rational, then why do we educate girls equally and allow men to become the artistic elite? Societal demands are much more situational than simple dichotomous categories can provide. Women are permitted to express emotions of a specific kind (e.g., crying) in some situations where men are supposed to repress emotions (e.g., upon hearing a painful reprimand). Nevertheless, men are not prescribed from all expression of emotions. Thus the way we treat one another with regard to gender is much more complicated than ideas hold. Everyday references to "the weaker sex" or "he-men" only point the direction of some expectations and do not describe the *pervasiveness* of the expectation. I will argue here that actual gender expectations are not so pervasive as may be thought.

Another way of identifying gender expectations is to look at the overall socialization outcomes and ask whether there is more emphasis upon one sex reaching this outcome than another. Whiting et al. (1966) have argued that independence is the goal of childhood socialization, and that this involves eight separate components. Table 5-1 presents these eight outcomes as they might apply to sex roles. First, one must consider what the general value attached to each outcome is for American society. American culture has two major goals that weave together: (1) individual freedom to pursue happiness and (2) the concern for the general welfare of the society. Individualism is encouraged through emphasis upon achievement and self-reliance. However, one should not achieve thoughtlessly at the expense of others, so dominance is underplayed by means of an egalitarian ideology that all men are created equal. Also, obedience at the expense of individual satisfactions is expected whenever the general good requires it.

Table 5-1

Hypothesized Socialization Outcomes and Gender Specification

Outcome	Generalized Value	Male Specification	Female Specification
1. Succorance (await others' nuturance)	Discouraged	Prescribed	Tacitly prescribed
2. Achievement orientation	Strongly held	Prescribed	Indifferent attitudes
3. Self-reliance	Encouraged with limits	Prescribed, except in domestic area	Proscribed in many areas
4. Obedience	Value depends upon situation at hand	Contradictory pressures	Prescribed
5. Nuturance	Encouraged in a general "good will" sense	Encouraged in sense of team work, non-personal giving	Encouraged in terms of personal giving
6. Responsibility	Encouraged	Prescribed	Prescribed in domestic arena
7. Sociability	Strongly held	Emphasis on all-male activity	Prescribed in general terms
8. Dominance	Contradictory ideas; conflicts with good will values	Prescribed	Indifference or proscription

The ideals of brotherhood and good will can be observed in the patterns of sociability that are taken for granted by ourselves, yet often commented upon by foreign visitors. Nurturance means more than a very maternal, emotional activity; it includes any reaching out to meet others' needs. This falls readily under our ideals of good will. The only outcome that is underplayed, if not discouraged, is that of succorance. Very few categories of people in our society—namely the babies and the aged—may display this stance without rancor.

Several implications follow from these goals. One is that it is virtually impossible to satisfy them all. It would take an extraordinary person to manage to be highly successful *and* nurturant *and* self-reliant *and* equalitarian in stance. Contradictions are built in because of the "individual-general good" dichotomy and because society is so structured that it is difficult to achieve these goals. They are, in fact, ideals that parents, teachers, police, and friends have in mind when relating to children. Some goals will be emphasized over others depending upon the child's ethnicity, her race, her locality, her religion, and her gender.

The remainder of table 5-1 outlines some possible ways in which gender further specifies these general ideals. Succorance is discouraged for anyone in our society, but males will be discouraged more than females, who may be taught subtle lessons to encourage it. Achievement orientation is pressed upon both sexes, but a boy learns that it is much more important for his identity than a girl does. Conversely, both will be encouraged to be nurturant. For boys it will be channeled into impersonal practices, such as organizational operations or teamwork, while for girls it will be channeled into personal relationships. Self-reliance is difficult in many areas of our complicated society; but to the extent that it is possible, boys will be encouraged to be so in all areas but domestic ones, while the girls will have only the domestic area to control. Obedience is complicated, as we shall see in later discussions, because boys are pressured to succeed yet more often punished for some types of achievement than girls. Girls are taught less punitively to obey authorities and the obedience applies to more situations. Both are encouraged to be responsible for decisions, though the arena of decision-making will be different. Both will be taught to be sociable. For boys this means adjusting to the patterns of the all-male friendship groups, while for girls it is a more generalized pattern. Finally, while dominance is not encouraged to be a primary ideal, it is often displayed as such to boys in some settings.

These distinctions are purely hypothetical and meant only to sketch out what the general direction of socialization *may* be in our society. It has not been the model that many social scientists have used in studying this process. The typical model is much simpler. Frequently, the research-er will pick out one activity, such as aggressive play, and ask whether or not there are sex differences. If boys more likely engage in aggressive play, then this is labelled as "masculine" and girls who do the same are called "masculine" girls. This labelling causes logical confusions, for the char-acteristics of the *group* of boys are applied to individual girls. Too often the sex differences are present yet not very important. More boys than girls may participate in aggressive play, but it may also be the case that only a minority of boys do so. Researchers frequently overlook this type of find-ing in drawing conclusions. Consequently, focusing on one or two small outcomes and too quickly labelling them as "masculine" or "feminine," investigators encourage a model of socialization to gender expectations that permits nothing except the male-female dichotomous model.

Related to these research practices is the tendency of social scientists to consider as important only those findings that produce "differences." Doubtless studies of boys and girls exist where the researcher found no differences in behavior and thus considered the study to be a failure. This should not be the case, and would not be, had the investigator included a theoretical model that permitted that fact of no differences. In reviewing some research for this chapter, the author discovered that numerous studies exist in which the only data considered to be important by the investigator are those where differences occur. Yet it is the *similarities* in boys' and girls' responses that challenge our ideas about gender and sex roles. For example, boys and girls have very different aspirations with regard to oc-cupations, yet they are similar in their motivations and interests concerning work.

In a study of sex differences, we must be as much aware of the *shared* traits of boys and girls as well as the differing ones. Only then can one say anything about the pervasiveness and distinctions of gender ex-pectations in society.

A third difference in the approach others have taken is that the models of socialization have an *androcentric bias*. The outcomes important for making so-called strong males are emphasized, while those values attached more to girls are relatively ignored. An extensive, even exhausting, litera-ture on "achievement orientation" fills what seems to be the bulk of the literature on childhood socialization. Also emphasized are the male fail-ures—delinquent boys—whose achievement comes by dubious means. Recent studies of nurturance are few. Achievement is defined narrowly to mean success in the school and work world, while logically it should in-clude interpersonal success and excellence in areas not rewarded publicly. Insidious labelling results again, such that a boy who does poorly at schoolwork will be thrown into a "low achiever" (read as "masculine failure") category, when in fact he may be extraordinarily successful in art or with machines. With regard to girls, less is known because fewer studies include girls. When they are studied, generally those who most resemble males are singled out for detailed analysis (Stoll 1972).

Finally, if one wants to find data to test this model, one is faced with the problem of insufficient data. This state of the literature is surprising because the topic of gender identity seems so obvious to anyone interested in socialization. Other authorities verified that hapless search of the literature was not without basis:

> There are very few studies of sex differences in child rearing practices in general, and existing data, most of which were collected for other purposes, are subject to [many] limitations (Hoffman 1972, p. 133).

> A persual of the journals shows that many studies, which include both male and female S's [subjects] in the sample, do not make provisions for sex differences in hypotheses. Where sex differences are found they are, consequently, rationalized *post facto*. Moreover, often no statistical analysis of sex differences is performed (Lynn 1962, p. 555).

Given this situation, all that can be provided here is fragments of what must be a very complicated process. Nonetheless, what fragments are available will likely disturb your commonsense ideas enough to send you to journals or out to the schools and playgrounds for more information.

Early Childhood   Much thinking on sex role learning has been conservative, in that most writers have presumed that a child's gender has profound consequences for subsequent identity and life career. Linton's (1945, p. 63) dictum is reiterated throughout social science literature. "The division of the society's members into age-sex categories is perhaps the feature of greatest importance for establishing participation of the individual in culture." Theorists have taken sex roles for granted and developed simple models of how they are learned.

The *comparative psychologist's* approach, for example, argues essentially that biology is the basis of gender identity. Proponents of this view generalize from other species as one device for deducing causes of sex differences. Tiger and Fox's work, described earlier, is one example. Another is Harlow's (1971) studies of rhesus monkeys. He has noted how male monkeys of this species prefer rough-and-tumble play, while females prefer less active chase play. Harlow believes such data are proof of built-in biological gender roles. Other investigators of this sort study the role of hormones on the behavior of various species, and then generalize to humans.[1]

Some study only humans, while retaining a preference for the role of biology. Many psychologists, in noting repeatedly certain differences between female and male babies, are maintaining that these differences are rooted in physiology. Table 5-2 presents a summary of the findings in this area. Boys appear predisposed to activity, independence, and relating to objects. Girls appear predisposed to restful observation of a complex environment and relating to persons. Unfortunately for these two viewpoints, actual evidence that biology is the causal factor here is not strong. One important source of negative data is Money's research (described in chapter one) that showed how no one physiological measure predicts sex identity as well as the gender applied to a child at birth during the social typing process. Granted, there is sketchy evidence that hormones may predispose people to display certain behaviors, and some neurologists argue that men and women have different nervous systems. Yet there is no reason to either deny completely the role of biology in the formation of sex differences, nor is there proof that its contribution is a direct and strong one.

The other approaches to sex role socialization emphasize nurture, or the role of social learning. The *psychoanalytic* approach, though heavily grounded in biology, incorporates the interplay of family dynamics on personality as well. Freud's theory, though under dispute, nonetheless remains worth considering. Unlike the impersonal model of the comparative psychologists, Freud's view of children and sex roles is filled with passion. His children respond to the world with inner thought activities, feelings, and outward displays of self. He presumed further that sex identity and sex—erotic impulses—are intertwined. Freud believed in the sensuality of the young child, who passes through various developmental stages as she focuses upon various sources of gratification (the mouth, the anus, and the genitals).

Freud believed that this focusing of pleasure (libidinal energy) becomes attached to the parent of the opposite sex at four or five. During the phallic period, the boy becomes preoccupied with his penis and fears loss or harm to it by his father, his rival for the love of his mother. Since the boy cannot vanquish his father, he represses sexual feelings for his mother and "identifies with aggressor." He is bound to his mother vicariously now,

---

1. The comparative and psychological studies are too technical to describe here in more detail because they require acquaintance with medical terminology. A brief, well-balanced review of these studies is Sutton-Smith and Roberts (1972). Bardwick (1971) has premised her psychological theory of sex roles on these studies and describes them comprehensively, though not with a critical eye.

Table 5-2
Sex Differences in Infancy and Early Childhood

Boys	Girls

At Birth

Boys	Girls
Larger size and weight; more muscle mass	Greater motoric passivity
More activity	More sensitivity to stimuli; sensitivity to a greater number of stimuli
Correlation of low sensitivity with higher prone head reaction	Greater tactile and pain sensitivity; higher skin conductance, greater irritability during an anthropometric examination

6 Months

Boys	Girls
Better fixation response to a helix pattern of lights	Longer fixation time to visual stimuli, less motoric activity, and greater cardiac deceleration; better fixation to a human face; greater responsiveness to a social stimuli; more social orientation
Greatest cardiac deceleration (a measure of attention) to an intermittant tone	Greater cardiac deceleration to complex jazz music

13 Months

Boys	Girls
Maximum response to a verbal stimulus high in meaning and low in inflection	Maximum response to a verbal stimulus high in meaning and inflection, implies a response to a person
Preference for low complexity stimuli	Preference for high complexity stimuli; earlier language development, especially inflection
Possible better figure-ground differentiation	Greater field dependency—less likely to eliminate irrelevant stimuli, awareness of contextual relationships.

Source: Bardwick (1971, p. 93).

while identifying with the strength and competence of the father. Thus the Oedipal wishes of the boy resolve in his taking on a masculine model.

During the phallic period the girl notices the absence of a penis, and renounces her mother who also lacks one. She too transfers feelings to her father, but in realizing that she cannot have him fully, turns again toward the mother for love. Thus girls take on mothers as a referent for their self-concepts.

Freud's theory sees further differences in the dynamics of sex role development. Since for a boy the motive is castration anxiety, his Oedipal desires are effectively destroyed. His conscience develops rapidly so that he can make judgments for himself. However, for a girl castration has already occurred, so the fear of penis loss does not threaten her Oepidal wishes as much. Consequently, girls do not develop the independent superego or conscience of the boy.

Attacks of the psychoanalytic position have struck hard at Freud's preoccupation with the phallus. Certainly it is debatable that girls suffer trauma over recognition of their "castration" (Millet 1970). Certainly Freud's ideas were colored by his experiences in the male-dominated Victorian Viennese society of his time. And one must wonder whether children feel the depths of sensual passion he attributes to them. Nonetheless, some of Freud's observations retain sensibility today. He noted how both boys and girls perceive females as inferior. He observed how girls develop less independence. He recognized that the dynamics of sex role development are not identical for the boy or girl. Contemporary theorists have elaborated these themes.

In sociology, Parsons (1955) *functionalist role theory* continued the legacy of Freud, with some major revisions. First, he elaborated the role models that mother and father present to the child. The mother is the expressive or socioemotional leader of the family—the one who nurtures, and tends to the family members' needs within the domestic setting. The father, often absent from the home, links the external world to the family. To Parsons, each complements the other and the stability of the family hinges on this complementarity. The boy, in identifying with his father, requires an active, outward searching orientation toward the world, while the girl gains a personal, emotional worldview from her mother. Thus Parsons explains in more detail how the child acquires the sex role patterns of society.

Unlike Freud, who saw the girl's sex identity as more problematic, Parsons argues that it is the *boy* who will encounter more difficulties. The girl may internalize her father and what his masculinity represents, but she is still tied to the same parent (her mother) for self-identity. The boy, though, must break away from his mother with her emotional protection and identify with the unfamiliar, threatening father. Thus strains for boys are greater.

Given this process, the personality differences between the sexes are reflections of the total culture. Parsons qualifies that he is discussing only *potential* results of socialization in our society.

> Other things being equal, men would assume more technical, executive, and "judicial" roles, women more supportive, integrative, and "tension-managing" roles. However, this is at best an extremely broad formula and often other things very often are not equal.

This appears to be an academic qualification, for Parsons fails to discuss what those "other things" could be.

Critics have not ignored the missing elements. For example, Parsons' contention that mother and father play two different roles can be disputed. This is true only in the obvious sense that most fathers work and many mothers stay at home. Research on families (e.g., Blood and Wolfe 1960) shows that the roles do not always differentiate so clearly as Parsons suggests nor in the way he suggests. Indeed, one can argue that mothers are so busy meeting instrumental needs that they have little time to be "socioemotional." If Parsons is correct, the children with only one parent should not develop typical sex role behavior. This does not appear to be the case. Studies of one-parent families or mother-working families are notable for the paucity of differences they find between children of incomplete and two-parent families.[2] Sex role learning must come from other than the mere presence of two adults of the opposite sex.

Yet Parsons' notion that the boy has a harder time in constructing an identity has been extended by *social learning* theorists. Lynn (1966) and Kohlberg (1966) have given the most elaborate statements of this position, basing their ideas upon a synthesis of child development. The perspective separates what Parsons had left as one: namely, parental identification is viewed as distinct from sex role identification. A child may identify with masculine ideals while not identifying with or accepting the particular be-

---

2. One review of the literature (Yarrow 1964) notes that there has been no research at all on the effects of maternal separation on sex role development. Although there are a number of studies on families without a father, most study their effects on the sons. Many find differences between boys with fathers and those without them. However, none have had the type of research design that would show father's presence to be the crucial or determining variable in these differences. The one consistent finding is that boys without fathers may engage in "overcompensatory masculine behavior" (e.g., aggression, delinquency). This is not evidence for Parson's theory.

havior of his father. Similarly, he may identify with a father who is atypical of sex role expectations. This allows for a theory that incorporates models other than the parents. The media, teachers, and peers are also considered in the formation of sex role identity. The viewpoint also distinguishes sex role preference—the desire to adopt a behavior associated with one sex—from sex role identification—the actual incorporation of the expectations associated with one sex. A boy may desire to behave in feminine ways (preference) while exhibiting only masculine ways (identification).

This perspective is the most elaborate and specific of any, and it is difficult to summarize briefly. Lynn (1966, p. 470) has offered the following as a succinct statement of his view:

1. Males tend to identify with a culturally defined masculine role, whereas females tend to identify with their mothers.
2. Both males and females identify more closely with the mother than with the father.
3. The closer identification of males with their mothers than with their fathers will be revealed more frequently in personality variables which are not clearly sex-typed.
4. In learning the sex-typical identification, each sex is thereby acquiring separate methods of learning which are subsequently applied to learning tasks generally.
5. Males tend to have greater difficulty in achieving same-sex identification than females.
6. More males than females fail more or less completely in achieving same-sex identification but rather make an opposite-sex identification.
7. Males are more anxious regarding sex role identification than females.
8. Males tend to hold stronger feelings of hostility toward females than females toward males.
9. With increasing age, males become relatively more firmly identified with the masculine role.
10. With increasing age, males develop psychological disturbances at a more slowly accelerating rate than females.
11. A larger proportion of females than males show preference for the role of the opposite sex.
12. Where a discrepancy exists between sex role preference and identification, it will tend to be as follows:
    Males will tend to show same-sex role preference with underlying opposite-sex identification. Females will tend to show opposite-sex role preference with underlying same-sex identification.
13. A higher proportion of females than males adopt aspects of the role of the opposite sex.

Note how this approach emphasizes the problems for the male, as well as the prestige masculinity brings in our society. It is hard to become a male, buts its rewards are such that females prefer and identify with the male role.

Though this orientation is provocative and has a ring of reality to it, problems remain. One is that too little data exist to support the many conclusions. Second, the perspective perpetuates the view that there are only two sex roles, and one or the other must be tried. It is easy to incorporate "bisexual" or "androgynous" or "neuter" identities into the framework. For example, to say that many girls prefer the male role is to say that more girls are androgynous. So long as the theory retains undefined concepts of "male-female," then it retains a conservative outlook. Like all the previous theories, there is an implication that one clear-cut sex identity, the one fitting one's body, is the only one of value. We have only to look at the women and men around us to know that this is oversimplification.

In order to make sense of Lynn's approach, we must define what is meant by "masculine" or "feminine" activities. For Bardwick (1971) and Hoffman (1972), the answer would be that boys develop more achievement needs than girls, who develop more social or affiliation needs. Their independent reviews of the literature are similar in the way they synthesize the data. Both argue that boys and girls enter the world with a different constitutional makeup. Thus "nature" is the first variable to be considered. Because boy and girl babies differ, parents respond to them in different ways. These parental reactions direct, shape, and even change the infant's initial dispositions.

A variety of research studies illustrate the role of parental handling. Moss (1967) observed thirty firstborn children and their mothers for the first three months of life. Sex differences were apparent from the beginning. For example, female infants slept more and were less fussy or irritable than boys. Mothers of boys held and stimulated them more than mothers of girls. Moss found that irritability was a signal to the mother of the child's need for attention. By separating babies into "restful" or "irritable" types, it was discovered that the *type* of baby, *not its sex,* was the best predictor of mother's behavior. Thus irritable girls received as much handling as irritable boys. If it is true that boys are more irritable on the average, then we can see how early differential socialization by sex begins.

Bardwick argues that the boy's striving for mastery of the environment begins these early months. Since boys are more active, they are subject to more controls from their parents. A struggle for autonomy against parental pressure results in an earlier development of self-esteem. The boy learns to evaluate himself for his own control and achievement in the world. The girl, being less troublesome and more responsive to any parental controls, has a more secure environment. Why then should she give it up? Since social relations reward the young girl so well, she seeks further pleasure by developing a sense of interdependence, conformity, and subjectivity.

Herein, claims Bardwick, is the reason for male achievement and female affiliation. When females do achieve, as in school, they seem to do so more for the affiliation success brings than mastery of the task itself. Smart girls are rewarded with popularity in elementary school. Boys appear to strive for mastery in the absence of social approval. Boys try to "figure the task," while girls try to "figure the teacher."

Hoffman discusses other evidence as to how girls are provided less opportunity for skill acquisition and independence. For example, Collard (1964) asked mothers of four-year-olds the ages they would expect a child to perform certain behaviors (e.g., the use of sharp scissors without supervision). Mothers of girls stated later ages than mothers of boys. Similarly, Garai and Scheinfeld (1968) observed that parents think girls are more fragile, even though they are sturdier and more mature than boys of the same age. Parents are more protective and anxious of girls' activities. Thus girls may learn to be hesitant of new activities and settings.

Bardwick recognizes too that many boys are not predisposed to be active, achievement-oriented, just as many girl infants are not so responsive to social stimulation. She argues that no amount of permissiveness by society will encourage an essentially quiet boy to be aggressive, just as no amount of allowance for dependency will turn a basically confident, independent girl into a passive woman. The culture may redirect or inhibit the "inappropriate" behaviors (e.g., calling the boy a sissy, or the girl an upstart), but this sanctioning is most likely to result in the child's finding more suitable ways to express his inclinations. The boy goes out for track and seeks intellectual success. This has been borne out by longitudinal studies that trace the personality changes of the same persons for several decades.[3] High-dependent girls become high-dependent women, and low-dependent girls become low-dependent women. Boys who are not dependent become more independent men. Correspondingly, aggressiveness is a stable trait in men. If unaggressive as boys, they remain so as adults. With women, no clear pattern from childhood remains.

The social learning perspective has established the complexity of the sex role learning process, and in doing so marks a break from theories premised upon commonsense masculinist ideology. Different bodies do not alone result in different personalities. Little girls are not raised to be all "sugar and spice and everything nice." Little boys learn to be men from their mothers, brothers, and male friends, not solely from the presence of

---

3. Two relevant studies here are Kagan and Moss (1962) and Block (1971).

he-men fathers. Little girls may be discouraged from participating in some physical activities, but overall they likely have more freedom than little boys, who are discouraged from engaging in activities that could be labelled as "feminine." Little girls do achieve, though not for achievement's sake itself. These are just a few of the conclusions that conflict with everyday beliefs about sex role learning.

Many other issues are unexplored. What role do fathers play in child rearing? So far only one attempt at this question has been made (Benson 1968). How do children themselves form images of themselves that are gender specific? A few studies of language learning suggest that young children apply gender distinctions to many common objects in their lives. We don't know how these gender conceptions evolve or whether the child thinks them very important. And what of the many socialization outcomes that have been ignored to date while investigators have focused their studies on achievement and dominance? On what traits, skills, and attitudes are girls and boys in our society essentially similar? Children do learn sex roles, *and much more.* Our exploration of their world has just begun.

Play and Games

Empirically, there is strong evidence that peers are second to the family in importance for socialization. In the peer group practice in social relationships occurs which contributes to the child's developing self-concept as well as her attitudes and values concerning the world around her. The family and the peer groups either share or compete for the major role in the development of a capable, competent social being. However, social scientists have much overlooked the daily activities of peer groups. In the socialization literature, one will often find what seems to be a "carbon copy" model of peer influence. Theorists presume that peers have a monolithic force upon individual children. With regard to sex roles, for example, one will often read statements as to how boys pressure each other to be physically skillful and behave "like men."

Actually, there is a vast literature which suggests that the process of peer socialization is more complicated. Most peer activities prior to adolescence take the form of play and games. Both are *autotelic* activities, that is, engaged in for themselves, for fun's sake, and not for any life-serious purpose. We refer to them in everyday speech as "recreation," an apt designation, for they recreate activities from real life. Play is distinguished from games in being less structured and more open-ended with regard to outcomes. Games have some elements of repeatable patterns, oppositions, and outcomes. We are much less able to predict the course of events of children playing house than of their playing a game of hopscotch. The former lacks elaborate, explicit rules about the constraints under which the children are bound. No goals are apparent. Indeed, much play is a dialogue concerning the construction of rules, constraints, and goals in an attempt to mimic real-life counterpart situations. When the same children play hopscotch, they take on a ready-made structure. Disputes will arise not so much over what the rules are, as to how they are to be interpreted. All players accept that the activity is an individual competition surrounding physical skill.

Play is characteristic of young children's activities. As Stone (1965) has perceptively observed, the child's first experience is as a *plaything* of its mother. In time, the mother and the infant are mutually players and playthings, and the infant responds to play actions of the mother with those of her own. This play is the infant's first opportunity for the learning of social meanings and the practice of symbolic communication in areas other than the immediate fulfillment of sleep, food, or comfort. Play provides rich creative opportunities for a discourse upon which a vast social symbolism can be elaborated.

The heart of socialization for the individual is the emergence of what Cooley (1922) and Mead (1934) have called the *self,* a psychic entity through which the child defines her person. The child is able to see herself as an object as well as a subject; she can reflect upon herself. The self arises out of communication, for linguistic descriptions are needed to clarify distinctions between the self and other objects. By the age of two, most children have sufficient language to make self-designations. Soon after this time they begin to play beside and with children of their own age. The self is not simply a stable set of attitudes; rather, it can be viewed as a set of processes surrounding these beliefs. Cooley stressed three processes: the presentation of a self (How do I appear to others?), the interpretation of the other's reaction to that presentation (What do the others think of me?), and an emotional response to that interpretation (Is their reaction pleasurable?). According to this model of behavior, people act on the basis of what they perceive and what they take account of.

During play activities, children perceive and take account of sequences of role-playing dramas. By taking the role of others—parents, firemen, other children, shopkeepers, fairies—they can reflect on themselves as different from others. They are also able to comprehend the relatedness of persons and roles. Stone suggests that realistically based role-playing serves as *anticipatory socialization,* a means through which the child can prepare for the enactment of roles in later life. Fantastically based play, such as cowboys and indians, probably serves to maintain the myths, legends, villains, and heroes of a society's past.

Where do sex roles enter in? Obviously, a child's conception of his or her gender will be a major component around which the self can be organized. Given Cooley's statement on self processes, the following could be asked by a girl, Am I displaying myself in feminine ways? Do others see me as a girl? How does it feel to be viewed as a girl? Of course, the process is complicated because there can be discrepancies at any point. The child may not make a fuss about "being a girl," yet discover that others pick out those features of her self-presentation that are gender preferred. Or she may try to present herself as feminine from mistaken presumptions of what it means to be feminine, and not receive the reaction she expects. The learning theorists would suggest that girls in our society will learn to display femininity, yet receive reactions from others such that they do not learn to value femininity highly. Here is the start of the "low self-concept" one often reads 'about with regard to women. Similarly, boys will have more difficulty learning how to display masculininity, yet will value it as part of their selves once they accomplish its management.

In order to present masculine or feminine characteristics, children need a setting in which to express them. We should expect some sex differences in play behavior for two reasons. First, we would predict that socializing agents such a parents and nursery school teachers will attempt to teach sex role preferences by controlling the child's access to gender-specific settings, toys, and activities. Second, we should expect that given a range of activities, children will select freely those activities that provide for the expression of their gender characteristics. In everyday terms, do girls play with dolls, boys with trucks, each learning her or his place? The answer is not clear.

Stone has noted that boys more often engage in fantastic role-playing while girls have more realistic play (e.g., boys play cowboys while girls play mother or teacher). He suggests that this play repertoire "makes it difficult for boys to establish an early well-founded conception of adult life, and, consequently, hinders their assumption of an adult identity." When boys do play realistic roles, such as that of father, their activity often reflects their ignorance of male adult roles.

> For example, a colleague noticed a boy and girl playing house in a front yard. The little girl was very busy sweeping up the play area, rearranging furniture, moving dishes about, and caring for baby dolls. The boy, on the other hand, would leave the play area on his bicycle, disappear to the back of the (real) house, remain for a brief while, reappear in the play area, and lie down in a feigned

sleep. The little girl had a rather extensive knowledge of the mother role, but for the boy, a father was one who disappeared, reappeared, and slept, *ad infinitum* (Stone 1965, p. 30).

This example further illustrates how limited childrens' views of sex roles or expectations can be. Sexuality, sociability, and the economic features of family life are left out of the drama, though these are profound gender-specific spheres of activity.

Play behavior was a popular topic of study for child development investigators in the 20s and 30s who took to the playgrounds and nurseries to observe natural behavior. Unfortunately very little research has been done since then. The one consistent finding among these studies is that *similarities in the play of girls and boys in childhood are greater than the differences.* For example, studies of toy preference have repeatedly shown that the majority of boys and girls play with dolls. One of the few toys that is hightly gender specific seems to be the vehicle (cars, trains, trucks). Blocks, clay, crayons, sandboxes, and so on are used by both sexes. Of course, the way in which they are used may differ, but this has not been studied systematically. Another common finding is that boys play with more physical energy and touching than girls. Otherwise, we know very little about sex differences in play.[4]

Important missing data from the previous houseplaying example are the verbal exchanges between the "mother" and "father." These conversations are more elaborate than the simple behavioral expressions of roles the observer noted. To what extent did the children expect the "mother" and "father" to be behaving as they did? Were there any disputes and over what activities? When children argue during play they are constructing rules that they see governing the roles they are playing. Sociologists have only recently turned to the study of language learning and its role in the development of the self, so it will be some time before evidence with regard to play conversations and the formation of gender attitudes will be available.

If play is a free-form drama for the creation and practice of roles, then games represent microcosms of society in which the child can learn about her role in the social order. Mead places game experience as the final step in the development of the self. It is not enough that individuals understand the nature and content of others' roles well enough to act them out. Rather, for Mead, the self-conscious individual assumes the organized social attitudes of the group to which she belongs. In behavioral terms, the indi-

---

4. Those interested in play research will benefit by referring to Millar (1968) and Herron and Sutton-Smith (1971).

vidual would recognize that there is a general group opinion toward some issue, that she has certain rights and obligations toward others in meeting group goals, and that she will judge herself on the basis of group standards. Mead refers to ball as an illustration:

> The game has logic, so that such an organization of the self is rendered possible: there is a definite end to be obtained; the actions of the different individuals are all related to each other with reference to that end so that they do not conflict; one is not in conflict with himself in the attitude of another man on the team. If one has the attitude of the person throwing the ball he can also have the response of catching the ball. The two are related so that they further the purpose of the game itself. They are interrelated in a unitary, organic fashion. There is a definite unity, then, which is introduced into the organization of other selves when we reach such a stage as that of the game, as over against the situation of play where there is a simple succession of one role after another, a situation which is, of course, characteristic of the child's own personality. The child is one thing at one time and another at another, and what he is at one moment does not determine what he is at another. That is both the charm of childhood as well as its inadequacy. You cannot count on your child; you cannot assume that all the things he does are going to determine what he will do at any moment. He is not organized into a whole. The child has no definite character, no definite personality (Mead 1934, p. 236).

Game rules are organizations of reciprocal responses, and to the extent that the child grasps these rules, she understands and makes herself part of a system of organized roles.

In real life, social groups or communities have an organized character similar to the game. As the child plays games, she acquires the experience to generalize from the particular attitudes of persons ("Mary expects me to chase ground balls over there") to the attitudes of the group in general in given situations ("A good right fielder is supposed to cover that area of the field for grounders"). The child uses logic to deduce overall principles of behavior, and judges herself in terms of these principles. Once the child takes on the view of this "generalized other," Mead argues, the self is complete and fully a social product.

Games will be meaningful for sex role socialization in several ways. First, the general society may view some games as gender-specific. For example, football and other body contact sports are generally considered to be "masculine." To the extent that girls are omitted from such activities, they will not have the opportunity to deal with physical aggression and violence in the same way that boys do. Thus, the exclusion of one sex from a type of game means that it may not develop the same skills or attitudes as the other participating sex. Second, when children violate expectations and participate in games considered to be inappropriate, then they will have to resolve the situation with regard to the meaning of gender for themselves. Boys who prefer intellectual games such as chess must decide whether or not to accept some persons' belief that the game is not "manly." Third, games may provide opportunities to engage in activities that outside the game would be considered inappropriate for the player in the real world. Competitive games predominate in American society, so most girls have an extensive practice at competitive success situations on the playground that they are discouraged from in other settings. Finally, the everyday practices surrounding games may also reinforce, accelerate, or reverse the intentions of socializing agents. When teachers pick game leaders, they may do so often on the basis of gender and select a boy. When children freely do so apart from adult supervision, they may perpetuate sexist practices or break them. Play and games provide peers with an opportunity to develop their own standards, their own "generalized other." In this way, each generation is able to create its own rules for behavior.

Although we can list many ways in which games are important, again little research on sex roles is available. Fortunately, the data that exists has been the result of the efforts of one work group of experts. Their investigations over the past decade have moved from the simple question—do girls and boys play different games?—to intricate studies of the sex differences in game playing. That the same investigators have executed the research means that a consistency in methods and theory underlies the work. Let us examine the most important studies and see how they complement what has been said to this point.

Roberts and Sutton-Smith (1962) have studied the relationship between game structures and socialization outcomes. Three pure types of games are distinguished, though many games include several of these dimensions: (1) games of *physical skill,* where motor activities determine the outcome, (2) games of *chance,* where guesses or random events determine the course of events, and (3) games of *strategy,* where rational choices among possible courses of action determine the outcome. In studying the repertoire of games played in various societies, the investigators discovered the following:

1. Games of strategy prevail in cultures that emphasize obedience.
2. Games of chance prevail in cultures that encourage responsibility.
3. Games of physical skill-strategy combination prevail in cultures that reward achievement.

Given these results, the researchers wondered whether they could understand the differential socialization of boys and girls in America. They noted, as we did earlier, that boys receive more achievement training from parents, while girls receive more obedience and responsibility training. Could one then predict the game preferences of girls and boys? If their theory was correct, then the hypotheses would be:

1. Girls, with their higher obedience training, should show a greater preference for games of strategy than boys.
2. Girls, with their higher responsibility training, should show a greater preference for games of chance than boys.
3. Boys, with their higher training in achievement, should show a greater preference for physical skill than girls.

In one test of these hypotheses, Roberts and Sutton-Smith obtained a list of favorite games from 1,900 school children. The games were categorized according to their typology and tabulated by sex of the respondent. Table 5-3 presents the results. Overall, all three hypotheses were supported.

Table 5-3
Game Preferences by Sex

Game Classes	Nonsignificant	Favoring Girls*	Favoring Boys*
Strategy	N=8 (Dominoes, chess, parchesi, etc.)	N=5 (I've got a secret, I spy)	N=4
Chance	N=4 (Coin-matching, forfeits)	N=7 (Bingo, spin the bottle)	N=1 (Dice)
Physical-Strategy	N=5 (Handball, tennis, volleyball)	N=1 (Pick-up sticks)	N=11 (Marbles, wrestling, boxing)

*Games where preferences differ in stated direction at p= .05 or better. The Ns in the table refer to individual tests of the hypotheses for separate games.

Source: Roberts and Sutton-Smith (1962), Table 7.

Several other points are relevant. First, we are not sure of the reason for the game choices. Since Roberts and Sutton-Smith did not measure the children's evaluation of "obedience, responsibility, achievement," then we can only presume these to be operating. Second, we don't know whether children play the games because they are reinforcing already established ideals or because the games offer new ideals. Do boys desire to achieve and thus turn to games of physical strategy, or do boys play the games and consequently develop a sense of achievement? This remark reiterates a common social science dictum: *correlation doesn't mean casuality*. When two items are found to be related, we can't be sure which one, if either, is the "cause." The final issue is that these data demonstrate the overlap between experiences as well as the differences. In particular, note that no game of strategy is predominated by boys; most games of strategy are preferred by both sexes.

In another study, Rosenburg and Sutton-Smith (1960) examined the game preferences of children by sex and compared them to studies of children several decades before. Their list consisted of 181 games. Children were asked to mark the ones they had played and note whether they liked or disliked them. Sixty-six of the games were eliminated because of infrequent responses. Of the games remaining, here is the breakdown:

> 18 games were played more often by boys
> 40 games were played more often by girls
> 57 games were played by both

Many of the games traditionally seen as masculine (basketball, cowboys, racing, baseball, etc.) were among the "no difference" list. Why is this so? The researchers argue that we don't know about the actual *participation* rates of the students. This is true; however, research on game participation (Stoll et al. 1968) as well as that of Eiferman (1968) suggests that these preferences *are* fairly adequate reflections of participation.

Another reason is historical. When the investigators examined the game preferences of children in the past, they could identify a clear trend. First, girls are now playing a wider variety of games than in the past while the number of games boys play has been considerably reduced. Second, girls now show greater preference for what were once boys' games while boys have not developed any preferences for girls' games. In addition, girls are retaining their own distinctive play roles. This evidence supports the theory that girls in America have less constrictive expectations than boys who face many more proscriptions in their activities. In later studies (Sutton-Smith and Roberts 1964), this view was shown to be plausible.

The School

Virtually every child in America shares a minimum of ten years experience in public schools. These settings presumably exist to train children for both the technical skills they will need in adult roles and to inculcate them with the values, norms, and motivational underpinnings that will assure their commitment to the society. But who is to decide what technical skills any particular child shall learn? This decision is a political one for only some of the youngsters can be directed towards careers of distinction, high reward, and power. Furthermore, in a society such as ours conflicts occur among subcultures as to which norms and values are primary. Because schools are political bodies, certain groups have more influence than others over determining what occurs. Thus, schools are places for recruitment to occupational slots and for indoctrination to the world view of those with power to direct their policies.

Historically, schools in the United States have served to reinforce those who hold the following ideologies or positions—racism, sexism, capitalism, urbanism, sectarianism. Members of ethnic or racial subcultures have, from the point of view of educators, been "assimilated" to mainstream American political and economic values. In reality, persons belonging to these groups were tracked in various ways so that they were directed towards the less-valued positions in society.[5] At the same time they were introduced to considerable political indoctrination so that they accepted the goals of democracy, individualism, personal achievement, and capitalism, while being denied equal opportunity in fact. Many of these persons did not want to give up the values of their special membership groups; they were forced to remain confused, live two distinct lives, or try to succeed at both—all strategies fraught with personal problems and many personal failures as a result. This situation is changing as minorities have acquired sufficient political awareness and power in various localities to force changes in the schools' organization.

Many of the processes that affect the lives of poor nonwhite and powerless ethnic students apply to girls as well. For example, girls have been tracked by the curriculum designs into one set of occupations, while

5. This process is known as *cooling out*. Clark (1956) has described how failure is structured into schools such that those who fail do so without reacting to the school (or society) with blame. The features of this process include (1) alternative achievement goals are suggested; (2) disengagement from the goal of success is gradual; (3) record keeping and other impersonal procedures force the student to confront only herself instead of the organization when problems arise; (4) teachers and counselors function to console while redirecting the student toward lesser aspirations; (5) standards of performance are sufficiently ambiguous that authorities can readily find reasons why persons deserve less reward.

boys are tracked toward others. Many high schools have secretarial or business diplomas populated primarily by girls who will leave to fill low-paying clerical slots. A bright boy is much more likely to be encouraged to take college preparatory courses than a bright girl is. She is, after all, "going to get married." Race and ethnicity enter in here, such that a bright poor boy is also less likely to be directed toward college, and a bright poor girl may be directed toward a meaningless "general education" diploma that leaves her with no skills at all.

Doubtless too, girls suffer the consequences of similar insidious stereotyping that affects the lives of other out-of-the-mainstream students. Much research in education has considered the influence a teacher's expectations have on the way he will react toward a student. If the teacher expects the student to perform well, he will encourage, reward, and direct the child to succeed. The actual frequency and directness of interactions toward "good students" (as the teacher views them) is greater than toward the "poor students." This is one example of the feedback looping discussed in chapter three. It has been shown that teachers direct themselves more toward boys than toward girls. Furthermore, much of the feedback girls receive from teachers tends to dampen motivation. A bright girl may not only be ignored, she may be reminded that being bright is not so important for her. That some dampening occurs can be seen in the fact that girls' performances in school begin in first grade ahead of boys, then gradually fall behind; boys improve their performances with schooling. (Analogous trends and gaps in grades and test scores exist as well when one compares nonwhite and white students.)

It is known that one indicator of racism in a school system is the allocation of monies: the nonwhite schools in a school system often receive fewer supplies, support budgets, maintenance, and so on. Similarly, programs for girls often gain less support. School athletics is the most obvious illustration. For decades, "sports" in school have been synonymous with "men's sports." Women's athletic facilities have been decidedly inferior and lacking. Consequently, few women have retained an interest in athletics, and those few that do have suffered the consequences of being deviant females. And because men's sports are so well nurtured, the unathletic young man has suffered as well. In another area, that of teacher's salaries, sexism persists in that female teachers are more poorly paid than comparable male counterparts and are much less likely to move up to administrative positions.

The issues of sexism is more complicated than these few processes indicate. A sophisticated observer of racism understands what is meant when some say that "the oppressor is also oppressed." With regard to sexism, some would argue that sexism hurts boys as well as girls. In fact, some educational researchers believe that boys lose out even more than girls at school. Finally, the role of schools in socialization must be placed in a larger perspective; otherwise it is very easy to oversimplify the scope of that role. Let us turn to several particular perspectives concerning schools and gender identity that illuminate these issues.

Teachers as Socializers   The most direct adult model available in the schools is the classroom teacher. Anyone interested in sex role socialization would naturally wonder what effects teachers have in creating and perpetuating identities based upon gender. One viewpoint popular among many educators and social scientists is that schools, especially at the elementary level, are populated by women teachers who espouse feminine values. Orderliness, self-discipline, and conformity are preferred to disarray, impulsiveness, and active disobedience. Feminine interests are emphasized—artistic works over machines. Consequently, the argument goes, girls perform well while boys are frustrated. A boy who succeeds at school becomes "feminized," just as a boy who fails is one who does so because he retains his masculine self-image of toughness and aggressiveness. The policy implication of this view is to press for more male teachers, as well as more masculine curricular materials.[6] The most complete statement of this argument is Sexton's thesis (1969) on *The Feminized Male*.

This argument can be found in other areas of society as well. It is premised upon the assumption that there are only two sex roles and that for society and personalities to function "healthfully," these roles must be maintained. Is this a sexist position? Sexton herself argues that what matters is that girls get their chances for success at the same time that boys are being femininized. Yet it is difficult to maintain that the sex roles should be perpetuated so long as rights and privileges are predominantly assigned to males.

In considering the details of this argument, one can understand why some opposing views have developed. First, it assumes that two sex roles are accepted throughout our society, regardless of social class, ethnicity, and race. Not only is there evidence lacking here, but the burden of proof seems to be on those who argue that only two sex roles exist. Consider how differently a blue collar male, a long-haired college student, and a Chicano farmworker would express their masculinity. There is no clear standard.

---

6. Stasz et al. (1972) have reviewed the literature on the effect of a teacher's sex upon student performance. They found the results of the studies to be inconclusive. In their own study, an experiment was designed to see whether boys or girls had better achievement with male or female teachers. They found that teacher or student sex did not correlate in any consistent way with student performance.

The blue-collar worker and the male college student would both argue that hair length is a necessary proof of their maleness, though one would have short hair and the other one long. There is, nonetheless, a mythology that *one* type of masculinity exists—white, middle-class, acquisitive, sociable, physically active, modestly dressed male. This view of masculinity is the one fostered in the schools and the minds of educators, though it clashes with the views of many young men in our society. Perhaps it is true that gender distinctions are necessary in any society. Need this imply that there can only be two sex roles of very different character? It happens not to be the case in America today, regardless of our mythological blinders. Many ideals of masculinity and femininity coexist.

Second, the argument errs in believing that because women occupy a social position, the character of that setting is "feminine." Sexton gives no evidence that women teachers espouse "feminine" values and norms. Similarly, there is no reason to presume that male teachers, by virtue of their gender, would somehow masculinize schools. Commitment to gender ideals, as the mythology presents them, varies considerably. In fact, Terman and Miles (1936) discovered that female schoolteachers scored lower on their measures of femininity than other occupational groups. More recent research on attitudes toward the myths concerning gender role has shown that as education increases, individuals are less likely to view themselves in gender-specific terms. (The error in the proposal here applies elsewhere. For example, the entry of women into medicine may not personalize the doctor-patient relationship, as some hope, because the type of woman who goes into medicine may not value interpersonal skills.)

Third, this argument ignores much hard data. As will be illustrated shortly, curriculum materials hardly ignore masculine pursuits and interests. In fact, it is girls who lose here. As for success in school, it is girls whose performance recedes, whose self-esteem decreases over the years. In addition, we have already seen how boys, if anything, are pushed too much into a constraining gender-identity, one less free for expression than girls. Boys who do well in school must also prove themselves on the athletic field in order to avoid taunts of being called a sissy. Girls have no comparable problem (until adolescence). If schools are hard on boys, it is in insisting upon their performing according to rigid middle-class views of masculinity, not in feminizing them.

The argument is valuable in reminding us that many young men do find school boring, that they do resort to activities that get them in serious difficulty with political authorities. The repression of young men by school and police, however, is focused at poor, nonwhite, and disenfranchised ethnic males—those whose views of masculinity conflict with that of men in power. Further support of this thesis is that in recent years privileged young men whose views of masculinity accommodate "feminine" ways (e.g., long hair, colorful dress) are being repressed as well. The problem is larger than one of providing young men with *machismo* teachers and books. It concerns privilege and power in society as a whole. It ignores how young women, though docile and not in trouble with authorities, are no less repressed by one group in society. Parenthetically, one might ask why certain groups of young women aren't getting in trouble as their brothers are. The answer may be that the girls, regardless of subculture, share the same fate as wives. The boys know that only some of them will "get the action" in adult positions.

Textbooks as Socializers   As was explained earlier, socialization agents need not be persons. They can take the form of structure of rules, as we saw with games, or be some cultural object that somehow directs and incites the socializee to respond. Given this, educators have examined textbooks in order to understand their role upon the formation of gender identity. Ideologies about the usefulness of gender-identity underlie research in the area.

On one hand, some investigators believe that young boys are not being given sufficient "masculine" (i.e., adventuresome, outspoken, rough) imagery in textbooks. Reviewing the literature, Austin et al. (1971) have noted that boys and girls arrive at school with the same verbal and reading skills. By the end of first grade the girls have moved ahead in achievement. They argue that the content of early readers is "feminine" because it emphasizes family life, art and music, poetry, and overlooks "boys" interests such as outdoor adventure and sports. Similarly, the language found in the readers more closely relates to the vocabulary used by girls than that used by boys. As the authors repeat throughout, "boys want to be boys" and the "unsexed" state of early textbooks is hampering their achievement in school. A variety of studies by another set of investigators (Zimet 1971) has reached similar conclusions about the nature of elementary textbooks.

Other investigators have concluded that the images (if any) presented in early texts and readers, present rigid sex-role portraits. In one study of 134 elementary readers (Women on Words and Images, 1972), ratios on the following themes occurred:

Boy-centered stories to girl-centered stories	5:2
Adult male main characters to adult female main characters	3:1
Male biographies to female biographies	6:1

Male folk or fantasy stories to female folk or fantasy stories	4:1
Male animal stories to female animal stories	2:1

In no one book were girls in appearance as frequently as boys. Also, whenever occupations were mentioned, females were participants of twenty-six "womanly" occupations, while men were participants in 147 different jobs.

Those stories in which boys or girls appeared as characters were analyzed for the traits the characters exhibited. These data hardly support the view that boys are being presented with "non-masculine" role models. Boys predominated when the following activities or traits occurred: cleverness and ingenuity, problem-solving success, strength and bravery, elective helpfulness, acquisition of skills, rewards, adventuresome or imaginative play, and altruism. In contrast, girls predominated as characters with regard to these themes: routine helpfulness, passivity, and pseudo-dependence, goal constriction and rehearsal for domesticity, victimization and humiliation. Only one theme—incompetence or mishaps—is the character likely to be of either sex.

In an examination of prizewinning picture books for young children, Weitzman et al. (1972) discovered similar patterns. Females were underrepresented by a ratio of eleven to one in the illustrations. Counting animals, the ratio increased to ninety-five male animals to every one female! Their analysis drew conclusions similar to those in the studies of readers.

Why are there such discrepant conclusions? One answer rests with the methods of research. All of the investigators resorted to *content analysis,* the categorization of printed material as a way of summarizing its messages to readers. The studies are not incompatible because the category schemes were so different. Those who find that boys lack masculine role images have looked at the settings of activities (Dick and Jane *do* spend a lot of time at home) and the language, which does omit words spoken frequently by boys. Those who find that rigid sex roles are present in the books have looked at the number of each sex present in stories and the activities each sex has exhibited. I would argue that the latter investigators are categorizing the content in a manner that is more meaningful for understanding the formation of gender-identity. The books *do* display persons of each gender behaving in gender-specific ways. This is not to discredit the value of the other research, for it may indeed be the case that boys would respond more to books were the material less domestic and artistic—but the *girls* might respond better too.

Both arguments are premised upon a theory of socialization that must be debated. Both sides presume that media content molds a child's mind. This is a simplistic prevalent view of media impact. It presumes that the reader is receiving the message accurately, that she accepts the message without change, and that she behaves in accord afterward. By now we have considerable social psychological research to discredit these presumptions. People approach new ideas with a preestablished set of attitudes. They tend to select out those ideas most consistent with their previous beliefs and reject or reinterpret material that is less consistent. We also know that attitudes are not necessarily good predictors of behavior. Consequently, the fact that the books present rigid sex roles is important in that students who hold such views will have them reinforced. There is less reason for arguing that media images *create* these roles. It should be remembered too that the books become part of a social activity. The teachers' responses to ideas presented in books may contradict the message being presented.

Fellow students as socializers.   In American schools, students progress in age cohorts. This practice encourages the formation of strong peer groups which may reinforce or compete with formal schooling systems. Prior to puberty, peer groups often have a single-sex character, and leisure activities in the form of games or social clubs are frequently all-girl or all-boy. At adolescence, physiological maturity brings sexuality into the fore and emotional maturity brings love-seeking into mind. The two sexes now have reasons to mix, and the youth culture becomes very strong as it organizes around these needs.

In *Adolescent Society,* Coleman (1961) studied the climate of values that underlie popularity in high school. By sampling twelve high schools from very different localities—affluent and working class, suburban and urban, large and small—he was able to identify themes from adolescence that seemed to occur regardless of the community or social background of the school. In identifying leaders, he was able to discern a variety of bases for popularity. Boys could be classified as scholars, athletes, athlete-scholars, and ladies' men, depending upon the basis for their reputation. Girls were categorized by other students as being popular for their looks or their school performance. Coleman wondered what the social consequences of various types of popularity would be. Table 5-4 shows one result: the average number of times a leader was chosen by name as being someone to be with and to like, who was a member of the leading crowd, or who was considered to be a close friend. This one table discloses considerable information on the adolescent subculture.

Table 5-4
Average Sociometric Choices Received by Boy and Girl Leaders and Non-leaders

	Be with and be like	"Leading crowd" designation	Chosen as close friend	Number of cases
Response received by:				
Boys				
Athlete-scholar	9.9	12.5	7.1	(54)
Athlete	4.6	6.6	5.9	(218)
Ladies' man	2.4	6.4	5.8	(138)
Scholar	1.9	3.1	4.4	(224)
All others	0.4	0.8	2.9	(3,480)
Girls				
"Beauty" types	5.6	9.3	6.6	(278)
"Brains" types	4.8	4.6	5.7	(380)
All others	1.2	2.5	4.1	(4,135)

Source: Coleman (1961), Tables 24, 26, and 31.

First, note that the athlete-scholar is the most popular of all boys, regardless of measure, and the girl noted for her beauty is the most desirable as well. Each of these types represents gender-specific attributes. Thus, one can say that scoring high on masculinity or femininity *in the mythological sense* is a basic element of popularity for these youths. However, boys and girls who achieve scholastically are rewarded highly as well. This performance is not tied so closely to sex stereotypes. In fact, many people might expect that brainy girls would be unpopular. Coleman's research showed the contrary: if a girl isn't beautiful, she does well by being smart.

Second, interesting differences in the variability of popularity between the sexes is present. Specifically, being a leader is much more necessary for social rewards for boys than for girls. Boys in the "other" or non-leader category (which means the vast majority of boys) receive fewer choices on the average than girls who are not leaders. In other words, the popularity system in high school seems much more rigid and restrictive with regard to the males. The few boys who make it big receive rich rewards, but most boys are "just average guys." Girls can be more secure in their social environment.

From this small piece of Coleman's data one can see how sex roles become a salient feature of the adolescent's self-definition. But it is not the only one. Coleman's research can be misleading because given the way he phrased his questions, student respondents had little choice but to label people as "athletes" or "brains." In other words, Coleman's own ideas about sex roles in adolescence shaped the way he collected his data. Another problem is that he focused upon the leaders—the small minority of students. What about the 85 percent of the boys who are not popular athletes or brains? Also, if so few boys can meet the masculine ideals of athletics and school achievement, then what of their sense of masculinity? Some of these boys are special in another way, as delinquents. Most young men, however, are neither outstanding leaders *nor* delinquents; their lives are yet uncharted for the rest of us to understand well.

One important study on adolescence has given us some insight on the "average" girl. Douvan and Adelson (1966) surveyed a national sample of adolescents in the mid-fifties. By separating the respondents into age categories, they were able to see how attitudes apparently change over time. What occurs in most terms is that girls and boys are not very different in early adolescence. Both hold similar attitudes with regard to their parents, jobs, future, education, marriage. Within a few years, however, the boy focuses much of his life-concern upon occupational success, while the girl turns more toward social and marital success.

The investigators realized that overall trends for girls as a group cannot be applied to girls as individuals. In order to better understand the variations in development of a feminine identity, they examined the individual responses on the following items:

1. Choice of a traditional masculine occupation
2. An active desire to be a boy
3. Belief that a boy's life is more desirable than a girl's
4. Rejection of marriage

Girls who scored positively on these goals or values rejected traditional feminine ideals. It appeared, however, that some girls did not fall easily into one "antifeminine" category. In further exploring the responses, Douvan and Adelson concluded that a variety of gender identities were evolving among the girls, as follows:

1. Unambivalent, feminine girls, who scored high on traditional feminine values and expressed no typically masculine preferences
2. Ambivalent feminine girls, who scored high on feminine items, yet made masculine preferences as well (androgynous girls)
3. Neutral girls, whose interests and goals did not stress either of the traditional sex role ideals

4. Boyish girls, who scored low on feminine measures and high on desire to engage in boys' pursuits
5. Achievement-oriented girls, who ignored feminine goals of marriage and family, and emphasized masculine occupational pursuits
6. Antifeminine girls, who did not want to marry (Perhaps more appropriately, they should be called male-rejecting.)

Douvan and Adelson's research reminds us that in spite of social pressures toward extreme masculine and feminine ideals, individuals choose whether or not these ideas are going to be meaningful for themselves. For many young women, femininity in the traditional sense is not considered to be the only life course to take. Most of these respondents likely did marry and follow the traditional path. It may not have been the one they preferred had they been given the freedom to choose other options. This research shows how in the fifties many young women had the potential interest in feminism; only the structures for expressing and acting upon that ideology were not yet present.

The investigators did not have a large enough sample of boys to perform a similar analysis. Possibly, boys who do not score high on masculinity fall into fewer subtypes than one finds for girls. Boys do not have the option of admitting that they enjoy feminine pursuits. Consequently, boys who do not score highly on traditional masculine practices may fall into an "ambivalent" or "neutral" category. Hypothetically, the average boy may not be as "masculine" as mythology would hold. The thrust of socialization research to date suggests very strongly that people do not slip their identities so readily into the cloaks provided by culture. Perhaps culture offers more than one cloak for each gender.

SUGGESTED PROJECTS

1. Textbook surveys necessarily simplify material. Explore one of the theorists described here (Freud, Parsons, Lynn, Kohlberg, Bardwick) in more detail. Did the author's description of their work ignore important points, distort the theorists' views, or misinterpret their ideas? Write a brief essay that you believe better captures their ideas on sex-role socialization.
2. For your own self-insight, analyze the components of your own gender-identity socialization, referring to the concepts from the model presented in the first part of this chapter. Keep in mind the ideals of "femininity" or masculinity" that existed in your social locality and any subcultures your family participated in.
3. Select an ethnic, religious, or racial group with a strong subculture. See how much you can learn about its definitions of femininity and masculinity from biographies, special interest media, and interviews. How do its definitions conflict with, specify, or reinforce those of the white middle class? Are its members aware of discrepancies?

REFERENCES

Austin, David; Clar, Velma B.; and Fitchett, Gladys. *Reading Rights for Boys.* New York: Appleton-Century-Crofts, 1971.

Bardwick, Judith. *Psychology of Women.* New York: Harper & Row, Publishers, 1971.

Benson, Leonard. *Fatherhood: A Sociological Perspective.* New York: Random House, 1968.

Block, Jack. *Lives through Time.* Berkeley, Calif.: Bancroft-Whitney Company, 1971.

Blood, Robert O., Jr., and Wolfe, Donald M. *Husbands and Wives.* New York: The Free Press, 1960.

Clark, Burton R. "The 'Cooling-out' Function in Higher Education." *American Journal of Sociology* 65(1956):569-76.

Coleman, James S. *Adolescent Society.* New York: The Free Press, 1961.

Collard, E. D. "Achievement Motive in the Four-year-old Child and Its Relationship to Achievement Expectancies of the Mother." Ph.D. dissertations, University of Michigan, 1964.

Cooley, Charles Horton. *Human Nature and the Social Order.* New York: Charles Scribner's Sons, 1922.

Douvan, Elizabeth, and Adelson, Joseph. *The Adolescent Experience.* New York: John Wiley & Sons, Inc., 1966.

Eiferman, Rivka R. *School Children's Games.* Washington, D.C.: US Department of Health, Education, and Welfare, 1968.

Freud, Sigmund. *Collected Papers of Sigmund Freud.* Edited by Ernest Jones. New York: Basic Books, 1959.

Garai, J. E., and Scheinfeld, A. "Sex Differences in Mental and Behavioral Traits." *Genetic Psychology Monographs* 77(1968):169-299.

Harlow, Harry F. *Learning to Love.* San Francisco: Albion Publishing Co., 1971.

Herron, R. E., and Sutton-Smith, Brian. *Child's Play.* New York: John Wiley & Sons, Inc., 1971.

Hoffman, Lois Wladis. "Early Childhood Experiences and Women's Achievement Motives." *Journal of Social Issues* 28(1972):129-55.

Kagan, J., and Moss, H. A. *Birth to Maturity.* New York: John Wiley & Sons, Inc., 1962.

Kohlberg, Lawrence. "A Cognitive-Developmental Analysis of Children's Sex-role Concepts and Attitudes." In *The Development of Sex Differences,* by Eleanor Maccoby. Stanford, Calif.: Stanford University Press.

Lynn, David B. "The Process of Learning Parental and Sex Role Identification." *Journal of Marriage and the Family* 28(1966):446-70.

Mead, George Herbert. *Mind, Self, and Society.* Edited by Charles W. Morris. Chicago: University of Chicago Press, 1934.

Millar, Susanna. *The Psychology of Play.* Baltimore: Penguin Books, Inc., 1968.

Millet, Kate. *Sexual Politics.* New York: Doubleday & Company, Inc., 1970.

Parsons, Talcott. *Family, Socialization, and Interaction Process.* New York: The Free Press, 1955.

Roberts, J. M.; Sutton-Smith, B.; and Kozelka, R. M. "Studies in an Elementary Game of Strategy." *Genetic Psychological Monograph* 75(1967):3-42.

Rosenberg, B. G., and Sutton-Smith, Brian. "Child Training and Game Involvement." *Ethnology* 1(1962):166-185.

————. "A Revised Conception of Masculine-Feminine Differences in Play Activities." *Journal of Genetic Psychology* 96(1960):165-70.

————. *Sex and Identity*. New York: Holt, Rinehart, and Winston, 1972.

Sexton, Patricia Cayo. *The Feminized Male*. New York: Random House, 1969.

Stasz, Cathleen; Weinberg, Susan; and McDonald, Frederick J. "The Influence of Sex of Student and Sex of Teachers on Students' Achievement and Evaluation of the Teacher." Princeton, N. J.: Educational Testing Service, 1972.

Stone Gregory. "The Play of Little Children." *Quest* 4(1965):23-31.

Stoll, Clarice S.; Inbar, Michael; and Fennessey, James. *Game Experience and Socialization: An Exploratory Study of Sex Differences*. Report No. 20. Baltimore, Md.: Center for Study of Social Organization of Schools, 1968.

Sutton-Smith, Brian. "Achievement and Strategic Competence." In *The Study of Games,* edited by Elliott Avedon and Brian Sutton-Smith. New York: John Wiley & Sons, Inc., 1971.

Sutton-Smith, Brian, and Roberts, John M. "Rubrics of Competitive Behavior." *Journal of Genetic Psychology* 105(1964):13-37.

Terman, Lewis M., and Miles, Catherine Cox. *Sex and Personality*. New York: Russell & Russell Publishers, 1936.

Weitzman, Leonore J.; Eifler, Deborah; Hokoda, Elizabeth; and Ross, Catherine. "Sex-role Socialization in Picture Books for Preschool Children." *American Journal of Sociology* 77(1972):1125-50.

Whiting, John W. M.; Childs, Irvin L.; and Lambert, William. *Field Guide for a Study of Socialization*. New York: John Wiley & Sons, Inc., 1966.

Women on Words and Images. *Dick and Jane as Victims*. Princeton, N. J.: Educational Testing Service, 1972.

Yarrow, Leon J. "Separation from Parents during Early Childhood." In *Review of Child Development Research,* by Martin L. Hoffman and Lois Wladis Hoffman. New York: John Wiley & Sons, Inc., 1964.

Zimet, Sara Goodman. *What Children Read in School*. New York: Grune & Stratton, Inc., 1971.

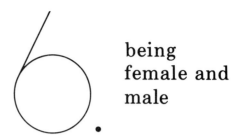

being
female and
male

It is futile to fuss over gender identities unless one can show that they make sense to everyday actors. Otherwise, as social scientists we are simply imposing our view of the world upon our subjects. How do persons conceive of themselves? How can we tell whether gender matters? One way would be to ask them to describe themselves. The simple question—"Who am I?"—placed at the top of a piece of paper with lines for twenty answers is the format of the Twenty Statements Test (TST). This measure of self-concept has been used in a variety of research investigations in social psychology. One of the most comprehensive studies, based upon a sample of all adult Iowa residents (Mulford and Salisbury 1964) is typical of the results found with other groups of respondents.

Table 6-1 provides the classification of responses for the total sample by sex of respondent. Many differences between men and women were found. First, note that a response of "I am male" or "I am female" occurred only moderately, though much more often for men than for women. This supports the thesis that gender identity is a more profound personal concern for the male in our society. Women can take for granted that they are female; it is a less problematic identifier. However, the most frequently mentioned roles for both sexes are those that are gender specific-marital identifications and other family roles. Almost all words that describe these positions in the English language specify gender. We are most likely to say "husband" or "wife" than "spouse," or "father" and "mother" than "parent." Women, though, use familial referents much more than the men. Similarly, most occupational identities are gender specific because most jobs in America are sex-segregated. The picture that emerges is as follows. The typical male respondent says, "I am an insurance salesman, a son, a

Table 6-1
Classification of TST Response by Sex
(in percentages)

| Types of Self-identity | One or more mentions | | |
	Total N=1208	Men N=572	Women N=631
1. Specific sex identity	17	25	10+
2. Age, specific, and categorical	11	12	9
3. Marital status and role	34	27	39+
4. All types of nuclear family status and role	60	43	74+
5. Extended family relationships	10	6	13+
6. Primary group identities	10	6	14+
7. Secondary group identities	14	12	16+
8. Religion			
a) Specific denomination	5	5	5
b) All types of religious self-identity	25	19	30+
9. Occupation			
a) Specific occupational identity	62	60	64
b) All types of work role identity	68	69	67
10. Ethnic group			
a) Identity as an American	6	9	4+
b) Other ethnic groups	1	1	
11. Education	3	3	3
12. Racial identity	1	1	1

* In a test of inter judge reliability there were 87.2 percent agreement on a sample of 256 responses.

+ Significant sex differences at the .05 level.

Source: Mulford and Salisbury (1964), Table 1.

husband, *and* a man." The typical female responds, "I am a housewife, a daughter, a sister, a wife, and a Methodist."

In further analysis, Mulford and Salisbury discovered that mention of sex identity remained fully constant regardless of age. In other words, although roles related to gender (marriage, parenthood, other familial obligations, work) change considerably over the life cycle, people are fairly consistent through time in their identification of themselves as male or female. In looking more closely at familial roles, they found that only 19 percent of the actual fathers described themselves as such, while 54 percent of the actual mothers did so. Thus, fatherhood is less salient as a basis of self-identification for men. Similarly, only 29 percent of the husbands called themselves such, while 41 percent of the wives did so. Being married is more salient for a woman's self-conception, though less so than mother-hood is. Furthermore, over time both sexes mention marital roles less; the longer one is married, the less likely it is a basis for self-description. With regard to occupation, most women in the sample were unemployed in the traditional sense, and 68 percent of these called themselves housewives. Similarly, about two-thirds of the men referred to their regular work status, regardless of the type of occupation they held. Thus women recognized their role as housekeepers, even though it is not one highly valued by so-ciety. Overall, research of this type indicates that people do describe themselves in terms of social categories, as Mead would have us predict. Also, while reference to one's self as "male" or "female" in explicit terms is not frequent, the roles one does refer to are typically gender-specific, so perhaps people feel that explicit mention of sex would be redundant.

Couch (1962) has used the TST to see whether there was a relation-ship between parental sex-role identification and self-gender identity. First, he had students describe the division of labor by sex roles in their own family. To do this they checked off which of their family members per-formed tasks such as grocery shopping, earning money for family needs, or displaying affection. This permitted him to identify students from families where tasks were allocated by gender from those where the sexes shared tasks. He predicted that in families with sex-role specialization, children will more likely describe themselves as "male" or "female." The results were surprising, as shown by the data in table 6-2. Males who identified themselves by sex on the TST also scored higher on measures of parental role specialization. For women, the opposite occurred. Those who referred to themselves as female had *lower* scores of parental role specialization.

Table 6-2

Mean Role-specialization Scores of Males and Females by Identification of Self by Sex

	Females Mean score of parental role-specialization (N)		Males Mean score of parental role-specialization (N)	
Self-identification by sex	13.83*	30	18.14	14
No self-identification by sex	17.88*	8	14.37	8

* Difference significant at the .05 level.

Source: Couch (1960), Table 1.

Couch retested the finding by using other procedures, which are too complicated to mention here. The same curious trend was always found. Couch's conclusions make sense in view of more recent developments (such as Lynn's theory discussed in the previous chapter) on sex-role socialization.

> It seems highly probable that those families with a high degree of role specializations are patriarchal families, in which high role specialization is associated with high evaluation of male and son statuses. This leads to self-identification as male or son by the males, for the value assigned to both statuses is consistent with the value placed upon the self as a general object. In contrast, females with a family background of high role specialization learn that the statuses of female and daughter are somewhat negatively evaluated. This is in conflict with the positive value placed upon the self as a general object. As a consequence, they think of themselves less frequently as daughters and as females than do females from families with low role specialization (Couch 1962, p. 121).

Couch implies that a woman's low self-esteem about being female may explain why many women do not describe themselves by gender. Evidence from other types of studies supports his interpretation.

Some of you might find the TST to be too superficial a measure of self. Do we often in our daily lives remind ourselves or others that we are males, mothers, or telephone linepersons? We do in certain circumstances, such as when we are acquainting other persons with ourselves, or others that in conversations where we are trying to account for our behavior. (Remember—"I'm a mother, too!") Cooley directs us to look for other manifestations of the self.

For many psychologists, the self is defined as a collection of motives and needs that emerge early in childhood. If certain motives are not well-developed, then as the individual encounters the opportunity to call on these motives, she will not use the opportunity. For example, a male whose motives do not include a need to be intimate or nuturant will not move readily into situations that call upon these needs. The young woman who has acquired a strong achievement drive will move toward and accept opportunities that challenge this drive.

A common research instrument in the charting of these needs has been the Thematic Apperception Test (TAT). This instrument consists of a series of ambiguous illustrations for which the subject is to provide a story. Various scoring systems have evolved for the interpretation of results, one of the most common being a measure of achievement devised by McClelland et al. (1953). The person who is achievement-motivated takes pride in his work when he is responsible for his actions, when there is some risk involved, and when there are criteria of performance. Clearly, this is an individual who is willing to take risks for a gain in self-esteem. One would expect that we could predict an individual's life achievements (in occupations) or performance on experimental tasks (risk-taking) were we to know his need to achieve. This happens to be true *for males only*. One problem is that most studies on achievement motives have used only male samples. Those that included women have found inconsistent results. Apparently, women with a need to achieve (those who define their self-esteem in terms of performance successes) do not seek to actualize that need. On the face of it, this is a most illogical position. Some women are avoiding the very situations that will leave them feeling proud and satisfied with themselves.

Several reasons for the discrepancy have been offered. Horner (1968) has suggested that women are raised with a fear of success. She developed a story-completion exercise that provided a way to measure respondents' use of success-avoidance statements. The basic cue was "At the end of first term finals Anne/John finds herself/himself at the top of her/his medical class." In several studies she discovered that women displayed much more fear of success than men and that very successful college women, those with high achievement needs, frequently expressed fears. Several variations of the study design allowed further insight into this need. For example, Weston and Mednick (1970) sampled black and white college women to test the hypothesis that the black women would fear success less. They argued that black women who can work are an economic asset in their subculture and less of a threat to black men. The results supported this hypothesis. Horner's own research on samples of students, black and white, female and male, provided similar results. The presence of fear-of-success imagery is as follows:

white men—10%	black men—67%
white women—64%	black women—29%

The high fear of success imagery for black men was taken to be a reflection of their belief that success is an unexpected event, unrelated to personal effort.

Some have argued that women's lesser accomplishments are not due simply to a fear of success. Katz (1972) has criticized this type of personality investigation for its failure to see how the social structure of sexism plays into the woman's life. She noted how Horner's hypothetical situation about Anne referred to success in a masculine setting. Katz replicated the earlier research with one twist. She included the following qualifiers before the stories, either "All of Anne's classmates in medical school are men," or "Half of Anne's classmates in medical school are women." The results were surprising, as table 6-3 indicates. First, women did not report high

Table 6-3

Success Avoidance by Success Situation and Sex of Respondent

Condition	Male	Female
Anne is in all-male class.	72% (76)	40% (49)*
Anne is in a mixed class.	46% (76)	35% (66)

* The difference for this condition, based upon a Chi-square test, is significant at $p < .01$.

Source: Katz (1973), Table 3.

amounts of fear-of-success imagery for either story. Instead, the *men* expressed considerable avoidance of Anne's success in the condition where she attended the all-male school. Katz interprets the results as follows. First, in just the several years since Horner's studies, young women have acquired much more interest in recognition of female achievement. Second, men are fearful of women succeeding in realms that are essentially masculine ones, perhaps because these are the prestigious areas of life in our society.

Katz's study demonstrates why simple measures of self-evaluation, needs, and feelings (those like the TST or TAT) are not in themselves sufficient grounds for explaining individual behavior. The self interacts with others, and its reactions or options are determined partly by the situation. Many men in our society may have been raised with a disapproval of women who succeed, yet they will change their evaluation if the woman's success is in certain settings. Similarly, although most women in our society have been raised to be anxious about success and power, historical changes are telling them that these fears are no longer a reason for avoiding success. The social meanings of activities change over time, so that a young woman who acquired a need to achieve as a youngster will less likely dampen that need as her older sister did a decade ago.

As a final point, one should remember that different needs or motives do not necessarily mean that people will behave differently. We know that men have a higher need to achieve than women, who have a greater need for affiliation. This does not mean that only those with high achievement

needs will seek success, for research suggests that many women will engage in achievement activities *provided those activities reward affiliation
needs.* Thus men might enter politics to gain self-esteem through electoral
success, while women might do so as a way to gain praise from individual
persons.

Another way to see how men and women differently conceive of
themselves is to ask them to check off specific feelings of descriptive
statements concerning a wide range of topics. This type of data was collected on a national sample of adults by Gurin et al. (1960). Strong sex
differences emerged on many items. These differences persisted control-
ing age and education. That is, the difference existed for a sample of young
college men and women or a sample of high school graduate middle-aged
men and women. Thus these self-attitudes cut across the lines of age and
class. Here are some of the major conclusions:

1. When asked to mention shortcomings, men were likely to stress ex-
    ternal failures and visible achievements, while women pointed to per-
    sonality shortcomings. Men were two to three times as likely to
    point to lack of education as a shortcoming.
2. In discussing personality deficiencies, women saw their flaws as being
    related to social skills.
3. Women expressed more concern over physical appearance.
4. In describing their strong points, men mentioned their jobs, while
    women responded "housekeeping." Women did *not* mention parent-
    hood or marital roles any more often than the men did. Thus both
    sexes share similar views as to which roles are the important ones.
5. Men consistently refer more often to moral virtues in describing them-
    selves; for example, honesty, loyalty, religious, dependability. (Gurin
    et al. interpret this use of popular adjectives as a sign that men are
    less introspective about themselves.)
6. Women more often mention nurturant characteristics as being a strong
    point in their personalities. However, men do not refer to achieve-
    ments, nor do women mention social skills in general. This suggests
    that achievement for men and social skills for women are negative mo-
    tivators. In other words, men achieve not to fail, and women are
    socially adept not to be rejected. Achievement and social skills are
    not viewed as positive goals, ways to achieve self-esteem. The pride
    comes in not failing.

Overall, women are more negative or ambivalent about themselves.
These data reiterate the themes that women develop less self-esteem and

are socially-oriented, while men orient toward the external world in a more personal way. However, it should be remembered that these differences are relative. A large overlap occurs for all of the items. *In no case were the majority of men one way and the women another.* For example, almost all men and women are satisfied with their physical appearance. If someone is not pleased with themselves, it is likely to be a woman. Less than 10 percent of women felt this way, however. *Most men and women share the same view of shortcomings and assets.*

Male and female bodies are different, so one should expect that the self-concepts concerning the body would exhibit gender-specific characteristics. All experience of the social world is mediated by body sensation. Research has shown that people develop maps of their bodies and evolve a repertoire of ideas to explain the events surrounding it. The body can become so much an object of one's self that the experience of depersonalization, a sensation that one's body is not one's own, are common, though infrequent occurrences. How we judge and define our body will be determined in terms of our society's general ideas concerning bodies. Our culture dramatizes the physical differences between men and women, and this emphasis appears in many forms as individual men and women relate to their own bodies.

Although we value men more in our society, the female body is the object of much excitation and attention. This interest is more than sexual, because women and homosexual males display the same interest as heterosexual men in admiration of the female form. In addition, the female body is represented as soft, passive, manipulable, while the male body is idealized to be one of strength and activity.

Freud suggested that the female perceives her body to be incomplete because she lacks a phallus. This phallus concern permeates many cultures, including ours. Genital display by males exists in primate and other mammal cultures as well as in human societies.[1] Breast development and exposure of breasts are focuses for our evaluation of female bodies. Although men lack breasts, they are not considered to be incomplete. Our society's view of the male body also overlooks the fact of its greater susceptibility to illness and injury.

Who feels more comfortable with their bodies, the woman or the man? With what we have seen about self-concepts so far, we might expect that women would feel inferior. This is not the case. Many studies point to women's greater security about their bodies, their more realistic appraisal

---

1. Ethnologists suggest that the origin of the phallus as a symbol of strength originates in the use of urine to mark off territory. In time, the visual display of the penis was sufficient warning to other members of one's species.

of them. Studies of children, for example, have noted that boys are more preoccupied with injury and pain during play, for their stories describe people being maimed and killed. This would follow from their greater exposure to physically dangerous activities. Consequently, the fact that small boys fight does not mean that they become comfortable with injury. If anything, violence arouses fears or bodily harm. Boys apparently participate in physical activities in spite of the pain, not because they are fearless.

Many clever experiments in adults by Fisher (1970, 1973) have detailed the ways in which men and women define their bodies. In one study subjects were placed in a darkened room with a light on their face alone. A series of masks, half feminine and half masculine, were placed on the subject, who was asked to describe how the face looked. The men had considerable difficulty in describing female masks, while the women had no trouble with male masks. One interpretation of this data is that men have difficulty accepting a feminine image. Fisher hypothesized instead that men had difficulty coping with body distortions, an interpretation borne out in further studies. Men were less comfortable when administered drugs that produce unusual body sensations. They coped less well with carnival-type mirrors that displayed misshapen images of themselves. They were fearful of threats that objects would penetrate their bodies. They were less clear about the boundaries of their bodies. Women were more adaptable, less threatened by threats of penetration, and more acceptable of distortions.

As Fisher explains, the body is the matrix for major life events in the woman. Her bodily attractiveness is a basis for life success on the marriage market. She is taught to be caretaker of her body, adjust to menstruation, pregnancy, and menopause. Women are thus more able than men to cope with body phenomena that are often considered disgusting, such as feces or blood. Being more sensitive to body feelings, she intuits choices on the basis of body sensations. Men have downplayed and degraded this sensitivity, for they fail to understand its roots. Males are raised to ignore and suppress these bodily cues. Not surprisingly, then, men and women differ in their focus upon body parts. Men are inclined to associate their self as residing in their head, while for women it resides in the chest and torso.

Bodily fears reflect cultural distinctions as well. Men identify masculinity with being large, and women identify femininity with being small. When asked what they would do with their bodies, men would make themselves larger, and women would reduce all but their breasts. Women also seem to have more anxiety about their legs, a symbol of mobility. Women actually have the opportunity to make changes on their bodies to be more fitting with social (and self) preferences, as we shall see shortly.

One other way we could measure self-conceptions would be to ask people about themselves with regard to their activities in the roles they play. Most women in America, married or not, are housekeepers. What does this mean for themselves? How does it shape their self-esteem? How does the role effect their feelings and attitudes outside of housewifery? In subsequent chapters we shall examine self-related attitudes of men and women at work, as parents, and as housewives. We shall see that many of the personality and style differences attributed to sex may be a result of the particular social roles each sex plays.

Sources of Self-presentation

Self-descriptions tell us how people conceive themselves as objects. The self is also part of the process, one that involves self-display, perceptions of others' responses, and reactions to those perceptions. How do people present themselves—through whatever means are available in the culture to make meaningful statements to others. Most obvious are the visual cues of dress and adornment. Many other ways of presenting an *appearance* are available. Consider language. The way a person speaks, in terms of accent, vocabulary, and grammar, provides clues to others as to her background, social class, and more. Another variable is body language—the way a person moves, locates her gaze, positions her arms. Related here is spatial position to others, how closely she approaches or avoids the presence of others in a room. These variants are among the resources immediately available to a social actor.

Resources in fact are disturbed prior to interaction by the culture and the already present system of meanings. In theory, men and women could dress any way that they wanted within their means. In fact, men do not wear dresses. Have you ever seen a men in a dress (outside of comedy programs)? There are no laws or informal punishments for wearing dresses and no man seems to have bothered to find out if there are any. It is simply taken for granted that men do not do so, and they don't. When women no longer took it for granted that they could do well in pants, there was some reaction (e.g., employer dress codes), but they made pants acceptable within a few years time. Women apparently have many more resources for self-expression than men. That is, a woman can be a woman regardless of her apparel. The point in this illustration is that dress is not a way a woman can well express her gender, *unless she wears a dress*. The dress is the invariant here. And in seeking ways of presenting one's self, it is the invariant cues, those that hold across many settings that are critical. So long as men don't wear dresses, the dress is a convenient symbol for making gender distinctions.

Why should gender matter in self-presentation? Where do the rules concerning modes of self-presentation come from? The answer rests with an understanding of how societies provide the basis for the ongoing negotiation of a social order upon which activities can be based. Note that it is not "The society provides an order." The rules and self-presentational outcomes we shall be discussing here are not fixed and determined. Society does not tell people how to act male or female. Individual males and females *are* society, and self-presentations emerge in particular situations, not in the abstract. This flux is most apparent in contemporary America, where the negotiations have become explicitly political and formalized.[2]

Many analyses of the woman's movement involve simplistic models of social order that overlook individual choice in action. For example, Figes (1970) has most astutely delineated the various strands of patriarchal and sexist belief systems that undercut Western religious, philosophical, and intellectual thought. Similarly, Greer (1971) has shown how these beliefs take meaning in the day-to-day lives of women, shaping their attitudes about their bodies and their selves. Implicit in such arguments is the proposal that a change in ideas will settle woman's problems. This type of analysis misses the meanings that mythologies provide for societal members, whether in the long run they are destructive ideas or not. Let us look at mythology more closely.

One curious illustration of the pervasiveness of sexist mythology occurs in a volume entitled *The Potential of Woman* (Farber and Wilson 1963). The collection includes a discussion among three male contributors, presumably concerned with the loss of woman's contributions to society. At the conclusion of this panel, the editor presented the question "What is a woman?" They responded:

> "I think she is a man's wife."
> "Shall I follow by saying she is also a man's mother."
> "And she is also a man's mistress."

In other words, a woman's self is defined by her relationship to a man. This response is part of the mythology that derogates single and divorced women and career women who seek self-esteem that is self-motivated. In short, "woman's place is in the home." This adage appears to be descriptive (i.e., says that women are domestic creatures). Yet this it not true; it is really a normative or *prescriptive* statement. Such statements are part

2. Much of the discussion in this section was inspired by Janeway's (1971) lucid discussion of female identity in America. This book has undeservedly been overlooked by many feminists and social scientists.

of the social mythology that defines sex roles (or gender presentations) and makes them easy to follow. Myths also provide an explanation for events in the "real world out there," thus helping each of us make sense of the complex swirl of activities surrounding us. We look out and see that many women are at home, while men are busy in other places. The myth says, "It's so that women are home because women belong there." Thus myths are often anchors that hold tendencies for change at bay. If several well-motivated males deeply concerned with changing sex roles could respond as they did above, then its reach must be deep in our minds indeed. In a sense these men are arguing that women have a great deal to lose by leaving the home. If a feminist were to respond that this is not true, as Friedan (1963) did in her *Feminine Mystique,* the mythological reply is simply, "It's the natural place for her to be." The myth is self-reinforcing and tautological.

Myths are imperatives for action, and any refusal to follow their dictates becomes a threat. Consequently, they are a basis for fostering social cohesion, though at the expense of personal convenience, social diversity, and change. On a personal level, myths are tied to needs, emotions, and desires, so logic alone does not persuade them. No matter how much is written to show that women need not be and has in history seldom been tied to the home, women will remain who cling to the ideology. To give it up would be to reject, in their terms, their husband and family, hence their selves. Unless they can find another reference for self-esteem, one that does not imply a break of ties with loved ones, such women can scarcely afford to break away from patriarchal patterns. To do so would be to commit a symbolic suicide, a serious disjuncture from the self. Myths are more than personal desires and rationalizations. Being public statements, they tie one's private feelings to an audience—assist in making an appearance. If a man rebukes his working wife by exclaiming, "A woman's place is in the home," he can count on others present to understand, and perhaps support, the implications of this statement. When invoked in this way, mythology becomes a rhetoric for social control.

Although a speaker, such as the husband above, may make his statement with an assertive tone, his inner feelings are not necessarily so assured. Were woman's place in the home, the imperative need never even be stated. Consider the dress example previously discussed. No popular adage exists concerning the wearing of dresses for men. A small boy who dresses up in a mother's dress might be told that it is sissy to do so. No mythological retort comes to mind however with regard to adult males because they don't violate the taken-for-granted beliefs condemning skirts. If expectations are always fulfilled—as anticipated by the myths—then social life would be ritualistic and ideas static, as happens to be the case for masculine dress preferences in the middle class today.

Out of ambiguities innovations are born. Mythologies are one response to ambiguity, as stated by those with sufficient power to mobilize people to accept the rhetoric put forth. (Women have long held secret mythologies concerning their place in the home, but lacked the collective consciousness or power to even turn these private feelings into public statements, let alone be listened to seriously.) What the myth-stater often overlooks is that the statement is double-edged. In proclaiming a rule, he may also provoke the bitterness, mistrust, malice, and injury that can spur the development of a counter mythology.

Myths support the roles that people are asked to play by others, though not in mechanistic sense. Roles can provide a "ready-made me," particularly in formal settings. They are proof that one has a place in the social system, and provide a moral compass for behavior. When we take on the roles that those in power prescribe and reward, then often material and personal satisfactions ensue. Furthermore, some of life can be trusted to others—those who are playing out ancillary or complementary roles in the system. Men and women can thus express their gender by playing out those roles that are gender-specific and by performing role activities in ways characteristic of their gender.

Role playing cannot be avoided, for it eases communications and provides a basis for trust. It makes strangers less threatening, keeps one out of trouble, and prevents situations from being too problematic. Roles are not masks or disguises, as some popularly claim; they are protective devices, instruments for action, and genuine elements of one's self.

Furthermore, roles are much less constraining than many writers imply. During everyday life, roles are improvised for they define only the skeleton of the structure of a relationship. They merely provide social boundaries as to the nature of the individuals we may interact with, in what way, and in what settings. Yet social life is certainly more elaborate than these few limitations imply. Also, in any particular situation, there is no perfect consensus as to what the roles entail. For some women in our society, being female does not necessitate being either in the home or attached to a man. For many men in our society, being masculine does not mean total devotion to the occupational role. Our age-category, race, ethnicity, personal biography, and even size, all interact to provide idiosyncratic meanings to the ones provided by society's "role expectations."

How does "society"—other people—provide a guide to self-presentation with regard to gender? Nowhere can one find a "book of roles" that is given to each individual at birth. The expectations are sometimes blatant, as when someone repeats an old adage about domesticity in women, but more often they are less apparent. Here are some of the places one would look to chart a society's mythology about sex roles:

The *popular media* are frequently accused by feminist women and men for perpetuating sexist mythology. In particular, advertising has been studied and analyzed for its presentation of women as either domestics or sex objects for men. Komisar (1971) has related this stereotyping to the organizational structure of Madison Avenue itself, wherein white upper-class males who are isolated from the true "average woman" create ad content. In other cases women are virtually ignored. Newspapers carry news of men's activities, as is indicated by the need for a special "Woman's Page." Movie critics in recent years have pointed to the virtual absence of women from major screen roles, and television has come under similar appraisal. There is no question that the media typically illustrate women in only the most extreme stereotypical ways, but what of men? Newspapers report on the news of men in power, not information relevant to the lives of most working men (i.e., blue-collar men). Only the sports pages are meaningful to males of any social class or background. The men appearing in movies and on television are either men in power, machismo adventure types, criminals, or family patriarchs who order their family members around.

I believe that it is too easy to blame the media as a cause for sex stereotypes. One problem is that once conscious of sexist ideology, it is difficult not to find it everywhere. (I can always pick out the sexist ads in a magazine and overlook the many more that are not clearly stereotypical.) Those of us who accuse the media are seldom objective in analyzing *all* that it presents. Second, the stereotypes are presented because they have not been upsetting to people, at least the people who count to the media business men. Few gains have been made to eliminite racism in media mainly because businessmen have not been convinced of the economic power of many blacks. Media images more often follow the public than lead it. (Radical ideologies do not sell dog food.) Third, one has to consider the consumer of information. Although 90 percent of the books I read as a youngster were very sexist, the only ones that were paid attention to were the exceptions, where the girls were self-motivating. Finally, one must put media in perspective with the other sources of role definitions. These other ones, as will become apparent shortly, are more powerful and difficult to change.

Orientational others, as Kuhn specifies them, are those persons one looks to when defining one's self. They have greater impact than media simply because they are personal sources of information. The directiveness and statements of people we are attached to or respect or fear reach us deeply through arousal of emotions, promises, of need fulfillment, and threats of rejection or punishment. What distinguishes orientational others from everyone else in one's social world is their salience for self-sustenance and change. They cannot be identified a priori; one must find out from each social actor just whose opinions matter most when they think of themselves.

Very little research is available here with regard to sex differences. For example, Denzin (1966) asked college students to name those individuals "whose evaluation of you as a person concerns you most." The three most frequent persons named for both sexes were family, friends, or faculty. Males were slightly more likely to mention friends. About 20 percent of both males and females mentioned religious persons. Few sex differences resulted.

Clearly we need more information here. If women are raised to be socially oriented, then do others have a greater impact on a woman's self-definition? Do the comments of males carry more weight? Who do men look to in defining their masculinity? We don't know.

Situations are bounded by an *invariant structuring of opportunities* that limit our role performances. One reason why women behave in "feminine ways" in some situations is that they have no choice. The essential situational components of time and space come into play, for many space-time locations in our society are gender-specific, either in a taken-for-granted way or by regulation. A woman cannot announce her rejection of traditional feminine ways by using a men's room. A man in a laundromat is considered to be out of place by its female participants. Control over time and space carries considerable power, as shall be clear when we discuss work and family roles. These variables are often overlooked by sociologists and political activists, yet they are essential determinants of behavior, and ones very difficult to change.

Some of the other situational characteristics include such personal resources as props, scripts, and parts to play. Sometimes individuals play stereotypical roles unintentionally because they have no power to do otherwise. The Southern slave did not portray the happy darkie to her owner out of devotion of self-acceptance of the slave mythology. Most women and many men in our society lack the range of choices to express their character, those idiosyncratic appearances, mannerisms, habits, desires, and so on that they value in their own mind. Compromises are made, often for the sake of powerful significant others who are not orientational others. Much contemporary tragedy, as it appears in novels and dramas, concerns the self-abnegation called upon by situations we all share (e.g., child-parent conflict, worker-boss relationships). Freedom to act is in fact freedom to accomplish the self-expressions that one values.

Another type of invariant is the set of rituals, customs, and mythologies that can take control in a situation. Once put into action by one person, it can be cumbersome to break the setting and start a new definition of things. When a man opens a door for a woman, it is hardly efficient for her to wait until it closes and open it again herself. Yet such rituals are grounded into gender-specific meanings, so that a woman who disdains such "chivalry" is left to feel out of sorts with herself while the man can feel that he has contributed his small share to social order. Sometimes violating a seemingly trivial rule can have serious effects. Any women who walks alone in a city late at night is very unlikely to complete the walk without being stopped by some male, whether a policeman or someone who presumes her to be sexually available. There is virtually no defense against this custom, for many men are armed with a mythology to deny any claims the woman might make that she is not out alone for purposes of sexual encounter. Consequently, few women do go out alone and the mythology prevails in fact, for only "available" women are on the streets.

These hidden dimensions of situations are powerful because they are so out of mind. The life experiences of women and men who try to redefine their gender identities verifies this fact. One hears them mention how "hardly a day goes by without my seeing something else that oppresses me." Yet they do learn to identify their personal resources and shape situations so as not to compromise themselves. Others, more fortunate, are in situations where the limits on their interaction do not limit their self-expression. To accuse them of "role-playing" is to fail to understand their view of the world. The myths work for them, and are as real as the counter-mythologies.

Taken altogether—personal biography, cultural definitions, personal ties, interpersonal influences, situational constraints—an *individual opportunity structure* results for the expression of gender identity or sex roles. Some actions or behaviors simply never occur to us. Others are possible, but only at personal risk. Sometimes we aren't sure what is expected or what we are capable of doing. Ambiguities abound, and often it is most efficient to slip into ready-made solutions. Sometimes we portray the person we wish to be, disturbing people we care about in the process because their views of the world do not accommodate our real selves. As individual persons enter situations and make choices, patterns of social behavior are reinforced or threatened. Sometimes sufficient numbers of individuals will innovate independently of one another, and the accumulated response can result in a sweeping change. Certainly this is the case for women in

America today. Considerable changes are occurring, not so much because the media or male orientational others or situations have changed, but because individual women have chosen to risk themselves in situations where they hadn't in the past.

Self-presentation and Social Identity

In the first section of this chapter, we saw how there are differences in the ways adult females and males define themselves. Then we discussed how social mythology and structural arrangements provide a direction in the presentation of this self. In day-to-day interaction, the two components interact. An individual's self feelings shape her orientation as to how she should behave in particular situations, and the situations themselves provide cues, pathways, and obstacles to guide her self-expression. It becomes difficult to separate what comes first. Do women express themselves in culturally defined feminine ways because they want to, or do they do so because they see no other alternative? This may be the wrong question to ask, for there are actually two issues at play here.

One is the role gender identity plays as a social category. The sexist mythology supports a pattern of beliefs that men and women are different, that men deserve certain privileges and rights, that women have certain duties to men. Once the members of a situation are identified by gender, the mythology can take over with regard to the pattern of behaviors that follow. The importance of gender can be seen by the following situation that many have experienced. You are sitting in a room and see someone who is posed and dressed in such a way that their gender is not readily apparent. Very likely you will not have any reason to interact with this person, yet you puzzle until you resolve for yourself which category they belong to. This need to categorize by gender occurs almost automatically because we miss how it is a basis for the assignment of interactional sequences and events.

In looking for another's gender identity, we are seeking a basis for defining our own identity in the situation. At the same time, we are serving as a significant other for the person present, whether she is aware of our internal query or not. She may simultaneously be noting that we are obviously of one sex or the other. This sizing-up process with regard to gender seems to permeate the most trivial situations, and a similar sizing-up often occurs with regard to age and race categories as well. Just why are these categories so important to us, even in settings where no direct face-to-face interaction may occur?

Much of social order is grounded in the public displays of apparent strangers toward one another. These actions give individuals ready listings as to whether direct interaction is likely and what type of interaction may occur. Category identifications also give us the basis to choose rules so that we can control whether or not we will encounter the other individual, and in what guise we shall do so. These displays, shiftings, and manipulations are usually done on the basis of nonverbal behavior, with minimal verbal overlay. These behaviors include seating positions, eye gaze, torso orientations, touching, smiling, and so on.

Little is known yet about the way these gestures combine with the body social catgories of age, sex, and race to convey particular meanings to others. We don't know how gender predisposes individuals to present themselves in one pose instead of another. Here is a short list of some of the research findings that are relevant here:

1. When females interact with other females, the eye contact is longer than that found when males interact with males (Exline 1972).
2. When females interact with other females, they sit closer to one another than when males interact with males (Baxter 1970).
3. If females like other people in a setting, they are more likely to express these feelings tactilely. They act as if touching is one way to communicate liking (Mehrabian 1971).
4. When males touch other persons, it seems to express superiority over the person being touched. Superordinate males touch subordinate males, though not vice versa. Males touch females much more frequently than females touch males (Hensley 1970).
5. Males and females address their torsos in different ways, depending on whether or not they like the person they are addressing. Females orient directly toward someone they like, while males orient directly only when intense *dislike* is felt (Mehrabian 1968).

These data tell us only behavioral tendencies. We don't know whether the others in the situations studied interpreted the acts as the subjects meant them to be. In fact, we don't even know what the subjects' intentions were. (Women frequently take submissive positions in terms of seating arrangements or body displays, and then wonder why people "bother" them!)[3]

3. Films and photography promise to become a useful research tool here. Some students in my film class took slow motion pictures of people crossing intersections. Clear sex differences in self-display were apparent. Men often put a hand in one pocket and stood with feet askance. Women frequently folded arms over their chest and stood with one foot slightly in front of the other. The woman's posture, then, was one of defense with preparedness to flee. These posturings were similar across age and apparent class lines.

The data also hint at built-in conflicts with regard to female-male interaction. If males are used to touching as a basis for status display, and females view it as a means for affectional display, then misinterpretations are certain. Here may result the basis for women's frequent complaint that their loved ones are not affectionate enough, except in explicitly sexual situations. And perhaps women misinterpret the casual gesture of male status as a desire on the male's part for intimacy. Similarly, when women turn and use touching as a basis for status expression, the male is also likely to misinterpret the action as an intimate one, because it is out of place for women to do so. The background rules for men state that women touch for intimacy, not power. My argument here should be viewed as illustrative, for social scientists are only now beginning to explore this dimension of social control and self-presentation.)

Gender identity feeds into the on-going social process, and consequently back onto one's self-conception. We have just seen how in many ways it is not a problem for individuals themselves. Our bodies, our adornments, and our positionings tell one another "I am a male" or "I am a female." On questionnaires, people do not have to hesitate in checking the correct blank. Many of our major role identities in families and at work are further gender-specific cues to others and ourselves as to our gender. On another level, however, gender is problematic. Here we must distinguish presentation of ourselves for the purpose of social typing and self-evaluating by others.

Although most men and women know that they are such, there are situations where their "masculinity" and "femininity" is in doubt. Here we move into the area of *moral judgments* that people make of one another. Although our society is structured to reward some categories in preference to others (e.g., men over women), the system is not perfectly rational. For one, rewards are scarce. Also, other categories, such as race and performance, are added in the the formula, so that a highly skillful white woman can be judged more deserving than a poorly trained black male. To complicate matters, sex is one of the rewards of the system for both men and women, yet sexual performances can also be a means to other rewards. Out of these confusing restrictions, rules, and resources, comes some system for rating people so that the various scarce rewards can be dispensed "fairly," or according to the rules.

Just as gender has become one efficient category for establishing the flow of interaction, so have "masculinity" and "femininity" become useful cultural concepts for social and self-evaluation. We have already seen instances of this process in operation. Recall here Coleman's study of adolescent boys, where the few boys who could express the highly idealized principles of being "real men" were richly rewarded, while average boys went with fewer social contacts. Or one need only look at the popular media—the Dear Abby columns, the popular fiction, indeed much of the literature on womens' liberation—to see that many people take seriously whether they are "really men" or "really women." Too, current sensitivities and debates about homosexuality (viz., is it "normal" or not) reflects the problematic nature of gender identity.

We have, it seems, a paradox. In many situations gender can be taken for granted and used as a marker to others and one's self for action. At the same time, one expresses one's self and performs one's activities in light of the judgment of others. Given that there are multiple meanings of "masculinity" and "femininity" floating around our society, one can never be sure that this aspect of one's self will not be called into dispute. One is left to having to account for oneself, thus to be on the defensive. Gender identity is called into dispute very infrequently, but when done so, its consequences for the individual can be profound. Conscious of this scheme of things, many—perhaps most—persons hedge their bets and behave in order to avoid open disputes, yet even this strategy is not without its sacrifices. Let us now examine how persons work through and around this puzzle of being female and male.

SUGGESTED PROJECTS

1. Most of the examples in the section on "Sources of Self-presentation" discuss the mythologies that apply to women. Take the myths that apply to men and see whether the general theme still holds. Does this analysis provide any unexpected conclusions about the position of men in America? How could you check the conclusions with data?

2. Erving Goffman has written many books with analytical schemes that could be applicable to the understanding of gender identity and self-presentation. These include *Presentation of Self in Everyday Life* (New York: Doubleday & Co., Inc., 1959), *Stigma: Notes on the Management of Spoiled Identity* (Englewood Cliffs, N. J.: Prentice-Hall, Inc., 1963), *Behavior in Public Places* (New York: Free Press, 1963), and *Encounters* (New York: Bobbs-Merrill Co., 1961). Choosing one of these volumes, see whether or not Goffman's perspective is useful. Try to deduce some hypotheses from his work and suggest ways they could be tested.

3. Examine magazines from different subcultures (e.g., by social class of the reader), and analyze the images of women and men presented therein. To do this well, you will have to learn about "content analysis" from a social science research textbook. Or, for one example, see Cornelia Flora Butler, "The Passive Female," in *Journal of Marriage and the Family,* 33(1971):435-44.

130

Female and Male

REFERENCES

Baxter, J. C. "Interpersonal Spacing in Natural Settings." *Sociometry* 33 (1970):444-56.

Couch, Carl J. "Family Role Specialization and Self-attitudes in Children." *Sociological Quarterly* 3(1962):115-21.

Denzin, Norman K. "The Significant Others of a College Population." *Sociological Quarterly* 7(1966):298-310.

Exline, R. V. "Visual Interaction—The Glances of Power and Preference." In *Nebraska Symposium on Motivation,* edited by J. K. Cole. Lincoln, Neb.: University of Nebraska Press, 1972.

Figes, Eva. *Patriarchal Attitudes.* New York: Fawcett World Library, 1970.

Fisher, Seymour. *Body Experiences in Fantasy and Behavior.* New York: Appleton-Century-Crofts, 1970.

Body Consciousness. Englewood Cliffs, N. J.: Prentice-Hall, Inc., 1973.

Friedan, Betty. *The Feminine Mystique.* New York: Dell Publishing Co., Inc., 1963.

Greer, Germaine. *The Female Eunuch.* London, England: McKibbon and Kee, 1971.

Gurin, Gerald; Veroff, Joseph; and Field, Sheila. *Americans View Their Mental Health.* New York: Basic Books, 1960.

Hensley, Nancy. "Power, Sex, and Nonverbal Communication: The Politics of Touch." Unpublished manuscript, 1971.

Horner, Matina. "The Motive to Avoid Success and Changing Aspirations of College Women." In *Women on Campus: 1970.* Ann Arbor, Mich.: Center for Continuing Education of Women, 1970.

Janeway, Elizabeth. *Man's World: Woman's Place.* New York: Delta, 1971.

Katz, Marlaine Lockheed. *Female Motive to Avoid Success: A Psychological Barrier of a Response to Deviancy?* Princeton, N. J.: Educational Testing Service, 1973.

Komisar, Lucy. "The Image of Women in Advertising." In *Woman in Sexist Society,* by Vivian Gornick and Barbara K. Moran. New York: Basic Books, 1971.

McClelland, D. C.; Atkinson, J.; Clark, R.; and Lowell, E. *The Achievement Motive.* New York: Appleton-Century-Crofts, 1953.

Mehrabian, Albert. "Relationship of Attitude to Seated Posture, Orientation, and Distance." *Journal of Personality and Social Psychology* 10(1968): 26-30.

"Verbal and Nonverbal Interactions of Strangers in a Waiting Station." *Journal of Experimental Research in Personality* 5(1971):127-38.

Mulford, Harold A., and Salisbury, Winfield W., II. "Self-conceptions in a General Population." *Sociological Quarterly* 3(1964):115-21.

Weston, Peter J., and Mednick, Martha T. "Race, Social Class, and the Motive to Avoid Success in Women." *Journal of Cross-Cultural Psychology* 1(1970): 294-91.

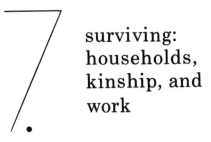

surviving: households, kinship, and work

At eighteen, the young woman or man in our society legally becomes an adult with all attendant rights and responsibilities. She can exercise the privilege to vote, purchase alcohol, bet, arrange credit, seek her own residence, and legally consent to certain sexual activities. In other words, she is free to meet her own needs without parental and community overview. Some of these needs are basic—food, shelter, and clothing. Closely related are auxiliary needs, such as the insurance of good health to enjoy life activities, and the resources to meet other needs that the person has learned bring self-fulfillment to herself. As a mature human being, she will have sexual preferences which in our society often interlink with the emotional needs that are satisfied best through intimacy with one person.

Gender will be relevant at this point in two ways. First, it will specify needs that a person feels are essential to achieving a satisfying adulthood. Most men in our society cannot conceive of life as very meaningful without a work attachment. Work has become the mainstay of male identity and responsibility. To be unemployed is to be less of a man, that is, not completely one's self. For women, the prospect of running one's own household and participating in a family of one's own creation, however small, is a basic goal. The incomplete woman is the one with no kin. Naturally, some people reach adulthood without investing their identities in gender-specific ways. Nonetheless, these models—man as breadwinner, woman as family manager—permeate all races, ethnic groups, and classes in our society.

This does not imply that men do not also desire a family or that women do not want to work. Nor does this imply that men believe themselves to be superior to women. It is on these additional issues (i.e., what else should a man and woman do, what is the power and resource arrangement between the sexes) that race, class, and ethnic differences appear. For example, Chicano women and men will express more gender-specific goals than white protestant women and men. Yet the latter are more likely to express beliefs that the male should have the final say in family decisions. The division of labor by gender in our society leaves many points open to debate and free choice, though we are often blinded by sexist mythology from recognizing the rich variations in gender subcultures that do exist.

Gender is also important in that the ongoing institutional arrangements will provide directions or obstacles that turn women and men toward different solutions for satisfying their needs. Each person must set out his life career within the political reality of his society. Most young adults enter the job market, but young women will find themselves in low-paying occupations that provide little mobility into higher status slots. This situation can help to dampen prior career motivations and make the possibility of economic dependence upon an adult male appear more attractive. Young men will find more challenge in the work world, yet they are hampered in other ways. They are not as well-trained to care for their own single household as the women are. Once working, men will also face pressures to become "complete" adults by marrying and having a family. Men do not have the option of having children apart from marriage in our society, and few men have seen this experience as a loss because childrearing has been denigrated as "woman's work." Nonetheless, in objective terms, it is clear that men are blocked from a considerable set of activities along with women. The ready-made solution is marriage. Women can have economic security; men can have household maintenance and family life.

Marriage in America means a legal heterosexual relationship. The partners agree to abide by the state regulations guiding such unions. They agree that only a legal decree can end the relationship. They accept that the man is the head of the household for purposes of determining family residency and for most economic transactions. They agree to be responsible for the welfare of any children that result from the union. They receive, in return, various rights, such as sexual ones, as well as promises from the state to assist the family at certain crisis points. They will receive other formal and extra-legal benefits that non-married couples can not obtain. For example, their taxes will be lower. They will have little difficulty in making economic transactions as a unit. Businesses will recognize the unit and give rights to a spouse that do not accrue to an unrelated partner. Life can be much simpler and economical for couples once their union is legalized, though they do so at the cost of accepting the state's terms and controls.

There are so many supports for legal marital unions in our society that most adults at one time or another do marry. Although we are raised to value independence and freedom, the society is so arranged that the solitary, self-supporting life is very difficult to manage at times. Numerous social activities are couple-centered and controlled. Single persons of both sexes experience many pressures to marry, so much so that at times people with little to gain through the act, such as homosexuals, do so for purposes of self-presentation. Marriage implies some security that another person will be around in case of crisis or trouble. As Slater (1970, p. 21) has noted, "Americans are forced into making more choices per day, with fewer 'givens,' more ambiguous criteria, less environmental stability, and less social structural support, than any people in history." They are encouraged to do this alone, to be autonomous and self-sufficient, in a society where interdependence is a requisite for survival. The consequences of pushing the denial of interdependence, claims Slater, are disconnection, boredom, loneliness, low self-esteem, and insecurity. No wonder, then, that most people who have experienced divorce remarry, and that most single parents seek out a legal spouse. In spite of all the pressures to "be one's own person," we admit to needs for others, develop trust, love, and desire to be intimate to someone who will reciprocate with similarly profound personal commitment.

Families headed by marital pairs are the preferred household form in our society. Communes, homosexual pairs, unrelated couples, group marriages, and other forms are few in number and often kept secret. Theoretically speaking, the household is a unit of residential propinquity and domestic functions, while the family is a kinship unit. The former has to do with economic needs, the latter with sexual and emotional ones. Because both units are virtually the same in our society, the work and intimacy worlds are intertwined. This means that from the point of view of individual persons, activities and decisions in one area of life are not easily separated from the other. We account for our behavior at home through reference to our work, and vice versa. Furthermore, the political structure of the society—laws and government regulations, as well as quasi-legal practices of businesses—ensures that the two worlds remain interconnected.

This perspective of family and work is not one found in either popular literature or social science. Rather, a simplistic role analysis underlies most literature on women and men, work and family. Popular theories are stated to the effect that American males are alienated from their work and suffer boredom and insecurity as a result. Presumably, men would be happier were their work conditions changed. More currently, we hear how domestic work is tedious and unrewarding, hence women should be allowed more entry into rewarding jobs, the very jobs that make men unhappy. What is wrong here? Essentially, there has been confusion with regard to levels of analysis. Studies that demonstrate worker unhappiness seem to speak about males because males happen to fill the roles being studied. The same can be said for women and household management. How are the economic roles to be changed? Will change bring happiness?

Another popular question concerns how we can achieve equality in marriage. This is premised on a belief that men have more power. As we shall see in chapter nine, considerable research has examined whether and in what ways the woman or man is dominant in the marital relationship. This model follows the traditional practice in the study of roles to examine the stratification of the role system. In one sense it is true that a couple can be studied in this way. However, the implication is that a change in the power relationship will improve life for the individual members, particularly the subordinate ones. (Others might argue that the power relationship contributes to the happiness of both and should continue.) The problem here is that marital couples are not isolated from other social relationships; furthermore, their own relationships are more than power arrangements.

In this complicated society, a role perspective provides a useful tool for making sense of the world. It helps to slice one sector of relationships that share something in common and examine them. Persons are not roles, however, and they recognize this fact. (Consider daily remarks such as "I hate to have to play that role.") Also, by focusing on particular roles apart from others, we can lose perspective on a problem. Although most American adults do marry, it is also the case that half of all adults at present are not married. To discuss the man-and-woman issue in terms solely of a married couple is to omit concern for a large proportion of adult life concerns. Role theory also tends to overlook the dynamic dimension of social relationships. The housewife role is really a series of roles throughout the life cycle of a family; it is also only one role that a woman plays during a day. Finally, an emphasis upon roles can lead one to ignore the interplay of other forces, notably social class and subcultural ones, upon individuals. Many of the early white, middle-class feminist speakers of the sixties were embarrassed to find themselves under attack for criticizing a type of feminine role that other groups of women in society valued. Women have since learned that there are many female realities in American society, each with its special set of problems (though similar causes underlie these diverse problems).

Much oversimplification results from a lack of historical perspective on work and families. It also follows from the tendency of social science scholarship to segment the two areas for purposes of investigation. Some recent studies provide direction for asking questions and seeking solutions to sex role problems that are premised upon a more holistic view of adult identity. Let us now try to correct some common misconceptions and tap into the lives of American women and men today as they view themselves, not as we wish to view them.

Historical Corrections

The contemporary iconic view of the American household as depicted in the mass media and popular literature consists of a male head, and a domestic female, and two children, one boy and one girl. This is the now notorious isolated nuclear family that has come under attack by some. It is also the image of the family that pervades social science investigations. The finest theoretical example of this view is Parsons' (1955) theory of family and socialization. As described, Parsons conceived of female and male in terms of the woman as emotional leader and the man as the instrumental and economic leader of the family.[1] Although family researchers were aware that this was not the only type of family, this iconic view was transformed in social science writings into an ideal. Family problems were defined as situations that deviated from this model. Thus single-parent families, divorce, and illegitimacy were viewed as "social problems" or "less than satisfactory life situations." Many topics—fatherhood, voluntary adultery, common-law marriage, singlehood—were virtually unexplored. To many social scientists in fact, the American household *was* the isolated nuclear family, however much they might protest for objectivity's sake in footnotes or prefaces.

Research on work suffered in similar ways. The iconic view of the American worker is only slightly more realistic. He is a professional (very likely a doctor), a white-collar worker, or a skilled blue-collar worker. She is a secretary or a stewardess. However, he or she do not have separate identities apart from work. They are devoted to their jobs and concerned with doing well, if not getting ahead. Social science reflected these views. Much of the prominent literature on work is from the so-called human relations approach, which attempted essentially to find out how to motivate workers to perform better on the job. Considerable investment of research has examined the occupational system and social mobility of males *only*. Women have been virtually ignored, even though 40 percent of the work force is female. On the other hand, many studies have also elaborated the meaning of work settings and careers for individual (male) identities. Yet

1. Ball (1972) has described in more detail how various definitions of "what is a family" give rise to particular catalogues of "family social problems." He recommends, as I do here, that one distinguish the household, a domestic living group bound by place, from the family, a group bound by kinship.

overall studies of the occupational realm have overlooked many categories of workers and have failed to examine the negative consequences of work on personal health, identity, and family life.

These criticisms cannot apply to the most recent developments in both specialties. During the sixties, the social sciences went through a period of self-examination that led to the uncovering of the implicit sexism, racism, and elitism that blinded researchers in their work. As one way of correcting these idealistic models of life, many social scientists turned back to history to gain more perspective on family, households, and work in America.

The roots of the American family are in Western Europe. Ariés (1962) has described how the European family until the end of the sixteenth century was quite different from the one we see today. The world of work and intimacy were interrelated. For the poor, houses were tiny hovels where the adults slept. The children were living elsewhere, and all family members spent their time on the streets or at work locations. For the more affluent families, the house was a social and business center. No room had a special function as it does today. Beds and tables were often portable, set up and taken down as the number of persons in the household fluctuated. Business associates were also friends or kin. These big houses were typical of affluent families in the early American colonies as well, particularly in the South, where the long distances required visitors to remain overnight. The categories that related persons to one another overlapped and were very indefinite and flexible.

Sullerot (1971) has described similarly how the power relationships among family members were formed. She believes that urbanization, which forced men out of the home, was especially favorable to patriarchy. As the home became more a refuge and isolated from other forms of social life, its value was lowered in men's eyes. Serious work occurred elsewhere. This contributed to the lowering of the status of women, who previously in many nonurban parts of Europe had shared in most societal responsibilities. Ariés concurs, and elaborates further that the formation of the school system separated child from adult. Consequently, the family split along another axis of authority, along generational lines as well as gender ones.

American immigrants brought with them the tradition of the English common law. According to this doctrine, unmarried females enjoyed equal legal status with single males. Single adult women were free to enter into contracts, own property, manage land, sue and be sued, and so on. Once married, the feudal doctrine of *couverture* was evoked, a model which argues that since woman and man are one, only one spokesperson is needed, the husband. The woman lost her property rights in exchange for a guarantee of some inheritance rights and the promise of her husband's continuing support. The woman lost her surname and adopted the residency of the husband.

Furstenberg (1966) studied the diaries of foreign travelers to America in the early 1800s and discovered the presence of the isolated nuclear family and female oppression even then, before the country industrialized. Young women were free to travel, leave home, and support themselves. Yet they were also under great pressure to marry at an early age and remain chaste until then. Once married, it was noted, a woman was as good as "put on the shelf." As Furstenberg explains, the women took on demanding domestic obligations and gave up any other activities such as occupations. To compensate for loss of power, men exhibited a compulsive chivalry toward women in public.

Smuts (1959) explored the role of women and work in 1890, a period when two-thirds of all families were on farms. Women provided all the necessities of the household: clothes, candles, butter, fuel. Men's work was the production of food to be sold; women cared for the home, garden, and dairy. In addition, they often earned much of the money that went into the development of the farm, not into their own or the family's pockets. Many women found themselves running farms as widows or sole survivors.

Male migrants to the city, whether from the farm or Europe, faced the prospect of a type of work that was unfamiliar to them. The woman continued to perform the same chores—growing food when possible, making candles, clothes, and so on. Most foods were unprocessed, so women preserved, pickled, canned, made jelly, and baked. Most of the family's medical care was provided by the woman, there being few doctors and nurses in the country. These women also sought ways to increase the family income, though opportunities were much more restricted than in rural areas. The man was no longer around the home, so married couples experienced far less companionship and assistance to one another.

What sort of work was available? Fortunate men were professionals or managers. Less fortunate ones were in manufacturing, low-skilled trades, or served as bookkeepers and clerks in dirty offices. Single or widowed women turned to the mills and the few manufacturing positions available or became salesclerks. A few fortunate women obtained teaching and nursing positions. The professions, commerce, and white-collar work all were closed to women. Oddly enough, twice as many girls than boys graduated from high school at that time, yet the boys were directed into careers. Keeping women at home was considered to be a mark of social standing, and a working woman was considered a sign of family problems.

Since 1890, several trends can be noted in the arena of work and household life. Men's occupations have expanded to include a large layer of white-collar positions. Many men in laboring and manufacturing jobs now have the advantages of union membership to protect the workers' rights. Women have experienced sharp increases in the availability of clerical and sales work, though most other job categories are still relatively closed. These positions typically are not unionized.

More important for the family is the labor force shift that allowed married women and mothers to enter the world of paid employment. (However, women work outside the home while retaining all domestic responsibilities within the home.) The demands of paid work have lightened. The work week has dropped from sixty to thirty-seven hours, and most workers receive paid holidays and vacations. Very arduous physical work has been alleviated by technology. Thus, family members can return home with energy remaining for their own pursuits.

It is important not to ignore the way the stratification of the occupational structure continues to shape the personal resources, life opportunities, and problems of individual workers. The occupational caste-like system places women in dead-end positions of low pay. Consequently, female household heads and single women cannot enjoy the standard of living and security of single men. On the other hand, men must face the consequences of the occupational class system, one that sorts many of them into tedious though secure jobs that compromise their self-worth. Many young men find themselves in positions better than those their fathers had, though trapped to go no further. Many married women accept the lowest-paying and most tedious jobs because their husbands do not earn sufficient money to meet family needs.

It appears too that four major types of household organization predominate. In metropolitan areas and among some ethnic groups, the *nuclear family embedded in a network of extended kin* provides the structure for meeting basic needs. Another group in our society, particularly the suburbanites and others who have been mobile, live in *isolated nuclear families.* These households may be supported by what may be called "fictive kin"—friends who fill in to provide the assistance that blood kin provided in the past. The third household type is that of the *mother-child nuclear family.* This type is often associated with blacks, but actually it is prevalent among the urban poor of all races, where marital stability is low. The fourth household is the *unattached adult,* one that has been virtually ignored by social scientists to date.

Most adults in our society experience several of these household forms during their lifetime. Many adults will become parents, but parenting will not consume their entire life. Many families in our society do fit the iconic image: father at work, mother at home, several dependent children. Yet this is not the only prevalent life-style, and those in this situation will likely experience other family-work structures during their life.

Although an extensive literature on the family exists, surprisingly few studies address themselves to the meanings of family life for women and men. The most popular topics of investigations are marital roles and marital success, mother-child relations, extended family and kin relations, marriage rates, sexual behavior, and fertility. The most popular sample in this research is that of college students, with middle-class married respondents composing much of the remainder (Heiskanen 1971). That sexist biases underlie much of the work is evidenced by the fact that the *Journal of Marriage and the Family* devoted two issues of its 1971 volume to the topic of sexism in research. Thus, in one article, Erlich (1971) stated how the six most popular texts on marriage described women as having "a natural maternal drive" and housewifery as "the proper woman's place in American society." With regard to sexuality, the texts encouraged the view that men (not women) need sex and can't help themselves when they rape or commit infidelities. Otherwise, the role of men is very much ignored, except as they enact the role of family decision-maker or patriarch.

This is not to imply that earlier work on the family and occupations is useless. Rather, the old data will have to be reevaluated in light of what we now know about sexism. For example, one can read between the lines of studies on extended families to infer how these relationships help or hinder women as housewives and how they contribute to women's self-definitions. Similarly, we need to take a second look at the numerous studies of social mobility to deduce how job careers and male family roles intersect and interact. This rewriting of the literature will take considerable effort on the part of social scientists concerned with sex roles.

In the meantime, research studies must take account of sexist bias. One simple way to correct and improve upon past work is to address commonplace myths about men and women and see whether they hold in fact. Commonsense is usually true to a point. The value of social science is in identifying the margin of error present in everyday explanations for events, and in sorting out the valid sayings from the false.

Another corrective is to explore topics overlooked by past researchers who were too blinded by the ideals to notice real, sizeable subgroup phenomena. The remainder of this chapter explores several lines of topics. The choice is idiosyncratic. Given the range of issues and ways of slicing the world of work-household-kinship, the author resorted to elaborating some of the questions and research that has caught her own attention.

1. True or false: Anyone can do a housewife's job. The housewife's lot is not an easy one. Housewives are passive, preoccupied with the mundane, unassertive, uncreative. "Koffee klatches" are a waste of time.
2. True or false: The blue-collar male is preoccupied with *machismo* values. He supports violence, disdains family life beyond being a breadwinner, spends his time with "the boys," and is unfaithful to his wife.

The Life Cycle of the Housewife

Almost all women in America experience the role of the housewife at some point in their lives. All women do housework, but only married women with responsibility for the domestic operation of the household are housewives. Married women who work retain the role as well. In spite of the fact that a considerable proportion of the adult population enacts this role, objective, substantive data is seldom available on them. As unpaid labor, housewives have never really fit in the stratification system. Their work has been so devalued that sociologists leave it out of their occupational ranking surveys. When asked, "What do you do?" by a television interviewer, many women respond, "Oh, I'm *just* a housewife." In recent years, some feminist writings have further contributed to the poor status of the position. Some argue that housewivery is beneath women, who should be seeking careers instead. Consequently the many women who lack resources and incentives for careers—women content with their role— feel further loss of self-esteem. *Everyone* seems to agree that the housewife's lot is not a happy one nor is it worth talking about. Woman's place is in the home.

One social scientist, Lopata (1971) did not accept these stereotypes and went to housewives themselves to see what their lives were really like, what their satisfactions and problems were *as they saw them.* Over several years she collected lengthy interview data on a sample of 279 suburban housewives, 192 nonworking urban housewives, and 100 working urban housewives of both white and minority races. The women lived in and around Chicago, covered a range of ages, and were both working class and middle class. Lopata discovered that there were many types of housewives, depending upon the stage of life they are in, their personal orientation toward the role, their personal satisfactions with the role. Looking at the major dimensions of the role, Lopata came to the following conclusions.

1. *Becoming a housewife:* in order to have a role, there must be at least two persons for roles evolve through the enactment of meanings, rights, and obligations between role partners. Marriage is the ceremony in our society that turns women into housewives in a symbolic way. They can now say "I am Mrs. ...." or "I am just a housewife." Becoming a housewife, however, lasts for some period of time afterward, and learning is not easy because the role is so complex.

   Figure 7-1 depicts the housewife's role and duties as Lopata discovered them. She must see to the maintenance of the household to keep it safe and clean, keep its supplies, assist family members in meeting their obligations, represent the family in social settings, and often raise children. Few women marry knowing what all these duties entail. Housework is considered to be trivial, thus many young women never learn how to perform the many technical skills that it calls upon. Women do not need to apply for the job—they get it along with the husband.

   Not surprisingly, this is a period of considerable life change. Many women in Lopata's study noted that it was time "to grow up" and stop behaving in girlish ways. They described the relational problems of learning to act "like a wife," which means having someone take care of them. Although women differed as to whether marriage meant more or less freedom, all agreed that their freedom was changed. Some women found the shift in status from responsible single adult to a dependent adult somewhat confusing.

   Few women felt prepared for their homemaking tasks. The higher a woman's education, the *less* adequate she felt her preparation. Her training is on the job. No one gives her a raise for good work nor can she be fired. Somehow she must seek out solutions and set standards for herself. She must learn from numerous unrelated sources: newspapers, magazines, mothers, friends. Few women can afford outside services in helping them meet their jobs. A maid is the dream of many suburban housewives, and money is seen as a means of acquiring products that would reduce work.

2. *Being a wife:* the young woman often enters marriage with an idealized view that she will be able to love her husband, have fun with him, and be with him. In fact, she will find that their respective work and the realities of survival make times of love and fun infrequent. In time, most women reassess their relationship with their spouse. Lopata asked, "What are the roles, in order of importance, of the man of the family?" Women responded in the following order: breadwinner, father, husband. Thus in time the romantic ideal is replaced by a more realistic evaluation.

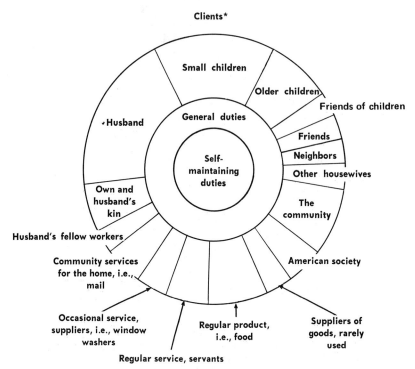

Clients*

Small children

Older children

Friends of children

General duties

Husband

Friends

Self-
maintaining
duties

Neighbors

Other housewives

Own and
husband's
kin

The
community

Husband's fellow workers

Community services
for the home, i.e.,
mail

American society

Occasional service,
suppliers, i.e., window
washers

Regular product,
i.e., food

Suppliers of
goods, rarely
used

Regular service, servants

* The size of the area represents its relative significance to the role. The way the role of housewife is performed by any particular woman depends on many factors, such as the presence of children in the household and the financial resources she has to obtain goods and services. Ideal standards of performance are available in all cultures.

Source: Lopata (1971) p. 138.

Figure 7-1. The social role of housewife.

Being a wife also means learning to relate to the husband's job and its demands. Many women felt it important to encourage men, provide a relaxing home situation, and provide social entertainment when useful. How did the men assist the women in their work? In about half of the families, certain tasks were the woman's alone: cooking, making beds, childcare, and laundry. Yet for many families, particularly those in the suburbs, men contributed to these and other areas of household work.

3. *Becoming and being a mother:* childrearing is another task for which virutally no traditional preparation is available. Women are supposed to be maternal by nature, hence their knowing everything about chil-

dren should follow naturally. On top of this, women are supposed to mother in a rational way in our society, that is, suppress many of the emotional features of the work. Even more complicating is the fact that the child is developing and changing over time. Consequently, new problems arise for which old solutions are not useful.

Motherhood begins once the woman knows that she is to be one. It is the major goal of most American girls including young working women. Yet, women who are mothers describe the fact in the passive voice as if they had no doing in the matter. They speak of how a "son was born" or a "baby came." Similarly, they describe the child with words of possession.

The arrival of the child sets off many changes in the self. Many women describe the event as causing an "identity crisis." Others found themselves overwhelmed by the additional number of skills and chores that made their previously efficient selves less capable of getting all the work done. A third consequence of children is a feeling of "being tied down" though this is not always viewed negatively. Another major modification was in the role of the wife. Although the child competes successfully for much time that had previously been given to the husband, the child's presence also provides a new base for companionship. Finally, motherhood causes changes in the physical environment that reflect back on the woman's self-feelings. Frequently, this is the point where a major move is made, say to the suburbs. Clearly, motherhood is an event that produces more immediate, profound changes in a woman's life than at any other point. Nonetheless, in spite of its challenges and sacrifices, motherhood is considered to be the most satisfying aspect of housewifery.

4. *Neighboring:* one feature of housewifery that often comes under criticism or humorous commentary is that of the "koffee klatch." By now it should be obvious that women must be doing more than just gossiping when they get together. These associations with other adult women are not trivial ones for they serve to help women meet the challenge of housework and childrearing. At different points in her life, a woman calls upon the neighbor relationship for help and satisfaction. For example, newlywed wives are usually too involved with work and their husbands to establish ties. With the entry of the child, however, the woman is left at home all day except for shopping and related trips. By meeting other women at parks and houses, housewives are able to establish information and helping patterns to make their job easier. Some people might consider some of the conversations to be useless (e.g., a comparison of detergent prices). These topics are

hardly useless to women charged with the smooth management of the household. The women must discuss such minutiae reflects on the society's poor organization of resources to assist them.

Overall, Lopata's work points to the competency and creativeness of women in meeting a most complicated and difficult job. Housewives are not the passive, dissatisfied, small-minded persons found in stereotypes. Many women find the tasks challenging, stimulating, and highly rewarding. Compared to the type of work they would have in the occupational world, they are likely realistic in their evaluations. Nonetheless, it is clear that they succeed with costs. What can it mean to one's self to work day after day with only self-motivation, self-rewards, little encouragement, few resources, no raises or vacations, and no chance of changing jobs without drastic changes in one's life?

Some critics might argue that Lopata's research only proves the oppression of these women as "happy slaves." This overlooks many of these women that have no other choice except to be unhappy. Many have deep affectional ties to their children and husbands that compensate for the other difficulties of their lot. Many have no recourse in the way of self-support or a job that will bring in money for domestic help. The problems of the housewife cannot be solved by giving women jobs. The food must be prepared, children raised, the house kept clean and safe regardless of other self-satisfactions. "Just housewives" accept this reality. Unfortunately, much of society does not, so the women go on day-to-day, rewarding themselves and one another in small ways.

Lopata's findings apply to women in different class positions, races, residences, and ethnicities, yet they exclude the impact of work. In 1970, about 42 percent of all adult women over sixteen were working. Motherhood and marriage depress this rate of participation only slightly. Most working mothers were in homes with the husband present. How did these women manage to meet the demands of the household and the working world?

Apparently, society provided little support or encouragement. Only 6 percent of the children affected were in childcare centers, simply because childcare centers are not available. The remainder were watched at home by babysitters and relatives or in rare cases, left alone. Also, working women apparently continued to put as much effort in domestic work. When a woman takes a job, her "real" job remains at home, and she contributes many hours labor to its maintenance. Many of these women were in low-paying jobs, so their work-related expenses consumed much of their income. Apparently, for many women and families, the small financial gain is felt to be worth the costs and additional problems.[2]

The Blue-collar Male at Work and Home

About half of all men work in the so-called blue-collar occupations—factory workers, construction workers, and other assorted laboring or crafts persons. Although the income of these men often matches that of white-collar men, a status difference exists between the occupational categories. White-collar jobs are "clean," nonphysical, mental activities. The majority of male white-collar jobs are professional, technical, and managerial. In other words, they are positions with authority and responsibility. In contrast, the blue-collar job is "dirty," physical, and not likely to be one of authority. Life-style differences separate the two groups of men, partly because the blue-collar male retains ties to ethnicity, race, and other subcultural influences.

Sexton (1971) has argued that both the media and the intellectuals have contributed to a fallacious negative stereotype of the blue-collar man. Both sources of information have encouraged a "myth of affluence," she claims, because the writers themselves are among those who have been mobile and successful in their lifetimes. The fact is that the true middle American household, one headed by a blue-collar worker, black or white, has a difficult time managing to meet basic family needs. A city worker, age thirty-eight, with a family of four, had to make more than $10,000 in 1970 in order to live a "modest but adequate standard of living." This budget allows for *no savings* at all and nothing that the affluent would consider to be luxuries. In order to live the "American standard of living," still one without savings, an additional $4000 would be required. What were workers actually earning? Table 7-1 presents the earnings distribution of year-round, full-time wage and salary workers. Additional breakdowns by race and union membership are included because these are important determinants of income level.

From this income data, the obvious conclusion is that most blue-collar males do not earn sufficient income to meet modest budgets. For only one category of worker, the white union craftsman or foreman, do more than half of the workers meet the $10,000 requirement. All blacks and nonunion whites have median incomes some distance from this goal. And un-

---

2. Kreps (1971) reviews the literature on women's labor force activity in order to answer why women take the same low-paying jobs year after year. Women leave the monotony of housework for the monotony of paid labor. Kreps argues that equal employment legislation will not be sufficient. Women must learn to apply for a more diversified set of jobs and demand work concomitant with their training.

Table 7-1

Median Incomes (1970) of Year-Round Full-Time Male Blue-Collar Workers by Race and Labor Union Membership

	Union Member		Nonunion Member	
	Income	Total (a)	Income	Total (a)
Black males				
Craftsmen, foreman	8,874	(383)	6,702	(222)
Operatives	7,512	(873)	5,493	(471)
Nonfarm laborers	7,192	(497)	4,690	(320)
White males				
Craftsmen, foremen	10,245	(6,473)	8,820	(3,633)
Operatives	8,663	(5,170)	6,865	(2,393)
Nonfarm laborers	8,048	(1,295)	5,627	(677)

a=In Thousands

Source: U.S. Department of Labor

like many white-collar workers, blue-collar men do not benefit from the tax regulations that allow various business deductions nor are they likely to have expense account and similar sources of hidden additional income. How do the families survive? The women and the young go to work as well in order to meet basic needs. The additional wage earners do not make anything close to the man's income, of course, because they are shunted into low-paying or part-time positions.

Sexton translates the meaning of such statistics for the daily lives of household members. This middle American family, black or white, is more likely to be in debt than those above or below them on the income ladder. They are often priced out of the housing market by land speculators and money lenders. Forced to own a car by the ordering of society, the middle American is very likely to be driving an old one, one kept past the limits of its planned life. And it was likely a used car to begin with. As for leisure, most middle Americans take no yearly vacation, except perhaps to visit relatives. Leisure money is spent on temporary events—sporting events, reading material, movies, and alcohol for socializing. The popularity of the television, however dull and repetitive its content, is understandable in view of these economic pressures. It truly is an entertainment bargain, particularly as a one-time purchase on installment.

Furthermore, blue-collar occupations are not organized in accord with the Horatio Alger myth. Whereas the white-collar man begins his mobility with advanced education and can face a career offering challenge and tests of self-worth, the blue-collar man is caught in a less fluid opportunity structure. In the most definitive study of occupations and mobility to date, Blau and Duncan (1967) have shown that blue-collar job entrants enjoy less mobility than other men, and that often their moves take them *down* in status as well as up. Consequently, many men end up years later at the same position on the status ladder as when they started out. Men who begin their jobs on the farm or in white-collar positions are much more likely to be upwardly mobile. Furthermore, Sexton has described how the blue-collar job peaks at an earlier age than other ones. By age forty, most blue-collar workers are frozen at the top salary they will ever receive. After this age they face job loss (due to injury or illness) and job demotion due to inability to perform adequately with younger men. Finally, while the hourly wages of those men in highly paid blue-collar positions, such as the auto workers, are often cited as an indication of the good fortune of blue-collar men, these workers seldom work year-round, are prone to sudden layoffs, and unlikely to have much in the way of retirement benefits. Workers in these high hourly wage categories still have a difficult time meeting the "modest budget" of the Bureau of Labor Statistics.

Another feature of the blue-collar worker is the media stereotype that argues him to be racist, conservative, and fond of violence. This view is ironic in light of the history of labor unions, where not too many years ago men were killed for their attempts to obtain what many today would call "radical" aims. During the Vietnam War, popular polls repeatedly showed the blue-collar worker to be more against the war than the white-collar man. Sexton suggests that there is a simple reason for it; the blue-collar son formed the bulk of the infantry while the white-collar son was on a college deferment. In a survey of attitudes toward violence, Stark and McEvoy (1970) found that white-collar workers and better educated men scored higher on many items. For example, the more educated a man is, the more likely he believes it proper to hit a wife for punishment. The blue-collar worker has traditionally been a Democrat and in support of social welfare programs. That some party defection has occurred in recent years may be because the social welfare programs seldom benefit workers when they are in need. Also, the blue-collar voter is becoming more sophisticated about welfare issues and policies.

Racial cleavages do beset blue-collar occupations. In the North, blacks have yet to break some unions in any numbers. In the South, racial discord has interfered with labor unionization, hence both blacks and whites suffer. Yet it is a mistake to cite data on union organization as evidence for blue-collar racism. More accurately, racism among white blue-collar workers is related to their ethnicity, their religion, and their residence within a city. For example, the Boston Irish Catholics were the last of that city's white ethnic group to suffer severe economic and social discrimination. Living closest in proximity to blacks, they sense the most visible threat to their own newly-acquired respectability. (Perhaps racist attitudes are encouraged by those in power as a way of defecting worker discontent from the real problem, which deals with economic issues that hurt both whites and blacks.)

The content of blue-collar work and its meaning for the worker is often romanticized. Working conditions are hardly as safe as that of the white-collar man. Factories are noisy, dirty, beset with chemicals, fumes, and dangerous machinery. Construction work can be arduous, even for the man in good shape, and it lacks the comfort of the controlled weather environment of the office. Few ties to the outside world, such as telephones by a desk, are present on the job. Lunch typically is brief and at one's work place. Outsiders do not come to the worker unless he is a foreman. The life of many blue-collar men, though out "in the real world," appears to be more remote and isolating than that of housewives. Consequently, like the women at home, the workers turn to those closest to them, fellow male workers.

Given this general overview of the average male worker, let us turn to his life as it incorporates both the world of work and home. The most insightful study of this type of man has been Sennett and Cobb's (1972) in-depth study of workingmen in Boston. The researchers lived in and studied working class neighborhoods, made lengthy interviews of family members, and held group discussions with persons. In the first report of their research, *The Hidden Injuries of Class,* Sennett and Cobb tried to discover how the blue-collar male measures his own value against the standards set by American society. What follows here is based upon their findings.

Workingmen aspire to dignity and the exercise of control over their lives. They see educated men as possessing the capability of being rational and emotionally restrained, and they also accept that white-collar work is valuable work. Yet they perceive blue-collar work as valuable because it is more than "pushing papers." Some blue-collar men aspire to better positions, though at the risk of feeling like imposters. Most stay at their jobs and suffer silently for *not* achieving the very jobs they do not actually desire. Thus blue-collar men appear to be in the damned-if-you-do-damned-if-you-don't payoff with regards to self-respect.

In America, ability has become the badge of an individual with IQ scores being the commodities in the mobility market. The workingman accepts the ideology that ability grants someone the right to transcend social origins and be free to control his own life. In fact, ability is measured so narrowly that most people are among the mass, which means they are "ordinary" and "average." How can one have a sense of dignity in this case?

The workingman is unaware of the biases in IQ tests and other ability measures so he believes that a person who fails has no right to complain. A reverse Horatio Alger myth serves to make sense of life: if a man hasn't gotten ahead, he must remain a member of the mass, suffer doubt and shame, lack the freedom to be unique and respected. This attitude permeates the everyday work world where workers readily accept the authority of their supervisors as legitimate. Workers do not see themselves as the hapless serfs of Marxian theory because they accept that another man has the right to take away their rights. In Sennett and Cobb's words, "whenever power becomes legitimate, whatever dignity a man accords to his rulers he must necessarily deny himself." Who holds legitimate power in the worker's eyes?—the man of ability, the one who has made it.

The worker's self-conception and behavior can be traced back to the urban school system he emerges from. There he learns early just who, in the school's terms, is going "to make something of himself." For the mass of boys, who are not included in this group, the reaction is often anger toward those who succeed. Masculinity is associated with the mass, not with the successful boys. School becomes a place to spend time, a blank space until it is time to get a job and make a living. School is not a place that can help them or give them dignity.

Outside of criminal activity, which few boys indulge in, the only source of power is sexual. Boys band together for purposes of sexual competition, rule-breaking, and other forms of status (just as the girls talk about clothes and boys). Teachers, parents, and police view these activities as disturbing of youths' chances to make something of themselves. What both the youth and the outsiders miss is how the social order of the school itself is a cause of the youths' reaction to life. The young men express their anger at individuals, not at the order of events; the adults express anger at the young men. If a young working class male achieves dignity, it is in the short run and at the expense of self-development. He must be tough, sexual, and troublesome and likely to suffer injuries, real or psychic, that lessen a chance of finding dignity as an adult. Consequently, the male gang provides practice in the class structure of the outside world. Class is defined in terms of personal responsibility. If you follow orders, you're lower than the person giving them, because you lack the inner resources to be independent.

As adults, workingmen bring the gang values to work with them, though in their less hostile form. It has been shown repeatedly in studies of workers that men develop systems of reciprocity and helping that shape the nature of work productivity. Most workers find themselves compromised at times between the values of hard work and fraternity. They want to be proud of their jobs, yet not make their buddies look bad by working too hard. To work at top speed means to deny the individuality—the depressions, the hangovers, the love affair's dreamings—that impede production. Consequently, the man who could be working faster or more skillfully feels inadequate and successful.

Family life is "real life" to these men, though the long hours of hard labor prevents them from enjoying their families. As single men, a blue-collar job provides a substantial income, one that allows a nice car and much leisure-time money. At marriage, however, the income becomes inadequate almost immediately. Many of these men are influenced by ethnic ties that favor nonworking wives and the desire for children, so family responsibilities increase at a rate far ahead of income. The economic facts of life require diligent, conscientious savings in order to purchase a modest house or send a child to a low-cost college. A blue-collar man must, like the housewife, develop a strong sense of self-motivation and strength in order to keep his household out of crisis.

Although the blue-collar man cares deeply about his family, he often finds that he must sacrifice family life in order to protect the household. Sennett and Cobb suggest that family problems result because these men fail to consult their families and see whether the sacrifices are wanted. The stereotype of the authoritarian father (the Archie Bunker) is rooted in the sense of ingratitude these men often feel coming from their loved ones. The wives feel put upon; the children view their fathers as autocrats. Male self-sacrifice is readily accompanied by an anger toward the others in the family and outside (e.g., blacks) who seem less virtuous and self-denying. Isolated on the job, rejected at home, many of these men become lonely, feel unappreciated, and grow confused. The speech of the working class man often reflects this alienation. Passive voice occurs frequently, and the personal "I" is avoided. This serves to demonstrate their fraternity with other men, yet it also suggests a self-denial that they can control the world.[3]

In spite of ties to other men at work or at the bars, workers devalue intimacy because it would mean a willingness to bare an inadequate self. Man talk is ritualized around matters of work and sports, not home, family, and love. It appears to men that this "cult of masculinity" is a convenient

3. Similar speech preferences have been found among middle-class women, thus suggesting that the patterns are correlated with inferior status or perhaps alienation. Female writing patterns appear more oriented toward others, and use verb forms less frequently than male patterns (Warshay 1971).

defense that enables workers to enact the facade of a successful self. The appurtenances of masculinity are easy to come by, being based upon dress (blue-collar clothes), speech patterns, a willingness to drink, and expressed interest in particular topics. "Being male" is the one sure way to hold on to self-respect, though for many it may be a solution by default.

In her study of blue-collar marriage, Komarovsky (1964) found that the demands of the working world significantly affected the communication between man and wife. The overlapping interests between blue-collar spouses in her sample was so low that intimacy was lacking in a large minority of cases. She discussed several reasons for this breakdown in relationships. Men do not "bring their jobs home" because they believe them to be too monotonous to discuss, that work and home should be separated, and that griping is "unmanly." This explanation is not satisfactory in view of Sennett and Cobb's research. True, these are the reasons men will state to others. Note, though, that the reasons blame themselves. We know that men do enjoy talking about work with each other, but that they are ashamed of their jobs with regard to outsiders. How can a maintenance man take pride in griping to his family when he is "just a maintenance man?"

Other of Komarovsky's data supports the notion that the workingman feels inadequate at home. She suggests that if he is authoritarian, it is because his decisions are often spontaneous, the result of emotional reactions. The workingman must not feel very potent otherwise because he has fewer complaints about his spouse than she does about him. Blue-collar wives expect their husbands to communicate more, reveal worries, and try to be understanding. The men make fewer such demands, which means that they inhibit emotional needs or perhaps fear what might result were they to express their worries and insecurities. In spite of a low degree of verbal intimacy (compared to white-collar couples), the blue-collar couple succeeds in the sexual arena. Both husbands and wives believe that women have a right to sexual fulfillment, and many of the couples feel that their own sexual patterns are satisfying.

The extreme isolation of blue-collar men is seen in the fact that over 60 percent could name no confidants outside of marriage, and contacts with nearby relatives were not as high as for the wives. Perhaps to compensate for the poor communications at home, blue-collar housewives have a high web of social ties. Almost two-thirds have an outside confidant, and relations with relatives are continued after marriage. The women have more frequent contacts with same-sex friends. Komarovsky also found that for those couples where the man "goes out with the boys" regularly, the wife also expects and gets a night out in return.

These few studies argue that the gruff masculine demeanor of the blue-collar male is not a reflection of a strong masculine self-image.[4] The inner-life of these men is filled with doubts, problems, and self-debasements. Work provides little fulfillment, and economic pressures allow little free time or resources to achieve self-security in other words. Reticence with regard to personal troubles and a strong sense of individualism helps to isolate these men from people who care deeply about them. Believing more than others in the myth of success and affluence, these men are trapped by the realities of the economic structure and their tendency to self-blame. One is hard-pressed to conclude that these men have much more power than their wives. Life in middle America, for both women and men, is fraught with many problems, threats of financial crisis, and little support for feelings of self-pride.

Work for white-collar men in government, business, and the professions may be less alienating because the jobs do allow greater mobility and opportunity. Exceptional talent, hard work, and drive *may* be rewarded (as are connections with the right people, personal style, and other characteristics). The white-collar family income is more likely to be within the "adequate standard of living" base. Yet great rewards accrue to just a few, so many white-collar men (e.g., sales personnel, lower-level management) are prone to feeling powerless or isolated. Though their jobs are safer and more humane than blue-collar ones, they lack the opportunity for much co-worker trust or fellowship. Ultimately, white-collar men are competitors who cannot seek comfort in one another's company. Those who do not compete find themselves in the more dronelike, repetitious jobs at the bottom of the hierarchy.

The family is important as a rationale and validation for the man's work. The house, with its apparent prosperity, and the family members themselves both serve as symbols of the male's relative success. When a wife serves on a committee or a child wins a game for the home team, the man's status in the community is reinforced. Consequently, the man is perhaps held more responsible than the blue-collar worker for events within his home. Cut off from close ties with other men or women, the family also provides the major resource for emotional growth and security. However, the business world, with its competitive ethos, ill-equips a man for the sensitivities of intimate family life. Thus the white-collar man, a bit more healthy and powerful, shares doubts and problems similar to the working class man he can look down upon.

---

4. For additional studies of blue-collar life, see Rainwater et al. (1959) and Shostak and Gomberg (1964).

Household Roles: A Model for Further Research

Given Lopata's work and the study of blue-collar males, one can work toward a more complete view of adult identity as it is influenced by gender. Lopata found that family roles, responsibilities, and major life concerns changed over time in a predictable way. That is, one can delineate what seems to be a "life cycle of household roles." Table 7-2 depicts such life cycles as they may occur in America. The description applying to women is deduced from Lopata's research. The description applying to men is much more hypothetical, representing the author's way of making sense of the man's role. Briefly, the American male is seen as having a series of learning experiences and adjustments similar to the woman's. Some of his problems match hers, such as settling into the role of spouse or becoming a parent. In the early years of adulthood, however, much of his self is invested in his work and in the meeting of family financial needs. As the man reaches middle age, he must face the realities of his work life as it actually is and face more emotional demands from the family.

The woman's cycle is more discontinuous. Marriage, the birth of a child, the departure of a family member, the entry to a job—all mark sudden changes in daily demands, responsibilities, and satisfactions. Women have a rich unwritten folklore to guide them through these changes, and society provides reinforcing rituals at many of these transition points. The woman's world is one of flux, one that calls on adaptability, and a willingness to accept the unexpected. The man's world is supposed to be marked off by similar transitional steps, as defined by his career. In fact, most work lives are not in line with the career mythology, and men vest a large portion of themselves in their families, however taciturn they may be about their feelings. Their domestic roles change in predictable ways, as with the housewives, but their social contacts do not provide the comparable guidelines for action that women find. Their work lives will present precipitous changes—promotions, hirings, firings—that similarly present men with mysterious changes. American men are thus forced to be more individualistic in dealing with their life problems and self-development. Unless they are fortunate enough to be on the upwardly-mobile, affluent ladder, which few of them are, their life situations seem idiosyncratic to them. The basis for sharing is there, but the men apparently do not build upon it as the women have done.

This model as charted has some apparent problems, for it is based on the modal situation in America today. As has been noted at many points throughout the book, the model case is not often one that a simple majority of the population experience in toto. It is really a type of statistical artifact caused by the summing up of many various individual life experiences.

Table 7-2

Hypothetical Life Cycle of Household Roles

Stage	Female	Male
Entry: Marriage or cohabitation	Becoming a housewife: Change to depending status Acquire domestic skills Redefine self as "mature"	Becoming a husband: Change to responsibility status Redefine self as "full adult"
Expanding circle: childbirth	Becoming a mother: Acquire childcare skills Restrictions on many activities Major self-redefinitions Change in spouse role	Becoming a father: Increased support responsibilities Change in self-definition Readjustments in spouse role
Full-house plateau: completed family	Self-development: Increased community involvement Work force participation Acquire childrearing skills	Self-resignation: Major redefinition of self to work Acquire fathering skills
Shrinking circle: departure of children	Search for new roles: Becoming a grandmother Return to work-education Reorient to spouse Change in self re-sexuality and femininity	Self-change: Change in self regarding sexuality and "masculinity" Disengagement from work Acquire leisure pursuits
Disengagement:	Widowhood, divorcee: Increased economic responsibility Becoming a potential spouse Change to independent status	Widowed, divorced: Becoming a potential spouse Acquiring domestic skills Change to independent status
(Remarriage):	Change to dependency status: Being a wife, stepmother	Change to responsibility status: Being a husband, stepfather

For a more sophisticated view of adult identity and gender, one should break this case down into the more realistic components.

First, this model focuses upon marriage or cohabitation as the basic household bond, when in fact we know that most adults in our society will experience the single state either before marriage, or after divorce or death of a spouse, in place of marriage. In 1973, of all adults under thirty-five, the age which traditionally has had a high incidence of marriage, half were single. Certainly the daily concerns of these persons are quite different from those of their married kin. Yet singles as a category of focus have been ignored by social scientists. Except for scattered studies like Goode's (1956) survey of women after divorce, few investigations seem to have taken the single state as a serious one in itself, apart from its being a temporary place before marriage. Mythology has it that being single is a very good place to be, one free from the economic pressures of family life, one open to sexual exploration, and one providing many opportunities to explore. On the surface, it would seem that single people should have fewer economic worries. Then why do so many people look for a mate and divorced heterosexual people remarry? We have much to learn about the intimate bond by studying those who are alone.

Second, age undercuts many of the identity changes listed. Youth, sexuality, and sex identity interact in our society, such that some women and men perceive age as a threat to their sexuality, hence their selves, Similarly, many changes listed in table 7-2 (p. 154) are related to maturational changes. Obviously, motherhood is a possibility only to women within a particular age span. Less apparent, age influences the man's chances of job change, promotion, and firing. There appears to be a point in our society where old women are no longer women, thus in a sense are freed from the restrictions of being female. Accordingly, older men, being retired, lose status because they are no longer working. This relationship of maturation to gender identity is one that researchers are now taking interest in, perhaps because there are sufficient numbers of older persons to study.

At present, most women in our society have work experience during adulthood, but they do not invest themselves in their work in the sense that men do. That is, being unemployed would not have the profound personal loss that it would bring to a man. This is not true of all women, however, and will likely be even less so in the future. Younger women appear to be staking themselves more on external productivity and success. It will be interesting to see whether these women share the same social-psychological experiences that men do with regard to work. Also, most working women are in positions akin to blue-collar work, in that they take orders and perform the repetitive or tedious tasks of selling or clerical work. Unlike blue-collar jobs, much of women's work involves a public display. Women are the major intermediaries between clients and managers, professionals, and bureaucrats. Although many provocative personal statements about the demeaning nature of this work can be found in feminist literature, there has been a lack of interest in the study of these positions by social scientists. Studies analogous to those of blue-collar men—the nature of women's jobs, their meanings, and their effects upon household roles—seem necessary for understanding what it is like to be an adult female in America.

While the modal household in our society has dependent children, couples do not necessarily extend their family beyond two adults. As in the case of single people, one can't help but ask why so few couples remain childless; most of those who do apparently do unwittingly as a result of sterility. On the other hand, in recent years the feminist literature has had personal accounts by women who have remained childless by choice without loss of self-esteem. (In the past, only men could admit to not wanting children.) Again, the relationship between fertility and gender identity needs to be explored beyond the simplistic view that women feel inadequate if childless and men have no particular interest in parenting. Are men really so unconcerned with family procreation? Why do they leave birth control to women? Although it takes two persons to conceive a child, social scientists often presume that only one, the woman, matters in the decision.

As was implicit in the discussion of the blue-collar men, class differences undercut the world of work and home in essential ways. For example, work failure for the blue-collar man means his family will suffer, while for the white-collar man it more likely means that he personally will suffer. The latter has more resources for surviving the economic losses attached to a job, but he is also more committed to work as a basis for meaning and selfhood. Similarly, the working class housewife is more likely to take on the additional responsibilities of a job, while the white-collar wife finds herself just as committed to the demands of community or volunteer work. Overall, there is no denying that money is better for life satisfaction. Surveys repeatedly show that education and income *do* result in greater expression of psychic pleasure and greater health. The personal, individualized neuroses or guilt of white-collar people are the small price for affluence and success, one that cannot match the troubles of less advantage, less skilled, less resourceful persons in society. Attitudes about masculinity, femininity, and sex roles are likely differentiated more by this variable than any other.

The modal experience in America by definition is a white, Protestant one. We have not yet sufficient data to separate true ethnic and race patterns apart from class ones. For example, studies of middle American black couples show them to display interaction patterns and attitudes similar to those of middle American whites. However, poorer urban blacks and whites seem more dissimilar. In fact, ethnic whites differ much from one another with regard to such values as patriarchy, maternity, parenthood, and sexual standards. In some subcultures gender is a more salient basis for identity than in others. Other subcultures emphasize the importance of gender to the same extent, yet define the meanings attached to gender in opposite ways. The influences of ethnicity and race are probably less profound in their effect upon adult identity than class or age, but they are present for many persons in that at least they present obstacles to overcome. Thus an adult with Catholic upbringing may reject some of the church's standards on sexual norms, but this attitude comes after first dealing with the restrictions. Ethnic or religious pressures are easier to ignore than the other influences, but this does not mean they are forgotten easily.

A final problem with emphasis upon the modal pattern is that it is often among the most conservative one in society, so signs of social change are overlooked. Feminism has been an active movement in this country for over a century, and women's rights have gradually increased during this period. Although women may not be satisfied with the rate of progress, the fact is that it has not been seriously reversed. Women now spend more time out of the home, have more economic resources, more education, and fewer familial responsibilities during their lifetime than earlier American women experienced. Correspondingly, men are spending less time at work, more time at home, and have fewer familial responsibilities. Although most persons experience marriage during adulthood, they also experience other states, such as divorcehood, marriage with outside sexual freedom, periods of homosexual bonding, celibacy, and so on. Given the variety in household and family arrangements that are possible, work takes on another basis for security. It used to be that one's personal life could be taken for granted after a marriage ceremony. This no longer being the case, people are evolving other forms of self-anchorage.

In summary, it is true that gender does direct adult identity in a very general way. Most women experience the housewife role, and a majority of men experience blue-collar work situations. "Only" women can be mothers in fact and in mythology. "Only" men can move into careers for the accumulation of wealth and power. At the same time, the personal meanings of these life situations are mediated by other social pressures—

the socialization influences of childhood religion and ethnic beliefs, one's social class position, physical maturation along with its social meanings, the economic situation, and so on. These differences make it impossible to speak of "American women" or "American man" in other than the most superficial way. Although women as a group (or men as a group) are channelled into a particular set of life opportunities, actual life circumstances exhibit great variability. Consequently, there are many forms of "woman's lot" or "man's fate" to be studied. We can now turn to some of the consequences of these separate fates.

SUGGESTED PROJECTS

1. Can you sketch a view of the white-collar man? Three volumes, though old, are still useful: C. Wright Mills, *White Collar* (New York: Oxford Univ. Press Inc., 1956), William H. Whyte, Jr., *The Organization Man* (New York: Simon & Schuster, Inc., 1956), Myron Brenton, *The American Male* (New York: Fawcett World Library, 1970). Community Studies are also an important source here, such as Herbert Gans, *The Levittowners* (New York: Random House, 1969), and John Seeley, R. Alexander Sim, and Elizabeth W. Loosley, *Crestwood Heights* (Toronto, Canada: Univ. of Toronto Press, 1956).

2. What are the consequences to the family structure when women work? Some places to start are F. Ivan Nye and Lois Wladis Hoffman, *The Employed Mother in America* (New York: Rand McNally & Co., 1963), Rhonda Rapoport and Robert N. Rapoport, *The Dual Career Family* Baltimore, Md.: Penguin Books, Inc., 1972), and Jessie Bernard, *Academic Women* (University Park, Pa.: Penn. State Univ. Press, 1964) The answer requires care in defining "consequences" and ways of measuring them.

3. Does work affect the personal lives of single women and men as it does those with families? What will happen as changes in the occupational world are made to accommodate the needs of working spouses (e.g., salary equity between sexes, equal opportunity employment, more part-time labor)? Will the lives of single people benefit as well? Interview or survey single people in these regards.

REFERENCES

Ariés, Phillippe. *Centuries of Childhood*. New York: Random House, 1962.

Ball, Donald W. "The Family as a Sociological Problem: Conceptualization of the Taken-for-Granted as Prologue to Social Problems Analysis." *Social Problems* 19(1972):295-308.

Blau, Peter, and Duncan, Otis Dudley. *The American Occupational Structure*. New York: John Wiley & Sons, Inc., 1967.

Erlich, Carol. "The Male Sociologist's Burden: The Place of Women in Marriage and the Family Texts." *Journal of Marriage and the Family* 33(1971): 421-30.

Furstenburg, Frank F., Jr. "Industrialization and the American Family: A Look Backward." *American Sociological Review* 31(1966):326-37.

Goode, William. *Women in Divorce*. New York: The Free Press, 1956.

Heiskanen, Veronica Stolte. "The Myth of the Middle Class Family in American Sociology." *American Sociologist* 6(1971):14-18.

Komarovsky, Mirra. *Blue-Collar Marriage.* New York: The Free Press, 1962.

Kreps, Juanita. *Sex in the Marketplace.* Baltimore, Md.: Johns Hopkins University Press, 1971.

Lopata, Helena Znaniecki. *Occupation: Housewife.* New York: Oxford University Press, 1970.

Rainwater, Lee; Coleman, Richard P.; and Handel, Gerald. *Workingman's Wife.* New York: Oceana, 1959.

Sennett, Jonathan, and Cobb, Richard. *The Hidden Injuries of Class.* New York: Random House, 1973.

Sexton, Patricia Cayo. *Blue Collars and Hard Hats.* New York: Vintage, 1972.

Shostak, Arthur B., and Gomberg, William. *Blue-Collar World.* Englewood Cliffs, N. J.: Prentice-Hall, 1964.

Slater, Philip. *The Pursuit of Loneliness.* Boston: Beacon, 1970.

Smuts, Robert W. *Women and Work in America.* New York: Schocken, 1971.

Stark, Rodney, and McEvoy, James. "Middle-class Violence." *Psychology Today,* November 1970.

Sullerot, Evelyne. *Woman, Society, and Change.* New York: McGraw-Hill, 1971.

Warshay, Diana W. "Sex Differences in Language Style." In *Toward a Sociology of Women,* by Constantina Safilios-Rothschild. Lexington, Mass.: Xerox, 1972.

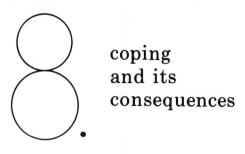

coping
and its
consequences

What does the search for love, football games, armed robbery, lung cancer, and suicide have in common? American males are more likely to be involved with these phenomena than females. Indeed, it is here, and not on personality inventories or attitude tests, that one might conclude that men and women are different. Some of the differences are quite impressive as we shall see. Overall, these differences are hints to indicators of the differential quality of life for various categories of women and men in our society. They speak of everyday pleasures, challenges, and pains—the costs and consequences of having been born female or male in our society.

These experiences are not trivial for the persons involved. They reflect on one's self-evaluation and opportunities in ways that multiply. For example, the state of being in love and personally secure makes a difference in many everyday interactions that have nothing to do with the loved one. Illness and good health each influence many daily opportunities, for to be sick is to be more dependent upon others. To engage in illegal activities is to invite loss of personal and civil liberties. Although leisure time activities are considered nonserious by many of us, imagine what your life would be were you to give up your favorite activities for a month.

All of these phenomena are important for self-evaluation in several ways. First, they may prove ways of presenting the self one wants to receive approval from others for. A common interpretation of juvenile delinquency is that it is a young man's expression of masculinity through defiance of authority and expressions of courage to peers. Some delinquents do consciously participate in deviant acts in order to receive peer praise and recognition for being a "real guy." Much leisure activity appears to fall into this category as well. Second, events that are less consciously "in-order-to" for the participant take the form of social feedback. The victim, so to speak, makes meaning of why the event occurred and what it says about her as a person. The woman who finds that someone is in love with her can take the fact of that love as indicative of the type of appeal she presents to others. Third, many of these experiences alter our life situations in profound ways, by quickly shutting off or opening a system of opportunities and problems. The states of being in love or being sick or being an arrested criminal are subsequently different from their obverse conditions. Our society seems to have many either/or structures built into it, such that one is not-criminal, however many illegal activities one engages in, until some critical event, an arrest occurs. At that point, one becomes a "criminal," and the world becomes a very different place in both objective and subjective terms. We want to be in love or not sick or not arrested because we have some awareness of the consequences of these states.

Gender identity comes in here in corollative ways. First, women and men are differentially socialized to prefer certain fronts over others, to engage in certain behaviors over others, and to search out certain types of rewards. For example, we should expect men to be more interested in testing themselves against environmental challenges than women. They will gain more inherent pleasure from tests of physical skills because they have had more experience in perceiving the thrills and excitement in spite of personal danger. Second, the meaning of the same event will be different for women and men. The role of patient is one of dependency; consequently, we should expect men to see illness as more threatening than women will. Third, the opportunities opened and closed by events will be different for women and men. Traditionally, love and marriage for women have meant a career termination, though not so for men. In the remainder of this chapter we shall examine these phenomena and see how the data illuminate gender identity in America.

The Search for Intimacy

Adults in our society have many pressures causing a strong need for intimacy. We have typically been raised in small families where emotional relationships became intense. At maturity, the culture encourages household formation based upon the pair. The economic organization is so organized that two people working together manage more efficiently than one person meeting his needs alone. The social order is so shaped that urban life, bureaucratic organization, and the intricate division of labor make formation of intimate ties outside of kinship difficult for many. The best way to ensure some personal security in the face of segmented, often alienating daily encounters, is to form a household of one's own, through cohabitation or marriage.

Our society allows a free courtship system to govern household formation. The preferred form of household is based upon the married heterosexual couple, yet those who wish to form ties of other sorts are able to do so, though with more difficulty. Strong feelings also exist that love should be present in households even when the ties are nonsexual. Love is the personal indicator that the relationship is "right" and will be able to function in spite of temporary troubles.

With regard to heterosexual bonding, the matter is complicated by two ideological systems: romantic love and sexual beliefs. Romantic love refers to the existence of strong emotional ties between a couple that emphasize permanence, monogamy, and intensity of feeling. Unlike other societies where marriages are arranged on economic or religious grounds, romantic love allows adults choice over their marital future. Given the way the society is organized, it happens that people who marry for love often satisfy expectations that they should marry "within their class" or "one of their own." The opportunities for marrying outside one's "proper" group simply are not that strong, particularly in view of homogeneous residential living patterns and the class stratification implicit in the educational and occupational realms.

American sexual beliefs have built-in inconsistencies. Our Puritanical heritage emphasizes abstinence from intercourse prior to legal marriage. At the same time, our patriarchal heritage emphasizes the sexuality of the male and his right to sexual pleasure regardless of marital status. Socialization to sexuality is confusing, often inaccurate, and secret, yet the attractiveness of sexuality is broadcasted throughout the media. Sexuality in America lacks much sensuality. Touching is infrequent, and bodies are viewed as objects of one's self rather than as essential elements of one's self. As was discussed in chapter six, males are particularly encouraged to dissociate themselves from their bodies. Sexuality takes on more gamelike and manipulative features. The act of achieving intercourse is a goal, not the experience of the act itself. So confused are we about sexuality that studies (e.g., Reiss 1967) have found that adult Americans are guilty about sex even when they do *less* than they think is allowed. And most people do not violate their own stated standards, so strong is their development of self-control in the area. Men are not much less likely than women to feel this guilt, in spite of the existence of double standard beliefs that could excuse any bad feelings they might have.

The double standard encourages a view that male sexuality is strong, driving, and a bit out of the man's control. This contrasts with the physiological givens. As Masters and Johnson (1966, 1970) have shown, the male drive is quite dependent upon psychological factors, and the male erection is hardly an automatic reaction to desire. Men are raised to be sexual aggressors which means in fact that they face direct rejections more often than the woman does. They are expected to be adept sexually, yet receive no training in sexual skills. Consequently, it should not be surprising that the average American male is hardly the lustful playboy or leering chauvanist pig some stereotypes present him to be.

There appears to be a conspiracy of silence among men as to their true sexual feelings and behaviors. Evidence exists that women and men are more alike than they perceive themselves to be. One indication is from research like that done by Balswick and Andersen (1969). They surveyed college students concerning their attitudes about behavior on pick-up dates. Each respondent was asked what their own expectations were along with what they perceived the opposite sex's expectations were. The results showed that each sex expected the opposite sex to be more permissive than they were. Similarly, the female perceived males as expecting her to be more permissive than he actually expected her to be. The largest distortion, however, was in terms of the male role. The females more accurately read that males expected them to be permissive in a pick-up situation, while the males misread the amount of aggresiveness the women desired from them. Consequently, a bind results. The men will play up "being male," though the women do not want them to. Similarly, the women do not dispute that they can be "loose" in this setting. Neither can move freely without invoking some conflict in this situation.

Further evidence that men are not so supportive of double standard prescriptions comes from the Reiss (1967) survey based upon a national sample of adults. Reiss developed a scale of attitudes toward premarital sex based upon an individual's perceptions of what was acceptable for males and for females separately. He found that the subjects could be typed as to the degree of permissiveness they accepted and whether they applied the same degree to both sexes. The distribution of type is presented in table 8-1. Very few persons subscribe to double standard beliefs. The black male is highest in this regard, with 20 percent of the respondents expressing this attitude (he is also the most liberal—23 percent—in granting the female sexual freedom). Two-thirds of all white males hold that coitus prior to marriage is wrong for *both* sexes. The white female is most traditional in expressing the propriety of premarital abstinence, while small minorities of black women accept premarital sex for both sexes. Except for the black male, the majority of persons express restrictive beliefs.

We all know that beliefs and actions are two different phenomena. How do men behave? Unfortunately, surveys on sexual activity have obscured our knowledge here. Kinsey's (1949, 1953) surveys are still a

Table 8-1
Premarital Sexual Standards by Race and Sex

	White		Black	
	Male	Female	Male	Female
Standard:	594	622	57	72
1. Abstinence beliefs emphasized for both sexes	68	92	30	65
2. Double standard	13	4	20	8
3. Coitus acceptable with love for both sexes	7	2	21	13
4. Sexual freedom for both sexes	8	3	23	10
5. Ultra-feminist	5	1	7	6

Source: Reiss (1967), p. 27.

useful source of information on American sexuality, but the sampling procedures were such that the males and females are not comparable. Since the samples were not representative, the social backgrounds of the female and male samples are too different to allow one to compare their experiences. Many social scientists have investigated premarital sex among college students, such as the cross-cultural work of Christensen (1966) or Christensen and Gregg (1970). A consistent finding in these studies is that males claim to having more sexual experience than females. Yet these data are still not sufficient to argue that males are so highly sexual as the stereotypes claim. First, they are based upon self-reports, and we have already seen that males have a strong sense that they are expected to be sexually aggressive. Thus some overstatement on their part is likely. Second, the data do not deal properly with the frequency of experience. Typically, *one* act of coitus, homosexual experience, or whatever, is sufficient to type the person in the "experienced" category. It is very possible that many of the "experienced" men do not have sex on a regular basis. This is suggested by the fact that the majority of "experienced" men often do not approve of premarital sex, and that most of their own sexual encounters have been only with women that they loved or were engaged to.

The false image of the American male is indicated in the sexual problems that women encounter. Kinsey and others since his time have noted that large minorities of female samples express dissatisfaction over their sexual experiences in that they do not think they ever had an orgasm. Yet physiologically the human female is well-designed to experience sexual pleasure provided stimulation is not too brief. Until Masters and Johnson's research, female "frigidity" was interpreted to be an individual problem. Now it is known to be an interpersonal one, where the male's activities are as important as the woman's psychological state. But men are not trained or educated to be sexually adept, and women are not encouraged to express their needs to men. Similarly, men feel pressured to perform in spite of their feelings. The failures in the bedroom cannot be blamed simply upon a lack of good intentions on the part of either sex.

Surveys concerning romantic love further show how stereotypes exaggerate the real sex difference. Most people would expect women to be more romantic than men, who are often less concerned about their emotional life. This is apparently not true, at least if surveys of students are indicative. Broderick and Weaver (1968) presented children ages eleven through seventeen with cartoons of couples in various situations. They found that boys at every age level were more likely than girls to respond to the pictures in terms of romantic content. Boys were more optimistic about the pictures, and if they perceived conflict in the settings, believed that a successful solution would be found. Knox and Sporakowski's (1968) survey of students at one college found that the males scored higher on romantic love, while women scored higher on realistic and conjugal items. Kanin et al. (1970) studied another college to see whether males fell in love more readily than females as had been found in earlier samples. They discovered that this was true in their sample as well. However, females in love appeared to idealize the state more by expressing feelings of euphoria or of perceiving the partner as being free of defects.

Love, then, is not a woman's domain. That men are as involved does not seem so surprising when one considers that most persons who write about love—poets, playwrights, lyricists, novelists, and philosophers—are men. Overall, it would seem that problems with sexuality and intimacy in our society are grounded more in the social order and the system of expectations than in actual differences between women and men. Most women and men desire intimacy, respect the values of sexual exclusiveness, reject manipulative sexuality, and experience love as a viable psychological orientation. We need much more consideration of the structures that keep the sexes from meeting on this common ground, as well as studies of love and sexuality in noncollege samples.

Leisure Activities

The study of leisure is hardly a popular topic for social scientists, and those who do study it have done so with a definite male bias in mind. Readers on leisure are more readers on sports and other male activities than anything else. Have you ever seen a paper on the "Sociology of Knitting, Crocheting, and Needlepoint," even though millions of people are engaged in these activities? One of the few studies with data on sex differences is national outdoor recreation which provides much useful data. Though "women's activities" have been omitted from the research, as well as passive indoor pursuits or indoor sports, the results are informative nonetheless.

The study consisted of national samplings of the American population for ages twelve and over during four quarters of 1960. Table 8-2 presents

Table 8-2
Participation in Leisure Activities by Sex*

	Male		Female	
	Percentage participating	Days per person	Percentage participating	Days per person
Attending concerts, drama	8	.20	10	.23
Attending outdoor sports events	28	1.61	20	1.06
Bicycling	9	2.04	9	1.48
Motor boating	26	1.55	18	.91
Camping	10	.57	6	.36
Driving for pleasure	51	6.57	54	6.78
Fishing	40	3.04	19	1.02
Hiking	7	.33	5	.20
Horseback riding	7	.47	5	.38
Hunting	6	.38	1	.01
Nature walks	12	.76	17	.74
Picnics	41	1.98	56	2.28
Play outdoor games, sports	34	5.08	25	2.28
Sightseeing	39	2.03	45	2.35
Swimming	47	5.44	43	4.89
Walking for pleasure	28	3.76	38	4.87
Water skiing	8	.42	4	.19

* Survey covers months of June-August, 1960, with a sample base of persons aged 12 and over.

Source: National Recreation Survey (1962).

some of the data on differential participation in outdoor activities by sex during the *summer months only*. The men participate more frequently in many of these activities: attending outdoor sports events, motor boating, camping, fishing, hunting, outdoor games, and water skiing. The women participate more often in nature walks, picnics, sightseeing, and walking for pleasure. The sexes participate about equally in pleasure trips by car, swimming, and horseback riding. Overall, the men spend more days at outdoor leisure than the women do. Yet for few of the activities are the differences really great. Hunting and fishing are notable cases here.

The stereotype of men is that they participate in more active forms of leisure than women. This position is questionable. Motor boating and fishing are not strenuous activities and women do participate in many physical forms of leisure. Rather, it seems that men's activities are characterized by the need for special equipment (e.g., hunting, boating) or access to resources away from home (e.g., forests and lakes). Women's activities are not so dependent upon material location, or special skills. Is access to resources the reason for these participation patterns? (Is it the intervening variable?) No direct test is available here, though data suggest that this explanation may be valid. First, the most frequent reasons given for not participating in an activity were lack of time, lack of ability, or being too distant from required facilities. The survey did not break down these reasons by sex. However, one table in the study, shown in table 8-3, indicates

Table 8-3
Availability of Leisure (mean hours) Time by Sex

Age Group	Weekdays		Weekends	
	Male	Female	Male	Female
18-24	2.75	2.50	4.75	4.25
25-44	2.00	2.50	4.25	4.25
45-64	2.50	2.00	4.50	3.00
65-over	4.50	2.25	6.75	3.25

Source: National Recreation Survey (1962).

that women have less time available for outdoor leisure than men. Second, we know that women are inclined to view "their" money, whether their own income or from their husband, as something to spend on others and not for their own leisure. Expensive cameras, audio equipment, and gaming equipment in this country are bought more often by men for men's use, while few so-called feminine leisure pursuits incur costly equipment. (The exception, the sewing machine, is just as likely put to use as a necessary household tool than as a tool for relaxation.) Third, the women may be putting their time into indoor activities. Some surveys of special samples pursued, such as of aged persons, have shown that women read much more than men do.

This picture of outdoor leisure would be facilitated by knowing to what extent men spend time with other men and women with women. A popular theory among social scientists is that men band together much of the time, even away from work, with the consequence that women and men are very much segregated from work in our society; but we need more expanded surveys to study leisure participation, its meaning for women and men separately, and its consequences on their relating to one another.

Opportunity and Injury

Accidents are not exempt from scientific analysis of causes, in spite of their idiosyncratic or capricious features. Accidents are more likely to occur in some settings than others. To the extent that persons are allocated in systematic ways to these settings, then we can predict the existence of accident-prone subgroups. Overall, men in our country are more exposed potentially to dangerous settings than women are. Table 8-4 presents

Table 8-4
Accidental Death Rates by Accident, Race, and Sex (United States 1960)

Type of Accident	White		Black	
	Male	Female	Male	Female
Motor vehicle	31.5	11.2	34.4	10.1
Falls	10.7	11.4	8.9	5.0
Fire	4.0	2.7	11.8	11.6
Firearms	2.1	0.3	3.4	0.9
Inhalation	1.5	0.9	2.6	1.9
Machinery	2.2	0.1	1.9	0.0
Water transport	1.5	0.1	1.8	0.1
Electric current	1.1	0.1	0.8	0.0
Total*	70.0	31.5	95.0	38.7

* Includes other accident types not listed here.

Source: Public Health Service.

some of the major causes of accidental deaths by sex and race. With the exception of falls, males have the higher fatality rate. Black males have especially high rates for motor vehicle, fire, firearm, and inhalation accidents. Some of these deaths can be attributed to unsafe working conditions, especially those involving chemicals, gases, and machinery. Death by falling characteristically occurs in the home. Women are home more often than men, so the death rate for home accidents are higher for women. Many of the falls also involve childhood accidents, and young boys are more likely to die this way than young girls.

Motor vehicle-related deaths stand out in the statistics as being a major cause of death among young men (as data in chap. four indicated). A further breakdown (table 8-5) of these deaths by the California Highway

Table 8-5
Motor Vehicle Deaths in California 1971

	Male	Female
Pedestrian	542	248
Motor vehicle driver	1,534	348
Passenger	613	572
Bicyclist	76	19
Motorcyclist	426	48

Source: California Highway Patrol (1971).

Patrol (1971) suggests reasons for these accidents. Men greatly outnumber women (except for passenger deaths) as fatalities. Some of this differential can be explained in terms of participation. Certainly the state has many more male motorcycle drivers than female. But does it have twice as many pedestrians, five times as many men at the wheel, and four times as many bicyclists? Obviously, participation is not the only explanation here.

A further exploration of the accidents shows that age interacts in interesting ways. For example, automobile deaths for men are heavily weighted in the younger years. With maturity, the sex differential declines. However, with regard to bicycling, the opposite occurs. Young bicyclists of either sex have a similar death rate, while adult male bicyclists have an unusually high rate. In fact, no female over twenty-four died while bicycling during the year under study, one when cycling was quite popular in the state for both sexes. Age makes no difference with regard to motorcycle or pedestrian deaths. Men of all ages outnumber women. The pedestrian data are enlightening because they include a breakdown as to the exact location of the accident. It seems that most pedestrian deaths occur as a result of crossing mid-block, or walking in illegal pedestrian locations such as freeways. Many of the male deaths were located in these less safe settings.

In general, much of the excess in motor vehicle deaths among men can be related to their violation of laws or recommended safety procedures. This may be the penalty of being raised to take chances, to balk authority in trivial ways, and to display one's manliness to fellow males. Women survive at the cost of not experiencing the thrill of speed or a close call.

It will be interesting to see whether women's accident rates in this area increase as they become more mobile and turn to vehicles such as motorcycles. Or will their caution remain? Given how motor vehicles are defined as male objects of power at present, it seems unlikely that young women will so easily ape their brothers to an early death.

Addictions

One casual factor in many accidents is the presence of alcohol or some medication. Drinking has been related to a number of social losses, such as work-force loss, crime, and the personal loss of self-support, health, and kin ties. Vagrancy, disturbance of the peace, disorderly conduct—often all acts relating to alcoholism—compose almost *half* of the arrests in this country. Skid rows are predominantly male settings, partly because women can support themselves whatever their fate (by way of prostitution) while men who fail quickly lose support from family and community. But it also happens that men outnumber women as heavy drinkers by a conservative ratio of at least 4 to 1. This is one of the largest sex differences discussed anywhere in this volume. (Although the sex ratio has decreased in recent years, experts believe that it is due more to woman's willingness to admit the problem than in the past, not to an increase of alcoholism among women.)

What could account for this difference? The explanations offered to date do not seem sufficient (Chilman et al. 1966). We do know that boys start drinking earlier than girls do. Also, women do not seem so ego-involved in drinking as men. That is, drinking occurs more because of situational pressures upon women, where it occurs more out of a personal expression of needs for men. Surveys on drinking find that women disapprove of it more, particularly those from the lower economic strata. Recent research (Wilsnak 1973) on alcoholic women suggests that many of them, like alcoholic men, are persons who subscribe to sex stereotypes for self-definition, and that onset of alcoholism may occur when crisis events preclude living up to those stereotyped views. For example, alcoholic women seem to have more gynecological problems and fertility difficulties than nonalcoholic women. This theory, that sex identity is a feature of alcoholic dependency, is provocative, though not well-detailed or supported yet by strong evidence. We shall have to see. Furthermore, we cannot ignore the theory that physiology plays a role here, for evidence is accumulating that alcoholics' physiological response to alcohol is different from that of other drinkers.

Another dependency where large sex differences occur is cigarette smoking. Only 30 percent of male adults have never smoked as compared to 58 percent of women (Hedrick 1969). Over half of male adults are currently smokers against only one-third of women. Perhaps because smoking is not so visible a personal and social problem, its social and psychological correlates have not received the attention given to alcohol and other drugs. Yet the personal losses are indisputable. The number of deaths in men due to respiratory diseases, including lung cancer, has risen sharply for males in the past several decades, and cigarette smoking is known to be implicated in the etiology of these diseases.

With regard to cigarettes and illness, striking sex differences occur. Male smokers are much more likely than female smokers to be afflicted by respiratory diseases. Also, the death rates are proportionately much higher—in some age groups more than twice as high for men as that of women. These mortality and morbidity (illness) rates are not trivial in terms of personal and social loss. They represent one of a set of diseases at present that is responsible for the disability and premature death of the American male. Physiology may play a role here, as with alcoholism. However, we know that other elements enter into respiratory disease, such as auto exhaust, factory fumes and such. Very likely the greater exposure of the male to these unhealthy environments is a contributing cause as well to the excess male deaths. Yet, as with alcoholism, we can do little more at present than say, "Here is an important cost of being male in our society that needs to be explained."

The situation is quite different when we turn to pharmaceutical and illegal drug use. The National Commission on Marihuana and Drug Abuse (1973) did a national survey to study the use of the psychoactive drugs—tranquilizers, sedatives, and stimulants—that result in altered mood states. They found that women were more frequent users of such drugs. For example, almost half of all women surveyed had used these drugs in the previous year, compared to one-third of the men. Furthermore, one-fourth of the women had received a tranquilizer prescription during that period, compared to only 12 percent of the men. This drug usage is consistent with medical attitudes toward women. Drug advertisements in medical journals typically present these drugs as appropriate for the solution of "feminine" problems—anxiety, depression, and so forth. Apparently doctors are more ready to attribute a woman's complaints to psychological causes than they are for men (or perhaps men demand non-psychoactive drugs and treatment). Whatever the explanation, the result is that many women are being given a chemical solution to what is likely a sociological problem. For this reason, the extensive use of psychoactive drugs, though legally prescribed, can be interpreted as an addictive problem.

The situation with illegal psychoactive drugs—marihuana, LSD, heroin, cocaine—is more interesting. The National Commission discovered that a sex difference in marihuana use exists for adults though not for youth. The rate of adult male use is twice that of females. Surveys of drug use among youth in other locations and with other drugs has replicated this finding (McGlothin 1971; Lukoff et al. 1972; Barter 1971). Young women and men are *equally* likely to use illegal drugs. Why is this age difference present? One reason perhaps is that adult women already have access to legal psychoactive drugs. Another is that adult men have more access to illegal ones and are more ready to violate the laws. As with alcohol, adult men have more opportunity to acquire the addictive drug. These factors are less relevant for younger women and men. It would be interesting to compare illegal drug use versus illegal alcohol use among the young to see whether the sex difference is also small in the case of alcohol, and what role sex stereotypes play in usage of each.

It is easy to overlook the importance of addictive drugs in everyday life, for their consumption seems a personal matter. For many people, a drink, a cigarette, or a joint do meet important immediate needs, and people do control their intake of these substances. For many men, however, alcohol and cigarettes can become addictive and lead to consequences that disrupt health, love life, and work. For many women, psychoactive drugs can become a screen that isolates them from personal relationships and their problems, as well as deplete their health. Both legitimate and illegitimate economic forces encourage the use of these substances without supporting the services needed to rehabilitate those who fall victim to their cumulative effects. This is a rich and important topic for anyone interested in gender identity and some of its consequences.

Crime and Victimization

Sex status is of greater statistical significance in differentiating criminals from noncriminals than any other trait. This has been true of all recorded societies and nations. In 1960, women comprised only 11 percent of all arrests in the United States. This proportion remained through that decade, even though arrest reports became more accurate and the number of arrests had doubled by 1970. Eighty percent of delinquency cases are boys. Girl delinquents most likely have been picked up as runaways, incorrigibles, or sexual problems.

Table 8-6 presents the total national arrest rates for 1970 by crime. All seven of the major "serious" crimes are listed, along with the five most frequent less serious crimes. Drunkenness, disorderly conduct, and drunk

Table 8-6

Arrests by Sex 1970

Arrest for:	Percent male
Serious crimes	
Negligent manslaughter	89
Murder	85
Forcible rape	100
Aggravated assault	87
Burglary	95
Larceny-theft	72
Auto theft	86
Other crimes	
Drunkenness	93
Disorderly conduct	85
Drunk driving	93
Narcotic offenses	84
Assault	87

Source: FBI Crime Reports.

driving—all alcohol related arrests—compose about 40 percent of all arrests for the year. Although about nine out of ten of these arrests are of men, that tenth woman picked up accounts for many of the women arrested. As the table shows, all the major crimes are characteristically masculine. In fact, for only two crime categories—juvenile runaway and prostitution-vice— are fewer than 70 percent of the arrestees male. These arrest categories compose but a tiny amount of the total arrests.

Those factors that correlate with crime in men, such as race, urbanization, poverty, attenuate the sex differences. In other words, in a small town with white, middle-class residents, the sex difference will be much greater than the 8 to 1 ratio, while in a highly disorganized, poor, minority neighborhood, the ratio will be lower. Thus a woman's likelihood of being arrested is related to the general criminality of a setting.

Once arrested, women are even less likely to be reacted to strongly by officials than men are. The disposition of crimes is as follows. For every one woman, eight men are arrested; fifteen men are committed to institutions after arrest; twenty men are sent to prisons after sentencing. So few women are eventually sentenced that some states do not have separate women's institutions, but instead reserve a wing of a building of the men's prison for women prisoners. The deprived environment of state and federal prisons has been well-documented, but the local city and county jails are even worse. In a 1970 census it was found that 86 percent of these settings had no provision for exercise; 90 percent lacked educational facilities; 50 percent lacked medical facilities; and 25 percent lacked visiting facilities. Yet many men were serving sentences of longer than one year in these institutions.

What can explain these differences? Most criminologists appear to have taken them for granted. Indeed, one of the most popular textbooks on the topic argues that since most criminals are male, sex is not a variable in crime! The obvious illogic here is that most men are not ever arrested either. The usual explanation offered for the difference is that girls are supervised more and socialized more to respect authority. Also, boys have more opportunity to break laws. Some studies on delinquents have shown that delinquent girls are less supervised than nondelinquent ones. But can this explanation really satisfy us in an understanding of adult crime?

First, we must consider the political meanings of the criminal justice system. Those acts defined as crimes are those activities that most directly involve the disadvantaged in our society. The police jurisdiction is restricted to fairly public and visible acts of personal harm or dishonesty in the handling of property. The police do not intrude on the bureaucracies where deceit and dishonesty bring harm on large numbers of unsuspecting people. Furthermore, the justice system is not well-developed or organized for the efficient and sure judgment of white-collar crime. It is also predominately a masculine system. Male legislators make the laws, male policemen make arrests, and male judges pass sentence. Women are so well-excluded from this system that they need not be concerned with it, except as it affects men in their lives. "Looking out for cops" is a serious daily concern for many categories of men in our society—men who are not intent on doing harm. What we find then, is that the criminal justice system operates so that one group of men can intimidate and punish another group of men.

The system is more than a politically-expedient one, however, because some crimes do involve serious harm to individuals. The study of victims illuminates further why women are not involved so much in criminal activity. Reiss surveyed victimization in Chicago and discovered the following victimization rates. Out of 10,000 persons, the following number would likely be victimized by crimes:

Black males	195
Black females	138
White males	34
White females	17

Since most criminals are male, it follows that males victimize other males and females. Furthermore, victimization is within racial categories, so that a black male victimizes other blacks, and a white male victimizes whites. This is especially true when a woman is involved.

The setting is also relevant. Offenses occurring in public settings (bars or on the street) are very likely to involve man against man. Women are most likely to be victimized or be assailants in the home. Yet even in the home a man is more likely to be victimized by another man. When a woman does assault someone, it is usually a man, in the home, and with the assistance of a weapon. One might think that size would play a role in the low proportion of female-male assaults. If this were true, then large women would assault smaller ones, but women do not assault one another. Weapons are critical features of many of these acts. Most men assault one another with the aid of a weapon. Women assault other men when a weapon is available—usually at home where a knife or a gun is ready.

Now the role of socialization is clearer. Some men are socialized to use and obtain weapons, whereas this rarely occurs for women. Men have much more experience with physical aggression through body contact sports and military training. Recent evidence suggests that experience in aggression is just as likely to reward and encourage further aggression than as provide a "release valve." Men also have less body sensitivity than women do, so they can "block out" discomfort, as well as feel less empathy for any violence they incur upon others. Add to these influences the category of opportunity. Most men do not go around beating one another and other women up. Those men (and women) who do seldom do so more than episodically. They do so when passions are aroused and a weapon is handy. One reason why men do so more often is that their passions can be aroused by many reasons other than the ones that impel women to strike out. A woman will attack a men she has deep interpersonal ties to—only his actions can arouse her passion. A man can become passionately angry over his failure to eat and help his family to eat by the insult of another man or women he cares about. Note, incidentally that women do not commit crimes out of the passion of economic need. The man she cares about does so for her; the community, in the form of welfare, will see that she is fed (though not the adult male she cares about).

The political explanation can now be modified somewhat. If men commit crimes of violence more than women do, it can be related to their earlier experiences with aggression and the availability of weapons. If they commit crimes against property more than women, it may be because they are the ones held responsible—by themselves, the community, *and* women —to provide economic resources for self and kin. What we need to know is whether interpersonal violence occurs more in the middle classes than the arrest rates show. To the extent that this is true, then political forces are responsible as well for the appearance of the statistics. If this theory is correct, then can we expect an increase in female criminality in the future as women are raised to have more aggressive experiences? And as women develop structures that encourage more personal intimacy, will we find more crimes of passion where women strike out against other women?

Illness and Therapy

While men in our society can point to the oppression of men inherent in the criminal justice system, women can point to the medical profession for its oppressive treatment of women patients. Yet this is not a totally correct interpretation of the health system in America. It can be shown rather easily that men suffer as a result of poor health organization as well, though in a different way than women do.

It is well known that men have a higher mortality rate for every major disease in this country except diabetes. Although this differential occurs throughout the world, it is greater for American population than for many other countries. In the case of some diseases, such as heart failure, the death rate for men has increased sharply for men in recent decades. Contrary to popular belief, heart ailments and hypertension are not clearly diseases of the affluent; many categories of blue-collar workers have these diseases more often than would be expected (Syme and Reeder 1966). The American male suffers in smaller ways as well. For example, he is likely to lose his teeth at an earlier age than the woman.

One explanation for this difference is that men do not see doctors until an ailment has reached a stage where it is harder to correct. This is reflected in health utilization statistics. Women of all ages use doctors and dentists more than men do. Male utilization of hospitals is greater than female in spite of the higher female admission rate during childrearing years, and men stay in hospitals for longer periods of time. Thus they use health services less for preventive purposes.

Why is this so? A simple answer is that they think it "unmanly" to worry about their health. This oversimplifies the issue considerably. First, as boys, they learn to depend upon their mothers to oversee their medical care and arrange appointments. Women are raised more to be aware of home health care and the use of doctors. Thus unmarried men, who have no one to oversee their health, have higher mortality rates than married men. Second, we should not overlook that most doctors are men, who practice during the working hours of other men. Consequently, one has to wonder how much such a practicality as time plays in here. A sick man often has to choose between work time and getting well quickly. Third, many women see doctors throughout their early adulthood for pregnancy, and others see doctors regularly for check-ups relating to birth control and gynecological diseases. Thus, the special problems of female physiology provide a spur for general preventive checkups. Fourth, men may be less willing to give up the addictive satisfactions they know to be unhealthy. (Why go for a checkup when you know the doctor will advise you to cut back on alcohol and smoking?) Finally, we know that women are more attuned to problems with their body than are men. It may well be that women go to doctors earlier in the course of an illness because it takes less disturbance to tell them that something is wrong.

If these reasons are correct, then male mortality is not going to be reversed unless many changes occur in our society. Men will have to be given more opportunities to obtain preventive and therapeutic health care. Perhaps the availability of less physically harmful psychoactive substances will play a role—if those who make economic decisions are willing to shift to such materials. Young boys will have to be raised with a greater body awareness, as well as a greater sense of responsibility for the care of their bodies. They will have to learn to be unthreatened by proctological examinations and similar procedures, just as women have learned to overcome the embarrassment of gynecological examinations. Overall, men will need to gain more respect of their bodies, which may, incidentally, mean that they will then share the insecurities over their appearance that to date have been pervasive among women. Good health may have to come at the price of a more vulnerable self-image. This seems a small price to pay.

Although women go to doctors, they are not satisfied in many cases with the treatment they receive. One area of concern is that of female illnesses, which include all ailments prevalent among women (e.g., varicose veins). In recent years, women have noted that their male doctors lack sensitivity and even sensibility in discussing these problems. In the area of sexual dysfunction, one need only consider the absurdity of the claims by men that frigidity is solely a woman's personal difficulty and that orgasms are centered in the vagina. (Imagine women therapists telling men that their orgasms were not "genuine" unless they centered in the left testicle). Similarly, many doctors deny that the pain of dysmenorrhea, the nausea of pregnancy, and even labor pain are profound or real (Lenanne and Lenanne 1973). Medical textbooks typically discuss these difficulties as being "psychogenic" in origin, although evidence shows that this simply is not true in most cases. The pain is very real and it often signifies some abnormal condition. Yet doctors continue to deny the pain and fail to provide readily available relief. Finally, the doctor-patient relationship has frequently taken on such a paternalistic quality that women have even had children spaced on their doctor's instructions, not obtained the contraceptive or therapeutic care they asked for, and experienced considerable humiliation from the doctor during examinations. Many young women are taking their health care into their own hands in reaction to the inability to find a doctor who is compassionate about their problems and not paternalistic in attitude (Women's Health Collective 1973).

Another set of ailments where women apparently suffer at the hands of doctors are the psychological ailments and "mental illnesses." Until the early sixties, men were more likely to be institutionalized. Today, women outnumber men in many mental institutions, partly because they are aged and have outlived male patients. However, the institutionalized patient is the exception. When one looks at local outpatient services or private practice, where the bulk of cases are located, one finds that women predominate (Chesler 1972). Apparently, increasing numbers of American women see themselves as neurotic or sick, and the medical profession agrees with them.

Psychological distress is not disturbed evenly throughout a population. We know that happiness is correlated with wealth, education, and age (money, knowledge, and youth being the best combination). Looking at women and men, it is possible to identify an interacting variable—marriage —are a predictor of distress. Table 8-7 shows the results of a national

Table 8-7

Selected Symptoms of Psychological Distress by Sex and Household Roles

	Married Men	Never-married Men	Single Women	House-wives	Working Women
Nervous breakdown	− .76	+1.00	− .86	+1.16	−2.02
Nervousness	+ .31	−1.05	−3.04	+1.74	−2.29
Insomnia	−1.17	+1.92	−1.68	+1.27	−2.00
Nightmares	− .75	+1.28	−2.35	+ .68	−1.25
Perspiring hands	+ .55	−1.18	−1.18	+1.28	−2.55
Headaches	+ .80	−1.96	−1.63	+ .84	− .87
Heart palpitations	+ .02	−3.87	−3.43	+1.38	−1.56

Note: Read the figures as expectations. A plus figure occurs when the symptom occurs more frequently than expected; a minus figure when the symptom occurs less frequently. The zero point represents the expected frequency.

Source: National Center for Health Statistics. *Selected Symptoms of Psychological Distress,* 1970.

survey of common indicators of psychological distress. Whereas previous studies (such as Phillips and Wilson 1969) have shown that women have higher distress than men, this survey shows that only one group of women, the nonworking housewives, have considerable distress. In fact, working women and single women have less psychological discomfort than either married or single men. These reports from housewives may be partly because such women have more time with themselves to perceive discomfort, but it is also likely due to genuine feelings of distress. Perhaps too the men are too tired to perceive or unaware of the real pressures in their lives.

Since housewives perceive so many discomforts, they seek help. Because so many psychological discomforts take the form of physical ailments, they go to doctors. One reaction is a chemical cure, as is indicated by the high rate of psychoactive drug usage by women in our society. The other reaction is to send the woman to a psychologist or other therapist, who typically holds the belief that the woman herself is at fault. Many therapists discourage attitudes or behaviors that are at variance with the female stereotype of passivity, domesticity, and modesty, though they do not discourage the same behaviors in their male patients. Feminists have accused the various helping professions—psychologists, psychiatrists, and social workers—of neglecting women's real needs and encouraging the perpetuation of sexist attitudes. For example, a poor woman who confesses to her social worker that she does not really want the child she is bearing, until recently would be "counselled" to become more maternal instead of being offered the option of abortion.

It seems that troubled women in our society slip into the oppression of madness, while troubled men seek refuge in alcohol. Madness does not have the debilitating physical effects of addictions, and it may work effectively at getting women through crises. This is what one would conclude after studying the suicide statistics. Men die earlier through unintentional illnesses, and through intentional self-destruction as well. Table 8-8 presents recent suicide rates for California, a high suicide state, by race and sex. Whites kill themselves more frequently than blacks, and men more often than women. The patterns of suicide vary by age as well. The typical white deaths occur later in life, especially after age forty-five, while the typical black deaths occur in the twenties. Each die when frustration over success is most heightened—the young black, when attempts at making a living are continually blocked, and the older white, when illness, retirement, and admission of failure are apparent.

The procedures used are very different by sex. Women use poisonous solids, liquids, and gases; men use firearms. Suicide is the second leading cause of death in college students, and typically occurs when a young man

Table 8-8
Suicide Death Rates (California 1970) by Race and Sex

All Races	18.8
Males	23.4
Females	14.2
White	19.9
Male	24.9
Female	15.0
Black	10.4
Male	12.9
Female	8.1

Source: Allen (1973).

has a history of social isolation and a lack of sexual experience. During the high school years, a common setting for suicide among young males is one that involves hanging in the presence of erotic stimuli. This suicide for the young man may be an expression of concern over failure to be a man in the fullest sense.

Part of the sex differential in suicide may be a result of inaccurate reporting. Both Douglas (1967) and Dublin (1963) have criticized the unreliability of suicide statistics. Individual cases of deaths are defined as suicide only to the extent that certain social pressures do not intervene. For example, coroners seem less likely to label a clear case of self-induced death by a Catholic as such because of the religious meaning it has for the survivors. Possibly many female suicides are classified as accidental, particularly given that many involve the ingestion of pills. It is more difficult to dispute a firearm death. Also, one has to consider again the role of body percept. Are women less inclined to harm themselves because they feel more at one with their bodies? Are they more disciplined not to disfigure their bodies?

In his famous study of suicide in Europe of the nineteenth century, Durkheim (1951) found that marriage had what he called a "coefficient of protection" for the male, though not for the female. This interaction effect continues to occur in America. Unmarried males and married females have the higher rates within their sex category. In her analysis of recent California suicide trends, Allen (1973) found that this effect was becoming less true for women. Women's rates regardless of marital status seem to be closing in on the men's rates. Allen explains this new trend as a result of increased responsibilities women are receiving as the society opens up more opportunities to them. Whether this explanation is true or not will have to wait until more precise measures of women's status are included in such studies. Also, since the trend was within only a ten-year span, it might not represent a real change.

Afterword

In this trip from love to death, we have seen the women and men share certain problems—the search for intimacy and self-expression through leisure time—though not others. Given life difficulties, either sex has a ready set of solutions at hand, most of which seem to further complicate their fates. We have hinted how the larger social organization of health care, and the demands of work interfere with men's preventive medical care. The media, schools, and military foster images of masculinity that encourage young men to take accident risks. Racism and the structure of welfare give some men no options but the use of weapons and illegal means to meet their responsibilities. Certain businesses encourage men to seek addictive substances as solutions to personal or social problems. Many medical practitioners patronize women, ignore their real physical ailments, and misinterpret the meaning of their psychological problems. And so on.

It is a wonder that people survive these assaults and obstacles, but most of them do, though not without scars. Most of us are too busy meeting basic needs to recognize the source of our discomforts. In an individualistic society, we tend to blame ourselves. We use the solutions at hand—drugs, divorce, suicide. In recent years we have become conscious of the potential power of collective action. The minority and women's action groups have publicized the value of political criticism and responsive organization around demands. Let us conclude our study then with a look at power and sexism in America.

SUGGESTED PROJECTS

1. Given the data in this chapter, what can you prognosticate for yourself in the areas of intimacy, health, or crime within the next ten years? Why is this prediction necessarily a poor one? How can you improve on it?

2. Take one of the many topics discussed in this chapter and explore it in more detail. Locate more data on sex differences or similarities, and work up an explanatory scheme that incorporates elements from other chapters in this book: socialization, self-image, work, and household roles.

3. Fiction provides one of the few sources of data on private lives, in that the novelist must refer to the experiences of her readers' world. This is particularly true of love and intimacy. What are contemporary novelists writing about, the intimate relations of women and men, women together, and men together?

REFERENCES

Allen, Nancy H. *Suicide in California,* 1960-1970. Sacramento, Calif.: Department of Public Health, 1973.

Balwsick, Jack O., and Anderson, James A. "Role Definition in the Unarranged Date." *Journal of Marriage and the Family* 31(1969).

Barter, James T.; Mizner, George L.; and Werme, Paul. *Patterns of Drug Use among College Students in the Denver-Boulder Colorado Area.* Washington, D.C.: Bureau of Narcotics and Dangerous Drugs, 1971.

Chesler, Phyllis. *Women and Madness.* Garden City: Doubleday & Co., Inc., 1972.

Chilman, Catherine; Lagey, Joseph; Schiller, Jeffrey; and Johnson, Marjorie. *Social, Psychological, and Economic Aspects of Alcoholism.* Washington, D.C.: Department of Health, Education, and Welfare, 1966.

Christensen, Harold T. "Scandanavian and American Sex Norms." *Journal of Social Issues* 22(1966):60-75.

Christensen, Harold T., and Gregg, Christine F. "Changing Sex Norms in America and Scandanavia." *Journal of Marriage and the Family* 32(1970): 616-27.

Douglas, Jack D. *The Social Meanings of Suicide.* Princeton: Princeton University Press, 1967.

Dublin, Louis I. *Suicide: A Sociological and Statistical Study.* New York: Ronald Press, 1963.

Durkheim, Emile. *Suicide.* New York: The Free Press, 1951.

Law Enforcement Assistance Administration. *National Jail Census.* Washington, D.C.: National Criminal Justice Information and Statistics Service, 1970.

Lukoff, Irving F.; Quatrone, Debra; and Sardell, Alice. *Some Aspects of the Epidemiology of Heroin Use in a Ghetto Community.* Washington, D.C.: National Institute of Law Enforcement and Criminal Justice, 1972.

McGlothin, William H. *Marihuana: An Analysis of Use, Distribution, and Control.* Washington, D.C.: Bureau of Narcotics and Dangerous Drugs, 1970.

National Commission on Marihuana and Drug Abuse. *Drug Use in America.* Washington, D.C.: US Government Printing Office, 1973.

National Recreation Survey. *National Recreation Survey, Study Report No. 19.* Washington, D.C.: Outdoor Recreation Resources Review Commission, 1962.

Phillips, D., and Wilson, T. "Sexual Status and Psychiatric Symptoms." *American Sociological Review* 34(1969):58-72.

Reiss, Albert J., Jr. *Studies in Crime and Law Enforcement in Major Metropolitan Areas.* Washington, D.C.: President's Commission on Law Enforcement and Administration of Justice.

Reiss, Ida L. *Premarital Sexual Standards in America.* New York: The Free Press, 1967.

Syme, S. Leonard, and Reeder, Leo G. "Social Stress and Cardiovascular Disease." *The Milbank Memorial Fund Quarterly* 45, No. 2, Part 2, 1967.

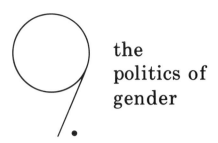

the
politics of
gender

The American colonies were settled in a way common to contemporary *colonialism* of underdeveloped countries.[1] Economic imperialism was as much the motive for early settlement arrangements as the religious and idealogical ones more commonly mentioned in history books. The first adventurers were males who, once settled, called back for women to care for domestic and reproductive needs so men could exploit and develop the land's economic resources. These women found themselves subordinated by both legal and religious precepts. English common law was adopted to regulate marriage. In effect, married women suffered "civil death": They could not own property or exist in any legal way apart from their husbands. This was not so great a loss to them during a period in our history when only propertied males were able to vote and participate in political processes. However, religious restrictions were more profound, though less apparent. Although the colonists were dissenters from the Church of England, the various sects accepted its precepts concerning woman's place. The Church taught that women were limited in mind and body as a punishment for the sin of Eve. The Almighty had compensated for these weaknesses by giving her virtues particularly suited to motherhood—modesty, meekness, compassion, and piety.

As the country developed, the colonial men needed more than wives and their children to perform the many jobs that were emerging. One answer was to import black slaves and white indentured servants. The latter were often brought in the same manner as the black slaves (through kidnapping) and the restrictions on their lives made them no less free than the plantation workers. The only difference between the two groups was that the indentured servant could hope to survive her tenure and be free to join the growing body of poor whites. If some men could afford slaves

1. The historical discussion here is based upon such important discussions of feminism as Flexner (1970), Catt and Schuler (1923), Sinclair (1965), O'Neill (1969).

and grow wealthy, then their wives would benefit as well. As the colony prospered, a small class of women—white women—enjoyed the benefits of the exploitation of the poor white and black workers. Thus the doctrine of white male supremacy expanded to include the idea of the supremacy of the white woman. The essential ideological cleavages of our society were established for the benefit of the moneyed group: white men over white woman over black man over black woman.[2]

In spite of these political patterns, women and blacks struck out in counterattack throughout American history. Women spoke out as individuals. For example, Anne Hutchinson challenged the Puritan church. Women joined together in politically based groups such as the Daughters of Liberty. Yet when the Constitution was being written, Abigail Adams futilely reminded her husband to "remember the ladies and be more generous and favorable to them than your ancestors."[3] He and the other writers did not, leaving the legal position of women a problem for the future generations to resolve. During the early 1800s, various women established schools to educate both women and slave children. By 1840, some women, such as the outspoken Grimké sisters, were devoted political activists for the cause of both slave and women's rights.

During the nineteenth century, woman's suffrage was entwined with two other movements—the antislavery and the antiliquor movements. All appealed to the humanitarian sympathies of the better educated women, and because clergymen were leaders in the latter two groups, more timid women participated as well. In 1840, the World Antislavery Convention rejected American women delegates, an act that spurred many women to speak out. During the remaining decade, state legislators began to debate the "women's question," and some states granted more legal economic rights to women. A Daughters of Temperance organization, modeled after the Sons of Temperance was formed; abolitionist groups excluding women were faced with public disruption. In 1848, the first Woman's Rights Convention was held, yet the feminists did not separate from the other interests. Rather, feminist leaders continued to push women's rights within and in conjunction with the other movements. Black and white women worked together. Certainly the most powerful speaker of the time was Sojourner Truth, an ex-slave, who at one woman's rights convention chided some antiabolitionist members:

2. I am not so sure that black women in fact had less power than black men or were considered inferior by black men. This stratification rule is the one established by those in power (white men), and is not meant to describe the specific historic relation of black women and men.

3. The letter from which this quote is taken is in Tanner (1971), an excellent collection of primary documents from the woman's movement.

Well, chilern, whar dar is so much racket dar must be something out o' kilter, I think dat; twixt de niggers of de Souf and de women at de Norf all a talkin' 'bout rights, de white men will be in a fix pretty soon. But what's all dis here talkin' 'bout? Dat man ober dar say dat women needs to be helped into carriages, and liften ober ditches, and to have de best place every whar. Nobody eber help me into carriages, or ober mud puddles, or gives me any best place (and raising herself to her full height and her voice to a pitch like rolling thunder, she asked), and ar'n't I a woman? Look at me! Look at my arm! (And she bared her right arm to the shoulder, showing her tremendous muscular power.) I have plowed, and planted, and gathered into barns, and no man could head me—and ar'n't I a woman? I could work as much and eat as much as a man (when I could get it), and bear de lash as well—and ar'n't I a woman? I have borne thirteen chilern and seen 'em mos' all sold off into slavery, and when I cried out with a mother's grief, none but Jesus heard—and ar'n't I a woman? Den dey talks 'bout dis ting in de head—what dis they call it? "Intellect," whispered someone near. "Dat's it honey. What's dat got to do with woman's rights or niggers' rights? If my cup won't hold but a pint and yourn holds a quart, wouldn't ye be mean not to let me have my little half-measure full? (Salper 1972, p. 79).

During the fifties, meetings devoted to the three topics of abolition, temperance, and woman's rights were commonplace.

After the Civil War, the political reality struck down two of the three groups—the women and the temperance people. In writing the fourteenth amendment, which guarantees certain rights and immunities to citizens, Congress used the word "male" three times. The fifteenth amendment, which guarantees suffrage in spite of prior servitude or race, omitted the word "sex." Women challenged the interpretation of these statements in courts repeatedly and Susan B. Anthony was actually arrested for voting. Yet after several years of legal battles, women failed to make any headway. It is important to understand here that the women lost more out of complicated power plays between the two major political parties at the time than as a result of genuine antifeminist feelings. For example, a number of judges interpreted the amendments in the women's favor, though were later overruled. Consequently, the stated meanings of these amendments were not so clearly antiwoman's rights either.

In subsequent years the movement splintered briefly into two groups, one devoted solely to the suffrage issue, and the other concerned with broader changes, such as in the institutions of marriage and family. This rift was closed again in 1890, by which time the movement had lost many working women to the labor cause. "Woman's rights," still aligned with temperance, had become respectable for middle-class women. During the decades up to 1920, the liquor industries campaigned to prevent woman's suffrage, because they feared prohibition would follow in consequence—a prognostication that proved correct. The statistics on the activity of the women during this fifty-year period are awesome. By one count (Catt and Schuler 1923), 56 campaigns of referenda were conducted; 480 campaigns to urge legislatures to consider suffrage legislation; 47 campaigns to induce state constitutional changes; 277 campaigns to persuade state party conventions to include woman suffrage planks; 30 campaigns to influence presidential party platforms to include the same; and 19 campaigns in 19 successive Congresses. The money to support these activities came primarily from small sums collected by women themselves. Several suffrage leaders also had the fortune of marrying sympathetic men of wealth and power.[4] But against the economic forces of the liquor industry and some religious groups, the struggle was extraordinary in retrospect. Were it not for the 1914 bequest of Frank Harris (a woman who had her name legally changed to a man's in order to manage her publishing empire more successfully), the suffrage movement might have gone well past the 1920 banner year.

Nevertheless, in the 1900s the suffrage movement lost its populist roots, neglecting minority and working women. Affluent white women co-operated with white male paternalism by developing women's clubs and volunteer agencies, that however well-intentioned, implicitly played a role in the failure of political leadership to solve large-scale social needs. When women went to college, they specialized in areas of their own and avoided the professions. Women of the time accepted the Victorian stereotype of female biological inferiority, and thus saw no reason to attempt entry into medicine, law, or politics. Few of these women wanted to live without husbands and children; many retained acceptance of patriarchal religious dicta, yet, they did support suffrage. Given that respectable women from the empowered class were behind so mild a desire as the right to vote, it is all the more striking that many years were needed to accomplish their end. (Such women would be dismayed by the changes of recent years—the politics of the Equal Opportunity Commission, the Supreme Court ruling on abortion.)

Most feminists prior to suffrage were pragmatic activists. That is, little energy was spent on the theoretical meanings and directions for their activities. They worked along with the abolitionists because they were

---

4. The history of feminism is not one solely of woman activists. Prominent men were involved in the movement from its inception; their political connections and money were invaluable resources to the women, whose vast army of supporting workers were not sufficient in themselves.

morally committed to antislavery. When they lost, they simply continued to hammer away in day-to-day terms through ceaseless lobbying, speech-making and legal challenges. The dominant theme was one of invoking legal reform to ameliorate the deficiencies in the existing social structure for women. For the most part, the personal realm was kept separate, so in this sense they were not "women's liberationists." That is, they were not too concerned with woman's identity, her social essence. Many wanted suffrage out of egalitarian concerns, not because they believed women to be as good as men. They did not think that the patriarchal ideals with regard to sex and the family were inconsistent with social reform in other realms.

Some persons during this period did take a longer view of events and wrote on a theoretical level. Two of these writers are worth discussing here because their theories are among the first cohesive analysis of sex roles in America. Though excluded from social science literature they belong there nonetheless and are worth any serious investigator's reading.

Charlotte Perkins Gilman wrote over twenty books, three of which are important contributions to the intellectual literature on sex roles. These are *Women and Economics* (1898), *The Home: Its Work and Influence* (1902), and *The Man-Made World* (1911). Though not very active in a political sense, Gilman was among the most popular writers for feminists during the turn of the century. Gilman elaborated the relationships between work, household, and female self-image. Without economic independence, she argued, women would never be free from intellectual and emotional dependency upon male kin or husbands. Yet the ethos of domesticity has so constraining an effect upon women's self-image, that they cannot imagine themselves suited for anything *except* a husband and a family.

In her analysis of the home, Gilman described how the home has changed little in its governing aspects compared to other institutions in society. At the same time it has lost many of its functions, such as those of defense or economic self-sufficiency. The home has a sense of sanctity attached to it, such that people think it more sacred to make a coat at home than to buy it or to teach a child at home than to let an educator handle it. This ideal view of the home conflicts with the fact that so many women are active in the economy and unable to satisfy the sacred concept.

Gilman points out that the home and the family are not the same. Our current handling of home (or household) is very inefficient. "Two people, happily mated, sympathetic physically and mentally, having many common interests and aspirations, proceed after marriage to enter upon the business of keeping house. This business is not marriage . . . not parentage . . . not child-culture. It is the running of the commissary and dormitory departments of life, with elaborate lavatory processes" (Gilman 1902, p. 70). Given the patriarchal ideology that subsums the familial unit, the man is responsible for the maintenance of this unit, while the woman must manage it. Gilman is one of the few commentators on the family to recognize costs of its patriarchal organization to the man. The husband is overwhelmed and taxed both by his job and the necessity to acquire "a bunch of ill-assorted trades" related to home maintenance. Housekeeping is so wasteful and unintegrated a set of tasks that the woman too has little time for the "real joys of family life." As Gilman observes, there is so much effort for both partners that they define rest or leisure as something that occurs outside the home!

The man at least can escape to the work world where there are some chances of meeting other interesting people, while the woman is limited to interactions with functionaries or superficial "company manners" inter-actions with other women.[5] Another advantage the man has is that he can feel satisfied with his role so long as he pays the bills, while the woman has more diffuse sources of self-esteem. Also, though she is dependent upon the man economically, she is not supposed to trouble him with her household problems apart from the bills. Finally, the woman is encouraged to focus her attention upon childcare—indeed this is the reason for her home bondage—yet household management is too time-consuming to allow her to satisfy the ideal expectations. Overall, the home

> hinders, by keeping woman a social idiot, by keeping the modern child under the tutelage of the primeval mother, by keeping the social conscience of the man crippled and stultified in the cling-ing grip of the domestic conscience of the woman. It hinders by its enormous expense: making the physical details of daily life a heavy burden to mankind, whereas, in our stage of civilization, they should have been long since reduced to a minor incident (Gilman 1902, p. 314).

Although only a small army of men is now needed to defend most of the country, virtually all the women are needed to maintain the domestic world.

Gilman's solutions did not include an elimination of the family. Rather, she urged changes in the social organization of the household—a more enlightened system of feeding, child-care by the state, and a more efficient organization of household care. This means that the structure of businesses would have to be redrawn to emphasize new industries or or-

---

5. Gilman's observations here can be disputed at points by studies such as those described in chapter seven. Gilman's view is colored by her experience with white, middle-class families of the time. Nonetheless, much of her analysis cuts across class and ethnic lines.

ganizations for meeting domestic needs, as well as to provide women with more interesting jobs in the labor market. With domestic burdens lifted, men would be relieved of many of their financial needs; women could utilize their talents and grow in real power and self-esteem; children would have more exciting and well-directed experiences and opportunities. Thus Gilman's solution is based upon her ability to see the details of how contemporary family life was so intertwined with the economic order. Her solution remains novel today as we shall see later.

Another prominent social theorist was Emma Goldman, who was so politically active that she was jailed three times (once for publicly displaying a contraceptive), and eventually exiled from the country as an alien "criminal anarchist." Goldman's anarchism led her to develop the first well-integrated discussion of women as a sex commodity (Goldman 1970). Gilman too had equated marriage with prostitution, in that the woman traded sexual services for financial security, but Goldman was not satisfied with Gilman's solution that a change in the economic and domestic order would necessarily improve woman's lot. As Gilman (1934) pointed out in her autobiography, she did not think she had ever suffered by not having the vote, but she knew she had suffered daily from being taken primarily as a sex object by the men around her.

In her essay on "The Traffic in Women," Goldman presaged the work of sociologists on prostitution that would follow fifty years later. She analyzed how the institution results from women's economic position, social inferiority, and religious ideologies. Women are thwarted and crippled because

> woman is being reared as a sex commodity, and yet she is kept in absolute ignorance of the meaning and importance of sex. Everything dealing with that subject is suppressed, and persons who attempt to bring light into this terrible darkness are persecuted and thrown into prison. Yet it is nevertheless true that so long as a girl is not to know how to take care of herself, not to know the function of the most important part of her life, we need not be surprised if she becomes an easy prey to prostitution, or *to any other form of relationship which degrades her to the position of an object for mere sex gratification* (Goldman 1970, p. 24, emphasis added).

Consequently, all women are as prostitutes, the difference being that the latter work in a setting that is considered to be immoral. No real change could come in eliminating prostitution unless the role of all women were changed.

In "Marriage and Sex," Goldman continues the discussion by describing how most women are ignorant of the mystery of sex, and thus bound by their ignorance. She condemns premarital chastity and marriage, patterns to be replaced by truly independent women and free love. Even the most decrepit of men, she notes, are able to survive without being parasites, while career women clutch forever to the hope of marriage. Women need work that is meaningful in the sense of fostering independence, but they also need the right to control their bodies.

How will women and men now relate? Through love. Gilman believed that the household should be redesigned to allow a couple's love to flourish, but Goldman argued that love would grow only if there were no religious or state controls on intimate relationships. This is, of course, an outcome of her anarchism, though it is prevalent today in some circles that disavow anarchism.

In "Woman Suffrage," Goldman criticizes the emphasis upon those legal reforms that urge woman's rights equal with man because this implies that women will become part of the social order that has already brought so much grief and corruption to society. In other words, women will not become free by aping men or by seeking a share in activities the men define as valuable. She notes how the suffrage states had granted equal rights to property, but most women could not earn enough to worry about property. Also, suffrage states were the ones women voted to establish lewdity or anti-prostitution laws. Thus Goldman was alert to the way the class and race systems cut women from one another, from making a genuine unity based upon the shared fate impossible.

Finally, Goldman points out that it is ludicrous to think that the male culture, with its centuries of experience in leadership, could be matched by the mere placement of woman in power. Men have accomplished because they worked hard to find solutions to problems in a "ceaseless struggle for self-assertion." The vote could not give women power—they would have to behave self-assertedly as well. By refusing to be treated as a sex object, by taking control of her body, and by asserting herself in opposition to public opinion, a woman would become free, as well as freeing man around her in the process.

Goldman's solutions are more simplistic than Gilman's, and do not follow well from her arguments. She does not explain how women are to become self-assertive, given their previous experiences and socialization. She fails to consider the implications of female claims for independence upon the men in power. And she does not elaborate how the search for equality will result in a greater increase in love relationships between men and women. Nonetheless, her analyses of woman's place are cogent, and her concern with woman's essence provides a link for understanding the way that social structure and personality become intertwined. In particular, her discussion of women as sex commodities shows an appreciation for the many forces that support this system, forces beyond the intentions of individual men. Also she shows how the class system separates women with the strongest power base from those with the most needs.

As has been well-substantiated in many places throughout this book, men suffer as a result of the current system of gender distinctions, too. Where are their supporters? One answer is that they express themselves implicitly in many activist groups, such as labor unions or similar special interest groups. While theoretically one can see how a labor union's charges and complaints are often attempts to redress problems that relate to gender distinctions, the unions do not make this relation in their rhetoric. Consequently, some groups in fact work for the solution of men's problems, but in no sense is there a consciousness that they are *men's* problems. Men see little reason to relate to their difficulties this way. The system is at face value one where men succeed, therefore how could problems exist as a result of being male? Furthermore, men have more resources for expressing their grievances, whether through the formal procedures of politics or the more informal ones of dissident action groups. Also, men have been socialized more strictly with regard to the values of individualism and competition, as well as face more serious consequences for deviance. Finally though men do have many all-male grouping experiences, the culture of these groupings reinforces attitudes that would inhibit the possibility of an ideology that sees men as a specifically oppressed group. Consequently, the attacks on sexism and gender categories in society have come from the women.

Politics: Private and Public

One debate about power continues among women and men today. Namely, who has the power in the family? Social scientists' attempts to answer this question have been considerably myopic.

One line of questioning has developed from the small-group research of Bales and Slater (1955). They brought together groups of strangers into small discussion groups and evolved a system for observing and measuring categories of interaction, such as "agrees, shows self-acceptance" or "gives suggestion, direction." One result of their work was the discovery that two types of roles seemed essential for the organization of the group: the "instrumental" or idea-person who directed and elaborated the group's work, and the "expressive" or well-liked person who responded with praise to others for their contributions. In mixed-sex groups, instrumental leaders were typically male. If women were leaders at all, it was in the expressive realm. This work was a major input to the work of Parsons discussed in chapter five.

Zelditch then expanded the notion to apply it to nuclear families in general. Basing his theory on biological factors, he predicted that women were tied down by reproduction, leaving men better suited to the demands of decision-making. In a survey of fifty-five societies with nuclear families, Zelditch found that in most the male head was responsible for the solution of family problems, for skills and decisions, and for being the ultimate source of parental discipline. Women were responsible for emotional support and tension release.

This research has many problems. First, the original Bales and Slater study placed women in situations that are not familiar ones. That they were not as assertive as the men is understandable in view of their infrequent experience with decision-making groups. Second, the Parsons and Zelditch conceptualizations presumed that some decisions and skills were more important than others. They did not consider the myriad of skills and decisions that housewives confront daily, such as meal choice, allocation of money or resources, particular child-rearing responses.[6] They seemed to exclude all decisions that did not relate to the linkage of the family to the external world. Third, they ignored that a man might make many instrumental decisions and still play many expressive roles within the family. (This emphasis on the male head as breadwinner no doubt accounts for much of the failure of researchers to study fatherhood.)

Other investigators have shown that varying degrees of division of labor exist in the American family. For example, Blood and Wolfe's survey (1966) of Detroit families uncovered norms whereby men were responsible for household repairs, lawn care, and snow shoveling, while women were responsible for making breakfast, doing dishes, and cleaning the living room. Thus men care for the house and its surroundings, while women care for the objects within the house. The latter work is more ritualized, in that it occurs daily and there are few problems to solve in meeting such domestic tasks. The men maintain the public image of the house; the women, the private. Komarovsky's study of blue-collar families included similar research, but she found too that some families had more sharing of tasks than others. Those families in which the couples were better-educated had less sex-role segregation. Some might interpret these studies so as to argue that high division of labor in the family would be more likely in patriarchal families, where the father is more concerned with "man's

---

6. More specifically, it is difficult to tell from Zelditch's paper exactly how he chose to label a role as instrumental or expressive. It appears that some preconception directed the work.

work." This does not follow, however, because we do not know how the couple evaluates these tasks and whether each member has the freedom to change or not. It is just as possible for an equalitarian form of household work to be dictated by one partner than be the result of a negotiation of equals.

This research on the division of labor serves as a reminder to the problems of studying power. Blood and Wolfe also studied decision-making more directly, by asking who made the decisions in a variety of areas, such as buying a car or a house, what doctor to select, and so on. The data in table 9-1 show that the husband's province are in the area of work and the automobile, while the wife makes decisions about her work and the food. Other decisions are shared. Note, though, that a full 26 percent of the husbands always make decisions about the wife's working, while only 1 percent of the wives have the reciprocal say.

A frequent criticism of this research is that we have no way of evaluating the importance of these decisions. It seems to me that a woman's decisions concerning her job would be much more important than daily food decisions, yet women have less control over the former activity. (Another problem less recognized in discussions of this research is that Blood and Wolfe interviewed only the wives, who may attribute more control over their lives than they have in fact.)

Scanzoni's (1971) study of middle-class black couples used a survey format that was within the context of the couples' own value system. He asked them to think about the one topic that caused the most arguments in the marriage, and which person usually got their way as a result. Scanzoni found that women were more likely to believe that a compromise was the result, while the husbands believed that they got their own way. Breaking the data down by status, husbands with higher status appear to have more power, both from their own and their spouse's point of view. This finding has been repeated in studies of white couples as well; external status means that the husband can make more claims of deference upon his wife. Consequently, Gilman and Goldman were correct: the politics of the family reflects the politics of society.

One can argue that studies of decision-making or division of labor are not sufficient proof for or against the existence of patriarchy. Certainly, social scientists have not accomplished much in the way of describing the emotional features of marriage. In some ways it is absurd to think of power as a salient dimension of a couple's intimate relationship. Many couples would agree, for the romantic ideal is one of equality, giving and sharing equally. Unfortunately, the romantics in America have been raised under a system of sexism and cannot reject its influences simply by arguing them

Table 9-1

Allocation of Power in Decision-making Areas
(731 Detroit Families)

Who Decides?				Decision				
	Husband's job	Car	Insurance	Vacation	House	Wife's job	Doctor	Food
Husband always (5)	90%	56%	31%	12%	12%	26%	7%	10%
Husband more than wife (4)	4	12	11	6	6	5	3	2
Husband and wife equally (3)	3	25	41	68	58	18	45	32
Wife more than husband (2)	0	2	4	4	10	9	11	11
Wife always (1)	1	3	10	7	13	39	31	41
N.A.	2	1	2	3	1	3	3	3
Total	100	99	99	100	100	100	100	99
Husband's mean power*	4.86	4.18	3.50	3.12	2.94	2.69	2.53	2.26

* The mean power for each column is computed on the basis of the weights shown, e.g., husband always (5).

Source: Blood and Wolfe (1960, p. 21).

away as unimportant. Many forces impede a couple's well-intentioned wishes to be equalitarian, avoid a patriarchal arrangement, and nourish a love and intimacy free from power struggles.

First, we have already seen that a husband's power is related to his status outside and his education. He expects more rights and his wife believes he deserves them. Despite beliefs to the contrary, the blue-collar couple is more likely to have a relationship with close to equal trade-offs than a pair of college graduates. The college graduate husband might help out more around the house, but he will also exert more control over family members' lives, and they will believe he has a right to his say.

Second, the legalities of the marriage contract place the wife in a dependent position vis-a-vis her husband (Kanowitz 1969). He has final say over the acquisition and disposal of property, even in so-called community property states. In many states, laws still discriminate against the woman such that she cannot own her own business or sign legal contracts on her own. In most states a woman cannot retain her husbands' name, even with his consent. The quasi-legal policies of banking and credit institutions also discriminate against the married woman by requiring her to receive her husband's consent for many actions or forcing him to be responsible for all of her activities. So in spite of equalitarian intentions, a couple cannot avoid being treated as one unit with the male as head.

Another way in which the system affects the intimate world is in the everyday expectations men and women have learned to acquire. For many situations in our society men have a "negative" authority"; that is, a woman is free to act so long as a man "allows" her freedom. Consequently, men can dominate a setting without appearing to do so, while the threats of loss of economic support or even physical coercion may be looming in the background upon the women. Since women are deprived of opportunities to be independent, these threats remain a viable force to be called into play whenever women seem to be "getting out of line." Of course, many women do not ever get out of line because they know their place so well and have little hope to change their lot if it seems disagreeable.

While the degree of patriarchy or equalitarianism in American marriages is open to dispute, the patriarchy of the economic and political structures is not. So pervasive is the masculine hold in these areas that social scientists have often overlooked how they are *masculine* preserves. For example, in sociology, two general views of power in America have been proposed. One invokes the notion of power élite, whereby a large number of organizations and governmental bodies are ruled by a small group of propertied persons. The other view, the pluralistic one, sees the country's direction determined by the negotiations and conflicts of diverse interest groups.

Whichever viewpoint one espouses, the fact is that men hold the decision-making positions, whether in the interlocking directorates or corporations or as the leaders of various interest groups.

It almost seems needless to document the extent of the exclusion of women from political life. Yet some statistics may be necessary if only to demonstrate its range:

1. Between 1917 and 1971, 69 women served in the House of Repre-sentatives; 10 served in the US Senate.
2. No woman has ever been President or Vice-President, only two wom-en have ever served at the Cabinet level. In recent years, figurehead positions have gone to women, such as Director of the Mint or Treas-urer. No woman has ever had a high administrative position in the areas of defense, labor, or state.
3. Although we currently have ambassadors in over 100 countries, only about a dozen women have ever served in this capacity.
4. No woman has ever been a Supreme Court Justice, and only a handful have made the top ranks of the judiciary.
5. Statistics on state level governments show similarly low rates of par-ticipation by women in all branches. Three women have been gov-ernors, all succeeding husbands who had preceded them in that post.

The last item in this list hints at the reasons for the the few women who have managed to acquire some political office or responsibility. They were there because they knew a powerful man who could support them, or they inherited the office from their husbands. Until the late 60s, virtually all women in the US Senate and House acquired their offices through the inheritance principle. More recently, women have run for offices without the benefit of these pre-established connections. A review of their cam-paigns shows certain similarities among them: marriage to a powerful man who encourages their political ambition; an earlier life experience as a mother with many community activities; a "grass roots" campaign that uti-lizes the efforts of local women to get a woman into office. Many of these women have had to run against their own party-sponsored candidates in primaries in order to make the final ticket. Consequently, many women lose because they lack the resources that seem necessary at this time to ensure a win over a man.

Women are also excluded from three other important sources of power in our society. They are omitted from the administrative ranks of major universities and research centers, who provide the intellectual leadership for the society. They are scarce among higher corporation management, and even much of middle management. And they are missing from the enormous military and defense conglomerate. Hopes that this might be changing as a result of equal opportunity rulings by the federal government are scant. The self-fulfilling prophecy comes full-circle. These organizations can point to the lack of available personnel to meet these jobs. They can also argue that women have not had sufficient business and decision-making responsibilities to fill these upper ranks. (This is true if one ignores the enormous amount of experience women have acquired in voluntary work or charitable organizations.) Educated women have degrees in the "wrong" areas—education and the humanities—it can be claimed. However, men with similar degrees are recruited into management jobs, while women are not. Other beliefs that prevent the hiring of women include fears about "company incest" (the effect of sex on work), beliefs that women will not make the commitment men do, and claims that men will not take orders from women.

Tiger (1970) has analyzed the ways in which men band together and exclude women from major societal decisions. His study includes cross-cultural data that suggest the process is pervasive in all types of societies, even those with egalitarian ideologies. For example, in Sweden, a country with the strongest rhetoric and public policy on sex roles, women are still scarce in the upper ranks of government and organizations. Data on the emerging nations of Africa have shown that women's participation in positions of power increases during the early stages of a country's national development, a time when all talented persons are needed, regardless of previous bias. However, once these nations establish themselves, an ideology of masculine supremacy emerges, and the participation of women declines. Tiger has also noted that the principle of inheritance applys in those few cases in other nations where women have taken major positions of power. And when women do reign, such as Golda Meir in Israel, the fact that they are women is a constant reminder.[7]

Tiger concludes further that women will continue to be subverted in their attempts to share the rule, even if they do manage to be elected and appointed to offices at a much higher rate than in the past. When women do begin to acquire power, however small, it seems that men find sub rosa ways to operate that exclude women. Decisions can be transferred to behind-the-scenes meetings that are typically in guise of social events, such as business lunches, golf dates, or gym activities. The structures of these settings already exclude women, so evidence that they are purposefully

7. As I write this, I recall reading a letter in *Time* magazine from Meir in which she chided them for mentioning that she was "a grandmother." She pointed out that no male leaders have been described as "grandfathers."

being left out of their rightful place is invisible. Furthermore, the social protocol of the ruling social classes and government capitals is one that separates men and women and is premised upon the view that women are attached to the powerful men. A woman in politics frequently finds herself in confusing social situations, such as when her co-working men congregate after dinner, while she is sent off with other women.

Tiger paints a pessimistic picture for women and other minorities who wish to break the propertied white male preserves. He may be too glum. For one, minorities are learning to develop their own power bases and use coalition politics to challenge traditional ways. Second, social mores are changing, and the number of male-exclusive social settings is decreasing. Also, women and other minorities are more sophisticated about the reality of politics and are learning ways to prevent, identify, and challenge sub rosa procedures. Women are also acquiring more skills in the use of parliamentary procedures and related techniques for exerting power. And they are becoming more confident in self-image to exert power without any accompanying guilt that it is "unfeminine" to do so. Nevertheless, the resources on the side of those in control are awesome, and the road of sharing of responsibility for the running of the society appears lengthy, filled with cul-de-sacs, ruts, and obstacles.

Contemporary Feminism

By the 1960s the American woman was ready for a new surge of feminist consciousness. She was well-educated, too well-educated for the type of job she found herself doing. Advances in birth control promised her more control over her body. If a mother, she was having fewer children at a younger age, and consequently had a long stretch of adulthood in the future unfettered by child-rearing demands. Changes in the distribution of health and illness meant that she could also anticipate her final years without her husband. The political tenor of the country changed from the relaxed domesticity of the Eisenhower years to the challenge of politicians like Kennedy, who inspired young women to participate in social change as well as men.

Already the recent movement is developing a history, much of which has been written by women who were active in radical or leftist groups in the sixties, and thus appears through their special experiences (e.g., Salper 1972). One can learn how women at the 1968 Students for a Democratic Society (SDS) convention were hissed at and thrown off the platform for demanding the inclusion of women's liberation goals in the general organizational doctrine. Stories abound of how radical male leaders relegated talented, resourceful women to clerical or domestic duties in leftist groups. Some of the women splintered off to form all-female radical organizations, forming groups known as the Women's Radical Action Group, the Redstockings, and local collectives devoted to women's causes. One of the early events causing nationwide coverage was the attendance of such a group as pickets at the 1968 Miss America Pageant. By 1970, many lesbian women active in these groups became so dissatisfied with the treatment they received by the movement's heterosexual woman that radical lesbian organizations emerged.

Though such events compose much of the written history of the movement, it is suspected that it was much more broadly based and that the grass roots nature of the phenomenon are more extensive than names of organizations and dates indicate. For one, Freidan's *Feminine Mystique,* was a bestseller in 1963. By 1966, Freidan found herself changed from a free-lance writer (who happened to write a book about women) to a political organizer and started the National Organization for Women (NOW). NOW's constituents were very much middle-class women and men of moderate political orientation, hardly the ones to be expected to move behind what is essentially a radical critique of society. Today, local NOW chapters and similar groups are quietly working at the drawn-out process of effecting legal and administrative changes, both in government and industry. Because such groups work within the framework of established legal or bureaucratic procedures, their results are not sensational or highly visible, but changes are occurring nonetheless.

Being a middle-class organization, NOW and others were under attack at one point for ignoring the needs of minority and poor women. Just as some lesbian women felt it necessary to work along with other lesbians, so too have other women broken off into special interest groups. The National Welfare Rights Organization provides welfare women with resources for "making it" on welfare, as well as a basis for acting to change welfare regulations. Since welfare in this country is virtually synonymous with the oppression of poor adult women (and by implication, their children and adult men), the organization is part of the women's movement as a whole. Similarly, in some localities, women's organizations have aimed at the needs and value-systems of particular racial, religious, and ethnic subcultures.

It appears that the movement is no longer dominated by moderate white middle-class interests, but is a conglomerate of special interest groups that form a block of people interested in improving the status of women. This is clear as one reads the numerous women's magazines, newspapers, and pamphlets that seem to be flooding the market. The diversity of opinion concerning goals and means is considerable. The one common denominator is that "women are oppressed." However, the reasons for the oppression, the actual way that oppression affects a woman, as well as the means for ending the oppression, are at times open to question. In general, it seems that most feminist women can agree on the ways that they are oppressed, i.e., economic and social discriminations. This is quite different from the earlier suffragettes, many of whom did not perceive that they were being treated unfairly. The tone of the contemporary feminist movement is more revolutionary. No longer does one question that changes are needed —it is the nature of the changes that are debated.

Just as the suffragist women encouraged theoretical formulations concerning sex roles, so too have contemporary feminists nourished a variety of intellectual analyses of woman's situation. The more popular writings on women cannot be included in this category. For example, Friedan (1963) and Bird (1969) essentially document material in support of the thesis that women are victims of discrimination. Another book that has inspired many feminists, men as well as women, is de Beauvoir's (1953) *The Second Sex*. Like the more provocative and sensational analysis of Greer's (1971) *Female Eunuch,* it is a discussion of the phenomenology of femininity—the way in which social order shapes the thoughts, needs, and motivations of women. Each provides powerful arguments that social discrimination has profound effects on the very being of women, their sense of self. Yet, however eloquently such popular books have alerted various women (and men) to become conscious of their plight, they furnish few useful guides for a well-organized movement. The rhetoric does not state much about practices a woman can count on as being effective in changing her situation.

Women from the more radical feminist circles have produced the bulk of theoretical material that examines the meanings of sexism beyond current statistics on discrimination or an analysis of female psychology. Having broken away from the leftist political groups of the sixties, these writers display stances that clearly extend from Engels. Yet, they clearly do not imitate him either, for they have had the benefit of another century's history, one that saw the vast urbanization of many countries, the technological growth that included the automobile and television, mass education, major health care improvements, two wars involving numerous countries, and woman's suffrage.

In *The Dialectic of Sex,* Firestone (1971) presents the most complete statement of what she calls "radical feminism." According to her analysis, contemporary feminism has three orientations. The "conservative feminists" (such as those belonging to NOW) are working for full equality with men rather than a freedom from sex roles as such. The "politicos" are women who align with the left, whether through unions, political groups, ethnic or racial organizations, and who work for women's issues within the context of these organizations. In practice, claims Firestone, this means that the women's claims are always pitted against those urged by male-dominated leadership. The "radical feminists" strive for liberation from sex roles and the traditional ways of defining gender identity. Consequently, they dispute the tactics of both of the other orientations for failing to reach into the system deeply enough.

Firestone locates the origins of women's oppression in biology. Early women were at the continual mercy of males for physical survival because the demands of reproduction, lactation, and female ailments limited their strength and mobility. Furthermore, human infants are dependent upon adults for a considerable amount of time, and consequently the mother-child interdependency is a universal and profound one. Finally, the natural reproductive differences furnished the basis for the information of female and male castes, as well as the first division of labor. These differences, though "natural," need no longer hold because humanity itself is the history of outgrowing nature.

According to Firestone, the modern family has meant "pseudo-emancipation" of women and children. Each has been set apart from the "real" world—the male world—and provided with segregating institutions that provide them with functionless activities and a myth of happiness. Both are considered inferior, incapable of handling important work, "cute," emotional, and deserving of a vacuous respect. The woman is isolated at home, and the child at school, while the man makes decisions. Consequently, any platform for freeing women from economic, physical, sexual, psychological, and educational oppression must take into account the oppression of children.

Firestone sees the love ideology as a cultural force behind oppression as well. Love results in parasitical female-male relationships: the female feeds off the man's economic bounty, while the man feeds off the woman's emotional strength. "Women live for love and men for work." Women know that men also need love, though they deny it. Firestone believes that there is such a phenomenon as love, one deserving of attainment, but that its current status is corrupted by an unequal balance of power. "Falling in love" is the way the couple idealizes one another so as to void the woman's class inferiority. Love can survive only if it is depoliticized.

The myth of romanticism, Firestone believes, emerged as woman became freed of the demands of biology. Consequently, romantic love is an artificial institution for the purpose of perpetuating male supremacy. A prime component of romanticism is eroticism, the emphasis upon the genital sexual encounter as the prime emotional need. This is supplemented by a "sex privatization" of a woman, which means that she is taught to confuse

her sexuality with her individuality. Thus, a woman is deceived from recognizing that the very quality of a lover admires in her—some feature of
her body—is shared by all women. In fact, her individuality is a false one,
based upon some tiny superficial physical characteristic that separates her
from other women. Finally, a woman is challenged by the Beauty Ideal,
which ironically drives her to make herself like other women, whom she
perceives as more attractive than herself and potential competitors for
"her" man. Firestone believes that these cultural pressures exploit men as
well because women also reify men and treat them as objects in return,
though not as sexual objects. Any attempts to challenge these various cultural pressures is complicated by the fact that "sex objects *are* beautiful."
Consequently, feminists can make the mistake of rejecting beauty as an
ideal altogether, when what should be rejected is a standard of beauty that
forces people to deny their humanity and become inanimate. Similarly,
eroticism in itself need not be rejected, but the context in which it occurs
should be redefined to eliminate the political meanings of the sex caste
system.

Other issues discussed in *The Dialectic of Sex* are racism; the lack of
female participation in arts, letters, and science; the recent concern with
ecology. Firestone views racism as a sexual battle between black and white
men, one that necessarily pits black and white women against one another.
Although culture has been dominated by male values, she predicts that it
will change toward an androgynous form as women are able to contribute
more to the arts and science. Finally, she argues that a feminist revolution
would contribute to the new ecological balance that seems called for, one
based upon fewer people, less consumption, less excessive use of technology
for technology's sake.

How would the feminist revolution actually occur? Four "minimal
demands" are suggested:

1. Women must be freed from the "tyranny of their biology," with tech-
    nology taking over the childbearing process and other children and
    men sharing equally in the child rearing process.
2. Women and children should be freed of their economic dependence
    upon men which implies a total reorganization of labor as we know
    it today.
3. Women and children should have "total integration" into society. This
    means that the concept of childhood with its special status would end.
    Correspondingly, women would be accepted as equal participants in
    all institutions.

4.   Sexual mores and love will change by overthrowing the structures that inhibit the development of real affection and communication, namely, agents of socialization and the media, both of whom encourage eroticism, the sexual privatization of women, and the beauty ideal. This is more important than insisting that we give up immediately our patterns of monogamy, incest, and other sexual taboos, practices that Firestone believes will not disappear in one generation.

In a similar statement, Mitchell (1971) analyzes the woman's situation as involved in four societal structures: production, reproduction, sexuality, and the socialization of children. Where Firestone emphasizes woman's private role, particularly her sexuality and freedom over her body, Mitchell believes that no one institutional area is primary. She cites historical cases whereby women have gained liberation in one area, only to face a new oppression in another. Thus women in modern China are being freed to contribute equally with men in the economic realm, but this has been complemented by a repression of sexuality and puritanism. Mitchell argues consequently that *all* four structures must be changed in order for women to break through discrimination. Her description of the role of women in England very much repeats many of the data on women in America, presented here, where,

> women are brought up to think of themselves primarily as mothers and wives; yet finding themselves despite this, nevertheless out at work, it is this family identification that determines their relationship to their job and their companions . . . Separated from her work companions by her dependence on her family, within this family she experiences a yet more fundamental division: that of herself and her husband—the original unity . . . Divided, individualized, isolate—a woman is yet, paradoxically, subjected to the most homogenizing, the most unindividual of ideologies—the nature of her so-called "womanhood," "femininity." "Women are alike the world over," "Just like a woman," "Oh women . . ." (Mitchell 1971, pp. 139-40).

After analyzing woman's place, Mitchell concludes that little change has occurred recently in three structures: production, reproduction, and socialization of children. However, in the area of sexuality, many signs of a new ideology are emerging. She claims that marriage in its traditional form is being threatened by the liberalization of relationships. This reflects the conversion of contemporary capitalism from a production-and-work ethos to a consumption-and-fun ethos. Though sexuality is the "weakest link" in the chain, women must press demands for changes in the other areas as well. Mitchell's recommendations are more detailed than Firestone's. For example, she argues that it is not the family that needs to be eliminated so much as the form in which people are allowed to organize and relate intimately to one another. At the same time, the movement should concentrate on women's right to earn a living and the right to equal work (not just equal pay). Unlike earlier socialists, Mitchell argues that emphasis upon economic changes cannot be isolated from demands that consider woman's role in the family and with children.

Firestone is reminiscent of Goldman, with her emphasis upon sexuality, the need for women to change things for themselves, and the concern with love and humanity. Mitchell is more precise and detailed in her analysis of the society she knows best, but discusses the problem in an abstract way that does not tie so easily to the daily lives of women and men. Both are provocative theories on sex roles in contemporary society, and worth studying in full, particularly for a prognostication as to what could occur in future generations.

Both of course have deficiencies.[8] Firestone, in particular makes sweeping generalizations about women and men that can be disputed at points by studies such as those discussed in this text. Both underestimate the role of the other commitments in life that tie us to one another—those of ethnic, racial, class, and ideological base. Consequently, their recommendations presume that women can organize solely as women, when these other commitments serve to separate women into groups with particular views of the world and particular needs. Both much oversimplify the life of men and the psychology of the male. Most curiously, both do not deal with *power,* except to state that the present power of male over female must be eliminated.

Where Are We Going?

We have shown here how any discussion of woman's rights, however personal, implies a political analysis. Then why do active feminists have so much trouble discussing power? Why is it so difficult for people to decide what goals should be set, what tactics utilized? Why did women's suffrage take a century of struggle? Why aren't many men cognizant of the profound restrictions and consequences the fact of "being male" can mean for their lives?

Power is an elusive concept to sociologists, who have failed to specify

---

8. Mitchell and Firestone do *not* represent the views of most feminists. Many varieties of feminism exist. For examples of other contemporary feminists arguments, see the numerous "women's" magazines and journals: *Ms., Aphra, Women: A Journal of Liberation, The Second Wave, Momma, The Lesbian Tide,* and so on.

its dimensions very clearly. They have developed methods for identifying people who are believed to be "powerful," i.e., those who manage to exert influence over others actions. They have identified types of authority, such as "legitimate" leadership or "charismatic leadership." Yet they have not addressed such questions as whether the amount of power in society is constant over time or whether various sources of power simply add up or multiply when located in the same individual.

In everyday lives, attitudes about power are just as confusing. Men are raised to search for power, though presumably only a few can grasp it. Power becomes identified with race and class as well. Consequently women, non-whites, and poorer people are believed to be "unfit" to hold power. Power implies a hierarchy, while it need not in fact do so. This is evident in the feminists' demands for more power to *become equal with men,* not superior to them. This threatens men possibly because they take for granted that women will "use up" some power, i.e., reduce the amount allocated to men. Social scientists are no help in answering whether this everyday model of power is true.

James S. Coleman (unpublished)[9] has criticized social scientists for ignoring that persons are not the only ones who hold power in society. Many interactions in industrialized society are marked by relationships between individuals and corporate actors. A transaction at a bank, a store, a hospital, may involve two individuals, but frequently one of the individuals is acting as the agent for a corporate entity, not for herself. Her power rests in the larger entity. People are now less tied down to the fixed, ascribed roles the family and small community once provided. Hence, they have more freedom to act in that these individual-corporate actor interactions are diffuse. People learn to play against the corporate entity for their own interest, doing things they would never do to persons (lie, steal, vandalize) as well as try to pit corporate entities against each other. However, Coleman reminds us, the corporate actor has the weight of resources on its side. So people become alienated because they cannot easily effect changes on their own behalf and there are many powerful corporate actors to contend with. Coleman suggests that we provide ways in which individuals can have more resources to influence the corporate actor, as well as have access to information about its activities. Thus, a campaign to end smoking should not work toward banning cigarettes, but rather seek ways to end the monopoly of company advertising. Every dollar spent on advertising would be matched by money spent on actions that would meet

9. Coleman has presented these ideas in speeches at Johns Hopkins University.

consumer interests (e.g., perhaps medical research or work on a less dangerous oral addictive).

Coleman's model is a first step toward a more elegant and realistic view of power, but it still oversimplifies the arrangements. For one, we know that personnel changes in positions of authority can make considerable difference in policy. It is still true that persons hold power, in that some people have a style, personality, and utilization of a position's resources that provide them with unique influence unattached to the office. Second, while Coleman believes that person-to-person power negotiations occur in everyday life, the feminists would argue that women are *always* tied in to the implicit caste system, always at a disadvantage, always with fewer resources. Similarly, a coalition of women for the purposes of changing or influencing corporate actors would automatically be starting from a position of weakness. Ten women would not be as influential as ten men, simply because the women's power base is smaller. Finally, Coleman omits the known bases of stratification that cross-cut these relationships. Very often the personal representative of a corporate actor is a woman, for women fill the mediating roles in the economy. Yet policy is prescribed by men, so women are asked to cooperate in the enactment of what may be policies that discriminate against themselves. Fourth, Coleman has not considered how our most intimate relationships have been intruded upon by actions of corporate actors—as is reflected in the statistics on household formation, health, leisure expression, mobility, and so on.

Coleman is optimistic that people can organize into small, efficient coalitions to exert sufficient pressure upon corporate entities for change. This is precisely what many feminist activists, female and male, are attempting to do through informal neighborhood groups, local chapters of large organizations, or the lobbying efforts of national bodies. The result is a piecemeal attack on many institutions. Although many activists believe that men will benefit if women are given more rights, the men have not been convinced. Men are now playing the role of conservators of society, a role once believed to be the woman's. Women have been able to build off the existing female patterns of friendship and helping networks for the purpose of political organization. But can they be effective if men remain apart, rejecting the thesis that being "male" can also mean being hurt or damaged or oppressed. Must they, as many feminist writers urge, give up their emotional dependency on one man and seek a life of more independence from permanent ties? Or must they emphasize their attack on the economic front? Should they try to get a 51 percent representation in all government bodies? Should they decry motherhood, or raise it to a new status of respect? Or should they press for the technological removal of the reproductive function from human bodies altogether?

These are difficult questions for women, and their answers necessarily implicate men, consequently all humanity. As Sullerot concludes in her book on the position of women around the world:

> The unwitting revenge of women in the world today is that they are essential to the solution of all its great political problems. Overpopulation, starvation, underdevelopment, illiteracy—all of these issues can only be solved with the assistance of women. The most powerful political leaders cannot impose policies of population control, of economic development and educational expansion without one positive contribution of women. Without this, politicians have only the power to destroy, not to create (1971, p. 248).

One can broaden the use of "politician" here to include all of the corporate actors and leaders outside of government itself as well.

In the meantime, individuals will be born, identified by gender, and live out the life consequences of such categorization. In America, women and men will believe that their lives are much more different than they actually are. The differences that do exist, however, will be profound ones that affect their self, their self-expression, their satisfactions, their problems, and eventually their way of death. Social scientists will chart, enumerate, and debate about these differences. Some women and men will challenge the previous norms, just enough to confuse the social scientists . . . and themselves. Where are we going? That is your choice, though some of you will have more power to effect your desires than others.

SUGGESTED PROJECTS

1. Take a political jurisdiction on which you have ready access to data— your state, county, or local government. Do an historical survey of elections to see whether women ran and how they fared. Then go to the newspaper files to see if you can interpret reasons for the events.

2. Based on your reactions to material presented in this book, draw up your own detailed political philosophy with regard to sex role change. What are your goals, priorities, preferred strategy, and tactics? How tentative or definite are you?

3. Read one feminist theoritician and analyze his or her argument in light of data presented in this book. In addition to those discussed here, you might select Kate Millett, *Sexual Politics* (New York: Doubleday & Co., Inc., 1970). Gene Marine, *A Male Guide to Women's Liberation* (New York: Holt, Rinehart & Winston, 1972), Eva Figes, *Patriarchal Attitudes* (New York: Stein & Day, 1970), Myron Brenton, *The American Male* (New York: Fawcett World, 1970).

4. Some argue that the elimination of sex roles will mean the downfall of so-
ciety. See, for example, Charles Winick, *The New People* (Indianapolis,
In.: Pegasus, 1968), or Karl Bedarnik, *The Male Crisis* (New York:
Alfred A. Knopf, 1970). How do you evaluate their arguments?

REFERENCES

Bird, Caroline. *Born Female.* New York: David McKay, 1968.

Blood, Robert O., Jr., and Wolfe, Donald M. *Husbands and Wives.* New York:
The Free Press, 1960.

Catt, Carrie Chapman, and Schuler, Nettie Rogers. *Woman Suffrage and
Politics.* New York: Charles C. Scribner, 1923.

de Beauvoir, Simone. *The Second Sex.* New York: Alfred A. Knopf, 1953.

Firestone, Shulamith. *The Dialectic of Sex.* New York: Bantam Books, 1970.

Flexnor, Eleanor. *Century of Struggle.* New York: Antheneum, 1970.

Friedan, Betty. *The Feminine Mystique.* New York: Dell, 1963.

Gilman, Charlotte Perkins. *The Home.* New York: McClure, 1902.

Goldman, Emma. *The Traffic in Woman.* Washington, N.J.: Times Change
Press, 1970.

Greer, Germaine. *The Female Eunuch.* London: Paladin, 1971.

Kanowitz, Leo. *Women and Law.* Albuquerque: University of New Mexico
Press, 1969.

Mitchell, Juliet. *Woman's Estate.* New York: Vintage, 1971.

O'Neill, William L. *Everyone Was Brave.* Chicago: Quadrangle, 1969.

Salper, Roberta. *Female Liberation.* New York: Alfred A. Knopf, 1972.

Scanzoni, John. *The Black Family in Modern Society.* Boston: Allyn and
Bacon, 1971.

Sinclair, Andrew. *The Emancipation of the American Woman.* New York:
Harper & Row, Publishers, 1965.

Sullerot, Evelyne. *Woman, Society and Change.* New York: World University
Library, 1971.

Tanner, Leslie B. *Voices from Women's Liberation.* New York: Signet, 1971.

Tiger, Lionel. *Men in Groups.* New York: Vintage, 1970.

epilogue

In *The Left Hand of Darkness* (New York: Ace Publishing Corp., 1972) Ursula LeGuin describes a world where sexist structures do not exist. Its inhabitants, the Gethenians, are sexually inactive and androgynous four-fifths of the month. The other fifth the hormones activate, and the individual enters *kemmer,* similar to estrus. The sexual drive becomes tremendously strong during this phase, and the individual seeks another person in kemmer as a sexual partner. At that point, each individual differentiates temporarily—one into a female phase, the other into male. Normal individuals have no predisposttion in this matter nor have they any choice.

The social consequences of this peculiar sex physiology are many. Monogamy is a "vigorous institution." Descent is reckoned through the mother, the "parent in the flesh." Incest among siblings is not prohibited, although it is between generations. Since coitus occurs only during fertility, contraceptive drugs and ritualized celibacy control the population rate. Everyone in kemmer is on holiday, regardless of their social status or position in society. Kemmerhouses—places for promiscuous sex—are similarly available to anyone in the society. Because everyone is liable to become a mother at some point in adulthood, no one is "tied down" in the sense that our women are. Burden and privilege are shared equally, consequently no one is quite as free as many of the males in the earth's societies. There is no rape or intercourse by force. Humanity is not divided into two categories such as strong-weak, active-passive, and so on. There are no games surrounding sexual-social interaction. "One is respected and judged only as a human being," writes an alien male visitor. "It is an appalling experience" to want one's masculinity to be well-regarded and have it totally ignored by these people.

Some of you may agree that ultimately it would take a physiological change for the problems of the sexes to be eliminated. However, a rule of ethology is that behavior precedes changes in a species' form, so (barring a genetic accident) we would have to will ourselves to change into Geth-enian-like forms. This possibility is not so far-fetched to many scientists as it may seem.

In a thoughtful essay on *Utopian Motherhood,* Fancoeur (1970) has considered the likelihood of various biological developments in reproduction. Scientists are working in the following areas and could make a breakthrough in any one of them: artificial wombs, surrogate mothers, the use of other species as mothers, cloning (asexual reproduction), virgin conception, and so on. However, the results of a national poll on these topics shows that most of the population is not favorable toward any changes in the reproductive realm. For example,

80 percent thought it wrong for women to avoid problems of pregnancy.

71 percent feared that the birth of a baby through love would end.

76 percent felt that men would be emasculated.

67 percent thought it wrong to breed for special characteristics.

What the scientists have missed is the importance of blood lines to Americans, even to those who do not themselves desire to reproduce. Remove reproduction, even as a potential, and you remove the very basis for bridging the female-male duality. Love is *not* enough. It is one thing to control reproduction within the body and quite another to remove it altogether. So long as Americans believe this way, female-male intimacy will remain, as will its accompanying problems.

In achieving utopian motherhood, the scientists would in effect create an androgynous population, similar (though not identical) to the Gethenians. No one would be mother, so how would descent be determined? Ultimately, the state would be mother, and that is an answer few Americans would accept. Also, presumably humans would continue to be sexually responsive at all times, so how would sexuality be controlled or regulated? Would it have to be? Apparently so, for women could still be raped. There would be no guarantee that freeing women from motherhood could free them from a denigrating position in society.

LeGuin's society reminds us that the entire realm of sexual physiology would have to change in order for sexual equality *by virtue of biology* to occur. Sexuality forms symbolic linkages to kinship, identity, intimacy, and other sources of deep meanings in culture. To remove reproduction from our bodies and leave our bodies the same cannot in itself provide the solution unless some of the ideas change as well. Indeed, some might argue that changing our ideas would make changes in our bodies unnecessary.

We have rooted our sexism in a false biology, for the facts argue that sex is a process, not a steady state. This is true with regard both to our bodies, as they mature and age, and to our minds, as our identities grow and adapt in response to nature and culture. It would be more difficult to speak of the fear of "emasculation" in a society where masculinity is whatever men in the broadest sense are. It would be meaningless to think it wrong for women to avoid the problems of pregnancy if women as a class were not expected to become pregnant in the first place.

Changes in consciousness are clearly a prerequisite for the social changes that have pervasive impact upon our lives as women and men. Yet I know how even "consciousness" is not easily attained, nor is it enough. In my sociologist's language, it refers to a change in identity and in the categories one uses to view the world. It is a change, as many women are finding, that requires loving support from others if one's will is to be accomplished. It is often painful, and in a world with much pain, it can be easier to forego the change. It is a change that intellect alone cannot direct nor control, unless that intellect respects individual passions and proclivities.

Feminist rhetoric can be very helpful in that it often indicates what a woman or man need not be and reminds us that our identities need not be fixed nor even totally consistent. But at the base of *my* identity, I am woman, and at times I am not sure what this means. The rhetoric tells me I need no longer must be a mother or a wife, yet these are still possibilities. Does it mean that woman must be whatever man has said she was not to be? Must she be strong, less emotional, assertive, independent, career oriented? Or would I not turn the identy of woman into man then—making everyone male in the process? Or are men supposed to become womanlike in return? It is difficult to be someone unless you know who you are becoming. Since the social changes concerning sex roles cut into the most predictable "becomings" in society, those of us participating in the challenge are particularly adrift at times.

Several other problems with consciousness-raising disturb me. One is that I do not see the seeds of consciousness nor the social support among men themselves to change significantly, let alone commit themselves to women's change. For example, whenever I present the relevant data on health or work or family life to men, I see very little recognition that the facts I am presenting have much meaning for their own private lives. They can acknowledge a certain "oppression of the male" in an intellectual sense, but that is the extent of their interest. They seem more interested in relegating the problems of sex stratification to the area of "women's problems" when this is clearly not the case. Presumably, this frees them of any social responsibility for change. Until some fellow social scientist can prove to me that there are seeds of brotherhood similar to the intimate patterns of support already present among women, then I must be pessimistic about the possibility that men in large numbers will contribute significantly to change in the near future.

Another problem in focusing upon consciousness alone is that a large part of one's world is composed of persons who have commitments to the existing system. It can happen in such small ways, as when a woman defers and lets a man help her with a coat, an act he would not do for a male. It happens every time someone asks "Is that Miss or Mrs.?" or "Is the man of the house in?" Or when she turns on the television to hear news only of men and men's topics, and goes to vote only to find these same men's names on the ballot. It happens when her daughter asks her why there isn't a building for the girls' club when there is a large one for the boys. Similar situations face the man who decides that he cares about parenthood, that he wants to share domestic upkeep with his family, that he does not want his son to be a great high school athlete. Too many other people are telling him that his values are wrong or improper or ridiculous.

What surprised me most in compiling the material for this book was the role of social structure in contrast to that of identity. It appears that women and men are not so different in identity and orientation as the mythology or much social science would have us believe. They would probably be more satisfied with a structure in which the gender-based distinctions were less arbitrary and final. Certainly men might live longer, and more importantly, have experiences of greater satisfaction than they are now permitted. Certainly women would feel more secure and sure of what they were for themselves, not in terms of what other people saw them to be. They have instead been divided by the economy and the polity, and given rare, often ritualized opportunities to come together as friends and partners. Their very similarity is a wonder in view of the different lives they lead. We could be, as the Gethenians, taken as human beings instead of separate breeds at war or unhappy compromise. I hope that this book has made a contribution in that direction.

REFERENCES

Francoeur, Robert T. *Utopian Motherhood.* Garden City, N.Y.: Doubleday & Company, Inc., 1970.

LeGuin, Ursula K. *The Left Hand of Darkness.* New York: Ace Books, 1969.

methodological appendix

The social science literature is replete with studies that include gender as a variable, though usually the researchers treat gender as secondary to an understanding of the topic at hand, or they may ignore what the data say about sex roles or gender identity. If you are interested in a topic (e.g., gender and religious behavior), you will probably find that many past studies of religious behavior already have the data you desire. From this point you can begin a secondary analysis of the data.

As was discussed in chapter one, one issue you will first want to examine is whether gender is important or not. Do men and women behave differently? Most social science data will come in conventional statistical formats. Frequently, there will be tables with percentage responses in them. Remember not to confuse statistical significance with the size of the difference. In very large samples, a 5 percent difference can be "statistically significant"; but you may not find such a difference meaningful for your purposes. That is, does it matter to you if 40 percent of the women pray once a day, in contrast to 35 percent of the men. It may, depending upon your research goal. Similarly, the data may contain mean scores from attitude scales. Look at the differences again as well as the significance tests. If you know anything about statistics, then see if a standard deviation or variance is given as well, using this information to deduce the distribution of the responses. Finally, some data will be in the form of a correlation. Many correlations in social science are moderate in size (.30-.60), so you should not expect extremely high ones before you are ready to accept the relationship as an important one. Remember too in your search that the fact of no difference or no correlation will be an important finding. Analysis can help us to move beyond the statistics, as I illustrate best in chapter eight.

Let us continue now with the case where we have studied some event of behavior and found that women and men participate in this event to

different degrees. In other words, gender identity and some events *are*
correlated. What does this mean?

First, we could argue that we have a *tautology;* that is, we have
measured essentially the same thing. In this case, we would say that the
event is so much an expression of gender identity that it is superfluous to
consider it apart from gender. In diagram form

$$Gender = Event$$

The use of cosmetics is an obvious illustration here. We don't ask
what "causes" the difference in cosmetic usage because the answer is
obvious. Women by definition use it and men don't. Such explanations
are not very likely in the case of gender identity, however, because it does
not reduce nearly so often. As we have illustrated many times here,
"female" and "male" are complex entities for which many conflicting
definitions exist in society. Consequently, we will not often find the degree
of sex difference—the high correlation—that would allow us to argue that
we have a tautology.

More likely, some difference exists, but there are overlaps; the correlation is moderate or even weak. Here we would consider how gender
identity acts as one of several causes of the event. Parenthetically, we must
point out, an analyst would also consider whether or not the event caused
the gender identity. For example,

$$Event \longrightarrow Gender\ identity$$

This possibility is logical, though not probable. Our usual measure of
gender is whether a person calls themself or is labelled by some authority
as belonging to one of two sex categories. Since these categories are virtually fixed from birth, it is absurd to think of them being a consequent of
some later act in life (other than a sex change operation). Only if one is
talking about subcultural meanings attached to gender identity, will this
possibility make sense. For example, one can imagine the following:
Self-image $_1 \longrightarrow$ Event $\longrightarrow$ Self-image $_2$, where, say, a woman's idea
of what it means to be "feminine" changes once she participates in contact
sports. This question is a very specific one of a type we shall not consider
further.

Gender identity can be considered, first, a direct cause.

$$Gender\ identity \longrightarrow Event$$

Many social epidemiologists, specialists who study how social position relates to health and disease, use this model. If more women than men are likely to be inflicted with some illness, then sex is included as a "cause" of the illness. This type of analysis is rather elementary, however, for it leaves out the question of why sex should make a difference. Unless one subscribes to the fact of inherent differences between the sexes and *can define those differences,* then this type of explanation is essentially a statistical one. It is not a useless one, however. Very possibly just knowing that there are sex differences will allow public health experts to distribute preventive aid accordingly. Simple statistical explanations may be all that is needed for policy makers for short-run practical purposes. They are not helpful for long-run understanding of the problem.

Most social scientists would want to go further in seeing how gender identity fits into the chain of events. One possibility is that gender identity precedes or causes another event which intervenes to cause the next one:

$$\text{Gender identity} \longrightarrow \text{Intervening event} \longrightarrow \text{Event}$$

We know that gender is a basis for differential socialization and many adult experiences, any of which may be direct links to the event we are studying. For example, some argue that boys have less parental supervision and are thus more likely to engage in illegal acts than girls. This is another way of saying that parental supervision, not gender, is a direct cause of delinquency. Gender is important so far as it leads to differences in parental treatment. Conceptually, we are saying,

$$\text{Gender} \longrightarrow \text{Parental supervision} \longrightarrow \text{Delinquency}$$

If this is true, then further data analysis would show that girls lacking parental supervision would be few in number, though likely to be delinquent. We would also understand why not all boys become delinquent. This explanation brings us closer to understanding the events surrounding delinquency as they apply to gender.

Another variation on this causal chain results in a more elaborate explanation. We may find that some event intervenes in such a way that the outcome is conditional upon *both* gender identity *and* the intervening event. The latter will specify the conditions under which a sex difference may or may not occur:

$$\text{Intervening event}_1$$
$$\text{Gender identity} \longrightarrow \text{Outcome event}$$
$$\text{Intervening event}_2$$
$$\text{Gender identity} \longrightarrow\!\!\!/\!\!\!\longrightarrow \text{Outcome event}$$

To take a hypothetical case, men and women in the same social class will have a certain level of free time and finances for leisure use. Marriage replaces restrictions on the use of resources, as well as increases the likelihood that marital partners will engage in activities together. Consequently, one might predict that sex differences in use of leisure time will be greater for single women and men, whose choices will be shaped more by self (gender) identity. If a married man owns a boat, then his wife is likely to boat as well. Among single persons, a boat purchaser is more likely to be a man. This example would show us:

Unmarried
Gender identity ⟶ Boating participation

Married
Gender identity ⟶/⟶ Boating participation

Though this is a trivial example, an investigator who found many examples of this chain of events could devlop a theory that marriage permits an expansion of experiences beyond those usually prescribed on the basis of gender.

Although a third chain of events is possible in logical terms, it does not make much sense with regard to the study of gender differences. This chain argues that some phenomenon exists prior to both gender identity and the outcome event, as follows:

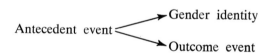

As we have already explained, unless "gender" is taken to mean specific definition of masculinity or femininity, it is always a prior variable. Consequently the most probable explanation for a correlation between gender and some event will involve the search for an intervening or specifying variable.

Let us also consider the case that *no* gender differences are found. Do we stop here and forget the data? Obviously not. First, the fact that no differences exist may be curious, unexpected, hence meaningful. As one sophisticated methodology teacher of mine once explained, "If you tested 100 mice and discovered that each had an IQ of 120, you wouldn't say the data were meaningless because you found no differences among the mice." Mice with IQ's of 120 are unheard of; so to do many social research studies produce "unheard of" results, in the sense that the results violate commonsense. If I collected data to show that men cried as often as women, many people's sense of order would be threatened for the mythology states that men cry less. In addition, it may be that we would find gender differences were we to locate the proper specifying variable. Age and physical changes directly shape the meaning of "female" and "male," just as social class, ethnicity, and race interact to provide various definitions of gender in our society. Consequently, it would not be surprising to learn that sex differences exist within certain of these subgroups and not in others. The more patriarchal subcultures automatically separate women from men and provide many more different experiences than those subcultures where gender is less a basis for social order. So wherever there are no differences, we need to think of cross-cutting categories that would interact with gender and produce differences.

A careful and clever social scientist will not be satisfied with the first explanation she considers. She will ask whether there might be a number of reasonable intervening or specifying variables. She will look around for data that supports one explanation instead of another. More is learned by considering alternate arguments than be relentlessly building up evidence for one point of view. In the examples in this book, I did not have space (or full imagination) to elaborate on the meanings of all the data that are presented. Join me in seeking out causal chains of your own.

glossary

Androcentric bias: Applies to a theory or approach that ignores women and women's activities; tends to generalize all behavior from the way males behave or think.

Androgen: One hormone that develops masculine secondary sex characteristics; present in both sexes, though larger proportion found in men.

Androgyny: Having "feminine" and "masculine" characteristics.

Aquatic theory: The theory that many secondary sex characteristics developed during a period in evolution when humans were forced to live as aquatic mammals.

Ascribed role: A role imposed upon an individual on the basis of personal qualities; similar to situs. The difference in the two concepts is that one would say that "there is an ascribed female role" rather than "women (a situs) more likely fill certain roles in society."

Authority: The power or dominance structure of a family; can be patriarchal, matriarchal, or shared.

Biogrammar: A repertoire of signals (postures, gestures, movements), genetically transmitted, that provide a basic communications system for a species; the "basic wiring" of an animal. Tiger and Fox believe human biogrammar is that of a hunting animal.

Bisexual: A person who can be sexually attracted by members of either sex; such a person need not be androgynous in personality.

"Buddy system": The practice whereby appointments, jobs, and grants are made on the basis of informal contacts. This practice results in the exclusion of persons unlike those in the in-group.

Caste: A hierarchy of divisions in which membership is ascribed at birth and unalterable. Marriage is to occur only within members of a division (endogamy). Women thus are not a caste, though in some ways they share characteristics of those who belong to subordinate castes.

Chromosomal sex: The attribution of persons to sex categories on the basis of chromosomal examination. The twenty-fourth pair of chromosomes in females is XX, in males, XY. However, not all individuals fit these two patterns.

Descent: The principles of family identification and inheritance; can be matrilineal, patrilineal, or bilineal.

Estrogen: The set of hormones responsible for promoting estrus and the development and maintenance of female secondary sex characteristics; present in both females and males.

Estrus: The regular recurrence of ovulation and sexual excitement in animals other than humans; also called "heat."

Ethnocentrism: Belief in the superiority of one's own culture; often implicit in social science theory and research, particularly in terms of racism and sexism.

Feminine: Cultural beliefs as to how females should appear and behave; varies by class, ethnicity, race, etc.

Feminization: Used to describe any process whereby the values and behaviors typically applied to females become typical of everyone in a situation, e.g., a belief that males would become "feminized" were they to do domestic work; often used to evaluate the event negatively.

Fear of success: A motive some psychologists believe accounts for the lesser achievement of women in American society; measured by a story-completion exercise.

Hermaphrodite: A person with sexual organs of both sexes who nonetheless is assigned to one sex at birth and will develop the gender identity of that sex.

Gender: A situs category that provides the basis for personal identity from birth.

Gender identity: One's self-concept as it includes (1) the sense of being a female or male and (2) evaluations of one's self in terms of the culture's expectations concerning feminity or masculinity.

Gonads: The sex glands (ovaries and testes).

Locus: Social positions that arise from the function an individual's performance provides for a group, e.g., the nurse in a medical unit.

M-F scale: A personality inventory used to classify people as "feminine" or "masculine" as determined by cultural stereotypes; usually presumes that people can be typed as one or the other.

Masculine: Cultural beliefs as to how males should appear and behave; varies by class, ethnicity, race, etc.

Masculinization: Used to describe situations whereby values or behaviors attached to males become typical of everyone in a situation, e.g., a belief that women are "masculinized" by working in outdoor occupations.

Minority group: A group singled out in a society for their physical or cultural characteristics, which is treated differently and unequally, and which regards itself as the object of discrimination.

Orientational others: Persons one looks to in defining one's self.

Parochialism: The refusal to see beyond one's own concerns, e.g., when a career woman writes about women in general without taking into account the lives of noncareer women.

Residence: Where newly-formed families locate their domicile; can be patrilocal, matrilocal, or neolocal.

Secondary sex characteristics: Any genetically transmitted anatomical, physiological, or behavioral characteristics (facial hair, breast development, voice changes) that appear at puberty. These differentiate the sexes without having any reproductive function. Being genetic, these are not identical from one culture to another.

Self: The psychic entity through which someone defines her person; includes self-presentation, the interpretation of others' responses to that presentation, and an emotional response to that interpretation.

Self-fulfilling prophecy: A false definition of a situation evoking behavior which makes the originally false conception come true.

Sex: The classification of persons into female and male categories on the basis of their reproductive functions; assigned at birth on the basis of external genital appearance, though this may not be a correct assignment in terms of later maturation.

Sex ratio: The proportion of males to females in a population multiplied by one hundred. Thus, a ratio of ninety-four indicates that there are six fewer males per hundred females in a group.

Sex roles: A loose term for the study of gender differences and gender stratification systems. Also, a particular approach to the sociology of gender that emphasizes the study of gender-specific roles, how they are learned, and how they are enacted, e.g., Lopata's study of housewives.

Sexism: Cultural beliefs and social practices premised upon the superiority of one sex, usually the male, and accompanying masculine values.

Situs: An aggregate of persons socially distinguished by any common characteristics (age, gender) other than status and locus. Belief systems provide a set of expectations concerning the probable behavior of members of these categories.

Social mythology: A system of explanations for events that serve as a basis for social cohesion while limiting personal opportunity, e.g., the feminine mystique.

Status: A hierarchial position, typically based upon power, prestige, or wealth.

Testosterone: A hormone that controls masculine secondary characteristics and plays a role in sexual drive. Present in both sexes.

Thematic Apperception Test (TAT): A measure of personality needs based upon a respondent's reactions to ambiguous illustrations; often used to measure achievement motive.

Transsexual: One who feels that he is trapped in the wrong body; may undergo surgical change of appearance to satisfy the desire to change gender.

Twenty Statements Test (TST): A measure of self-concept based upon a respondent's answer to the question, "Who am I?"

author index

Adorno, Theodore, 56
Allen, Nancy H., 180, 182
Anastasi, Anne, 6, 21
Anthony, Susan B., 185
Arendt, Hannah, 68, 74
Ariés, Phillippe, 136, 159
Austin, David, 102, 108

Bahr, Howard, 59, 74
Ball, Donald W., 135, 159
Balswick, Jack O., 163, 182
Bardwick, Judith, 12, 18, 21, 83-84, 88-89, 108
Barter, James T., 172, 182
Baxter, J.C., 127, 130
Bem, Sandra, 71, 74
Benoit-Smullyan, Emile, 41, 56
Benson, Leonard, 90, 108
Berreman, John, 45, 56
Bird, Caroline, 200, 208
Blau, Peter, 147, 159
Block, Jack, 89, 108
Blood, Robert O., 86, 108, 192-194, 208
Broom, Leonard, 68, 74
Broverman, 70, 74
Buyendijk, 15, 21

Catt, Carrie C., 183, 186, 208
Chesler, Phyllis, 178, 182
Chilman, Catherine, 170, 182
Christiansen, Harold T., 164, 172
Clark, Burton R., 98, 108
Coleman, James S., 104-106, 108, 205-206

Collard, E.D., 89, 108
Collins, Randall, 39
Cooley, Charles H., 91-92, 108, 113
Couch, Carl J., 112-113, 130
Cox, Ruby, 60

Davis, Elizabeth, 31, 39
de Beauvoir, Simone, 200, 208
Denzin, Norman K., 124, 130
de Ropp, Robert, 3, 15, 21
de Staël, Germaine, 59
Diamond, Milton, 17, 21
Diner, Helen, 31, 39
Douglas, Jack D., 180, 182
Douvan, Elizabeth, 106, 108
Dublin, Louis I., 180, 182
Durkheim, Emile, 180, 182

Eiferman, Rivka, 97, 108
Eisenberg, J.F., 14, 21
Engels, Friedrich, 30
Epstein, Cynthia Fuchs, 62, 74
Erikson, Erik, 70, 74
Erlich, Carol, 139, 159
Exline, R.V., 127, 130

Fava, Sylvia Geis, 64, 74
Figes, Eva, 37, 39, 120, 130
Firestone, Shulamith, 200-203, 208
Fisher, Seymour, 118, 130
Flexnor, Eleanor, 183, 208
Ford, Clellan, 35, 39
Francoeur, Robert, 210, 212
Frazier, E. Franklin, 59
Freud, Sigmund, 70, 83-85, 108, 117

Friedan, Betty, 121, 130, 199-200, 208
Furstenberg, Frank F., 137, 159

Garai, J.E., 89, 108
Gilman, Charlotte Perkins, 59, 187-189, 193, 208
Glenn, Norval, 60, 74
Goldberg, L.R., 71, 74
Goldman, Emma, 59, 189-191, 193, 204, 208
Goode, William, 155, 159
Gough, Kathleen, 39
Greer, Germaine, 120, 130, 200, 208
Grossack, Martin, 72
Gurin, Gerald, 116, 130

Hacker, Helen, 44, 46, 56, 59
Harlow, Harry, 82, 108
Heiskanen, Veronica S., 72, 74, 139, 159
Hensley, Nancy, 127, 130
Herron, R.E., 93, 108
Hoffman, Lois W., 82, 88-89, 108
Horner, Matina, 114, 130
Hutchinson, Anne, 184

Ivey, Melville, 10, 21

Jackson, Maurice, 65
Janeway, Elizabeth, 120, 130

Kagan, J., 89, 108
Kanowitz, Leo, 195, 208
Katz, Marlaine L., 114-116, 130
Kennedy, Robert E., 33, 39
Kohlberg, Lawrence, 86, 108
Komarovsky, Mirra, 151-152, 159
Komisar, Lucy, 123-130

Larson, Richard, 65, 74
La Sorte, Michael, 63, 74
Leavitt, Ruby, 35, 39
Le Guin, Ursula, 209-210
Lenney, Ellen, 71, 74
Lipset, Seymour M., 67, 74
Lopata, Helena Z., 47, 56, 140-144, 153, 159
Lukoff, Irving F., 172, 182
Lynn, David B., 82, 86-88, 108, 113

McClelland, David C., 114, 130
Maccoby, Eleanor, 6, 21
McGlothin, William H., 172, 182
MacLean, Paul D., 13, 21
Madigan, F.C., 13, 21
Mead, George H., 91, 93-94, 108, 112
Mead, Margaret, 32-33, 39
Mehrabian, Albert, 127, 130
Merton, Robert, 43, 56
Millar, Susanna, 93, 108
Millet, Kate, 85, 108
Mitchell, Juliet, 203-204, 208
Money, John, 3, 11, 17-18, 21, 83
Montagu, Ashley, 5, 21
Moore, Mary E., 13, 21
Morgan, Elaine, 28, 39
Morris, 26, 39
Morris, Desmond, 14, 22
Mulford, Harold, 110, 130
Murdock, George, 32, 39

Oakley, Annie, 33, 35, 39
O'Neill, William L., 183, 208

Paige, Karen, 10, 22
Parsons, Talcott, 67, 74, 85-86, 108
Paulme, Denise, 39
Phillips, D., 179, 182
Powdermaker, Florence, 59

Rainwater, Lee, 152, 159
Reed, Evelyn, 31, 39
Reiss, Albert J., Jr., 174, 182
Reiss, Ira L., 162-164, 182
Riley, Matilda W., 50, 56
Roberts, John M., 83, 95, 108
Rokeach, Milton, 56
Rosenberg, B.G., 22, 97, 108
Rossi, Alice, 61-62, 65, 75

Salper, Roberta, 185, 198, 208
Scanzoni, John, 193, 208
Sennett, Jonathan, 148-151, 159
Seward, Georgene, 39
Sexton, Patricia C., 100-101, 109, 145, 159
Shapiro, Michael, 47, 56
Shostak, Arthur B., 152, 159
Simon, Rita James, 61-62, 75
Sinclair, Andrew, 183, 208

Singer, Judith, 4-5, 22
Slater, Philip, 133, 159
Smuts, Robert W., 137, 159
Stark, Rodney, 147, 159
Stasz, Cathleen, 100, 109
Stoll, Clarice, 39, 67, 75, 82, 97, 109
Stoller, Robert, 17, 19, 22
Stone, Gregory, 91, 93, 109
Strainchamps, Ethel, 67, 75
Sullerot, Evelyne, 36, 39, 136, 159,
  207, 208
Sutton-Smith, Brian, 83, 95-97, 109
Syme, S. Leonard, 176-182

Tanner, Leslie B., 184, 208
Terman, Lewis, 71, 75, 101, 109

Thomas, William I., 43, 56
Tiger, Lionel, 14, 22, 25-27, 39, 82,
  197-198, 208
Truth, Sojourner, 184-185

Warshay, Diana W., 150, 159
Weisstein, Naomi, 70, 75
Weitzman, Leonore J., 103, 108
Weston, Peter J., 114, 130
Whiting, John W., 78, 109
Wickler, Wolfgang, 13, 22

Yarrow, Leon J., 86, 109

Zimet, Sara G., 102, 109

subject index

Accidents, 168-170
Achievement motive, 113-116
Achievement orientation
   learned in games, 95-97
   as socialization outcome, 79-80
Adornment, 119
Aggression
   development of, 89
   male, 12, 35
Alcoholism, 170-171
Amazons, 31
Androcentric bias, 81
Androgen. *See* Hormones
Androgyny, 71, 82
Animal research. *See* Ethology
Anticipatory socialization, 91
Aquatic theory, 28-29
Archeology, 23-40
Authority structure, 31
Auto accidents, 169-170

Bem Sex Role Inventory, 71
Biogrammar, 26
Biology. *See* Ethology, Hormones
Blue-collar males
   family life, 147-152
   income,145-146
   work environment, 146-152
Body language, 127-128
Breast feeding, 12, 33
Buddy system. *See* Male bonding

Caste
   characteristics, 43-44
   defined, 43
   women not members of, 45

Castelike characteristics
   as applied to race, 45
   as applied to women, 45
   illustrated, 46
Childbearing, 12, 33
Chromosomes
   diseases related to, 4-5
   as measures of gender, 17
   sex, 2-4
"Club context." *See* Male bonding
Colonialism, 183
Comparative psychology, 82-83
"Cooling out," 98
Correlation and causality, 97,
      210-217
Crime, 172-176

Descent, 3
Domesticity, 34
   in mythology, 120-126
Dominance
   and socialization, 79-80
Double standard, 163-164

Estrogen. *See* Hormones
Ethnocentrism
   defined, 66
Ethology
   defined, 13
   errors in interpretation, 14
   sex differences, 13-17
Experimenter bias, 71

Family
   and economy, 30-32
   Gilmore's theory, 187-189

225

Family *(continued)*
historical overview, 135-139
role in socialization, 82-90
structures, 31-32
and work worlds, 131-159
Femininity
relative status, 15
Feminism
contemporary, 198-201
early, 183-188
"Feminized male," 100-101
"Frigidity," 165
Functionalism, 85

Games
in socialization, 94-97
Gender
defined, 41
and social structure, 42
Gender differences
in accidents, 168-170
in addictions, 170-172
in adult self-image, 110-117
analysis of, 210-217
in body percept, 117-119
contemporary American, 47-54
in crime, 172-176
cultural, 23-40
defined, 2
early childhood, 4-9
economic, 34-35, 37
education, 52, 60
ethological data, 13-17
in high school, 104-106
historical, 36-39, 135-139
in illness, 176-179
income, 53, 63
in leisure, 165-168
in love, 165
measurement of, 8
occupation, 52-53
old age, 13, 54
physical, 2-14, 24-25
self-concept, 92
in sexuality, 162-164
sociologists, 60-64
in suicide, 179-181
values in study of, 47
in victimization, 174-175

Gender identity, 17. *Also see* Self-concept
adult expressions, 160-161
in adults, 111-119
measurement, 110-119
and parents' roles, 112-113
Generalized other, 94-95
"Great Mother" theories, 31-32

Health utilization, 176-177
Hermaphrodites, 15, 17, 25
Hormones, 83
female cycles, 10
male cycles, 11
as measures of gender, 17
old age, 12-13
puberty, 9
Household
defined, 135
role cycles, 153-158
structural forms, 50-51, 138
Housewife
role, 47
role cycle, 140-144

Identity
defined, 41-42

Leisure, 165-168
Locus
defined, 41
and self-definition, 42
Love, 161-165
Love ideology, 201-203

M-F inventories, 71
Male
status systems, 26-28
Male bonding, 67
in sociology, 63-66
Marijuana, 171-172
Marriage
legal requirements, 195
pressures toward, 133
Marriage forms, 31-32
Masculity
relative status, 15
Media
sexism in, 113

Menstruation, 10
Mental illness, 178-179
Minority group
   defined, 44-45
   men as, 44
   theories of, 56
   women as, 44-45
Mortality rates
   sex differences, 13, 49-50
Motherhood, 142-143

Nurturance, 79-80
   in adults, 115-116

Obedience
   learned in games, 95-97
   as socialization outcome, 79-80
Orientational others, 123

Parochialism
   defined, 66
Patriarchy, 31, 36-38
   in American history, 183-188
   in American ideology, 120-126
   historical roots, 136
   in marriage, 195-196
Physical size, 9, 24, 26, 33
Play
   in socialization, 90-94
Politics, 26, 196-197
Power, 202-207
Power inequalities
   in government, 195-198
   in marriage, 191-195
   in small groups, 192
Pre-industrial humans, 25-32
Prejudice, 44, 56
Prostitution, 189-190
Psychoanalytic model, 83-85

Race, 35
Race
   and identity, 42
   as situs, 41
Racial minorities
   as castes, 45
   similarities to women, 45
   in sociology, 65-66
   in unions, 145-148

Racism
   in schools, 98-99
Rape, 11
Residence, 31
Responsibility
   learned in games, 95-97
   as socialization outcome, 79-80
Role
   defined, 41
   and gender, 42
Role playing, 122-123

School
   role in socialization, 98-107
Scientific method
   described, 57
   sexism and, 58
   values and, 58
Secondary sex characteristics, 9, 24,
      26
Self
   defined, 91
   in socialization, 91-94
Self-concept
   in adolescence, 102-107
   in adults, 110-119
   body percepts, 117-119
Self-fulfilling prophecy, 43, 55
Self-identity
   and self-presentation, 126-129
   and social mythology, 120-126
Sex
   definitional problems, 16-19
Sex differences. *See* gender differences
Sexism
   in America, 47-54
   defined, 20, 220
   in everyday life, 120-129
   in government, 195-198
   in language, 67-68
   in marriage, 191-195
   in media, 113
   mythology of, 120-126
   as prejudice, 44
   in research design, 69-72
   in research sampling, 69-70
   in schools, 98-99
   in science, 57-59
   and scientific productivity, 60-63

Sexism *(Continued)*
  as a self-fulfilling prophecy, 43
  and social change, 55
  in social research, 139
  in social theory, 59, 68, 72
  in sociology, 59-75
Sex ratio, 48-49
  at birth, 3
Sex role
  measurement, 71
Sex roles
  defined, 41
  politics in research of, 47
Situs
  defined, 41
  and self-definition, 42
Smoking, 171-172
Sociability, 79-80
Social change
  and sexism, 55
Social class, 35
  and schooling, 99-101
Socialization
  adolescence, 104-107
  defined, 77
  early childhood, 82-90
  functionalist theory, 85-86
  play and games, 90-97
  psychoanalytic theory, 83-85
  research problems, 78-82
  role of peers, 104-107

role of school, 98-107
role of teachers, 100-102
role of textbooks, 102-104
social learning theory, 86-90, 92
theories of, 75-109
Social learning theory, 86-90
Social mythology
  and social control, 120-126
Socializers. *See* Socialization
Status
  defined, 41
  and gender, 42
  personal, 41
Stratification
  and gender, 42
Suffrage movements, 184-188
Suicide, 179-181

Temperance, 184-186
Testosterone. *See* Hormones
Thematic Apperception Test, 113-114
Transsexualism, 18-19
Twenty Statements Test (TST),
  110-112

Victimization, 174-175

Work
  and adult identity, 131-132
  and family, 131-159
  historical overview, 135-139
Working women, 144